Verguet's Sketchbook

Verguet's Sketchbook
A Marist Missionary Artist in 1840s Oceania

Mervyn Duffy & Alois Greiler

ATF PRESS

2014

Text copyright © 2014 with Mervyn Duffy, Alois Greiler and the Society of Mary.

The images in this volume are reproduced with permission from originals in the General Archives of the Society of Mary (APM). Permission for their further reproduction can be sought from there. The text of this volume is copyright to the Society of Mary.

The Marist Series
Through the Marist Series the Society of Mary (Marist Fathers) shares projects by Marists in the field of theology and history and works about the role of the Marists in the church, in particular in the Pacific.

Series Editor: Alois Greiler SM

1. *Catholic Beginnings in Oceania: Marist Missionary Perspectives*, 2009, edited by Alois Greiler SM.
2. *A Mission Too Far . . . Pacific Commitment and the Missions 1835–1841*, 2012, Jan Snijders SM.
3. *Thinking Things Through: Essays in Philosophy and Christian Faith*, 2102, Andrew Murray SM.

ISBN 9781921511264 paperback
ISBN 9781921511271 epub
ISBN 9781921511288 pdf

Cover and layout by Mervyn Duffy

An imprint of ATF Ltd. PO Box 504
Hindmarsh, SA 5007
ABN 90 116 359 963
www.atfpress.com

Contents

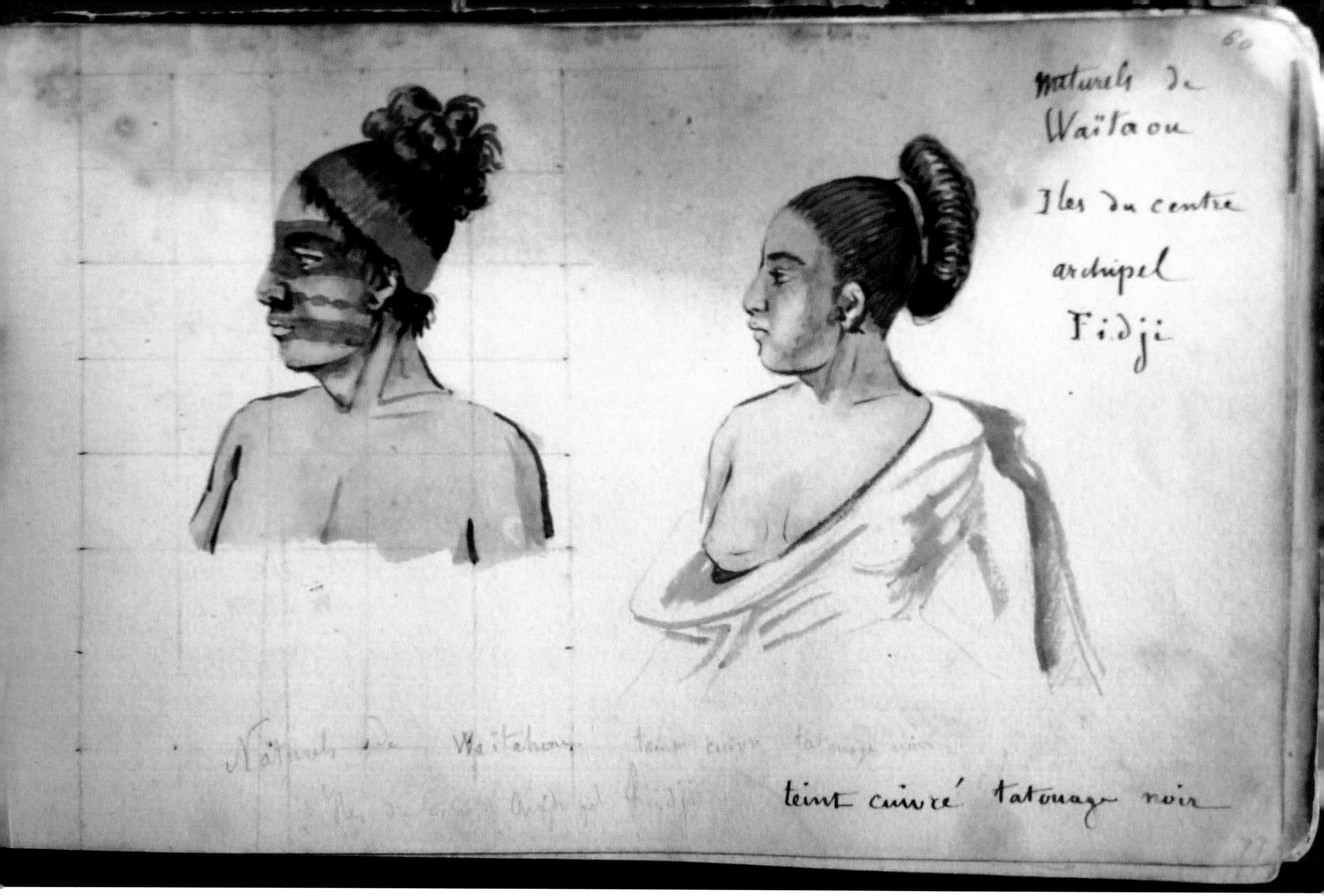
Naturels de
Waïtaou
Iles du centre
archipel
Fidji
teint cuivré tatouage noir

Foreword

Facing Page

A page from the sketchbook showing
a Fijian man and woman
identified as being from "Waitaou"
(possibly modern Waidau in Bureta,
western Ovalau)
in the Islands in the centre of
the archipelago of Fiji.

Verguet comments
"bronzed complexion with black tatoo"

This is a book to be welcomed without reservation. Indeed, it could usefully have been published decades (or even a century!) ago. So, current and future readers should be grateful to Duffy and Greiler for their efforts. Leopold Verguet may not be an 'important' historical figure: he did not hold high office, he was not central to dramatic events. But, he is highly 'significant' as an enduring recorder of first-hand observations, and experiences and impressions of a pioneering expedition to the south-west Pacific. As an 'eye-witness' he is invaluable, thanks to his artistic and literary remains.

Outstanding among the latter is a book published in 1854 about the unsuccessful Marist effort to evangelise the Solomon Islands in the mid-1840s. Not only is it a narrative of events but it also serves as an ethnographic study and as rich history of an episode in Pacific 'culture contact'. However, Verguet was also a gifted artist and the richest part of his legacy is an extensive archive-preserved corpus of paintings and sketches covering the full itinerary from France and back (1844-48). Some of these were used as illustrations in his writings, where they can be seen as hints of what was eventually to come into being in the form of this luxurious book.

It is an admirably contextualised work, with the pictures being set not only within an authorial commentary but amidst extensive quotations from Verguet's own writings. Were Fr Leopold Verguet able to meet Frs Mervyn Duffy and Alois Greiler he would surely say '*Merci beaucoup*'. Indeed anyone who perused it from 2014 onwards would be equally likely to say much the same thing.

Hugh Laracy (Solomon Islands Medal, first class)

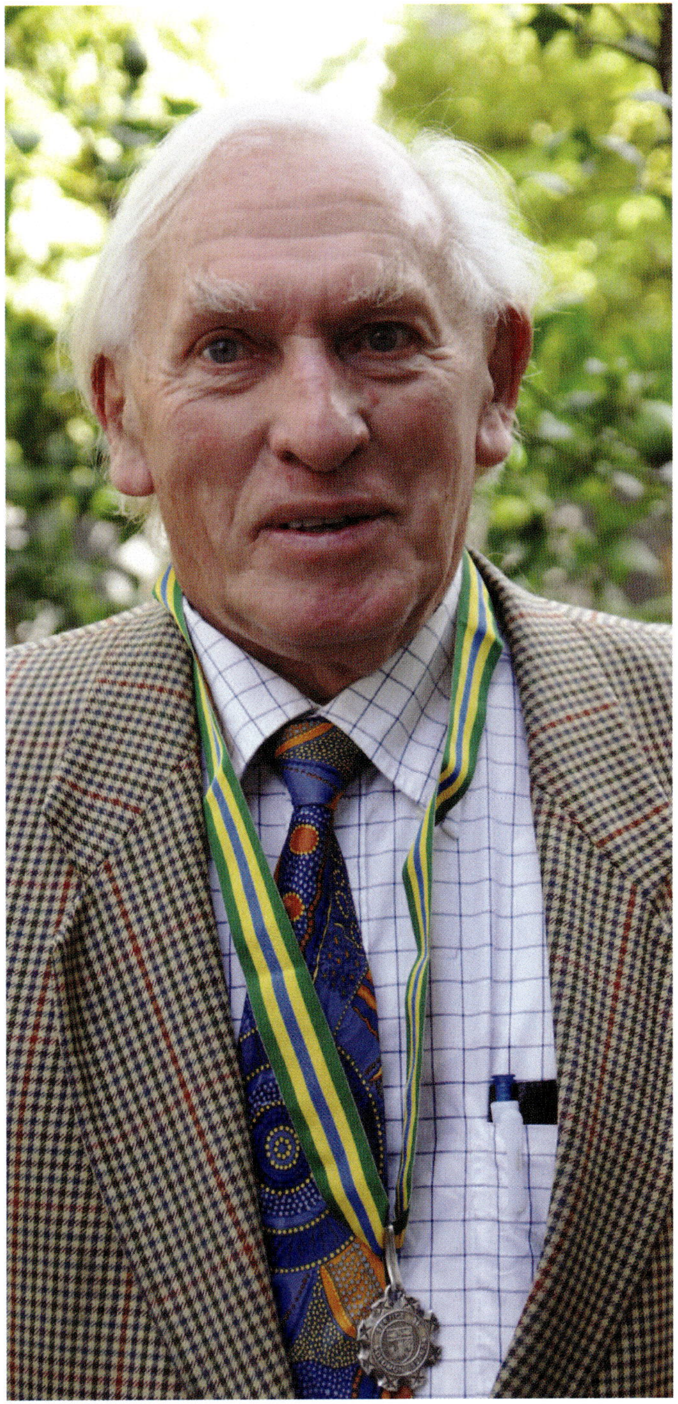

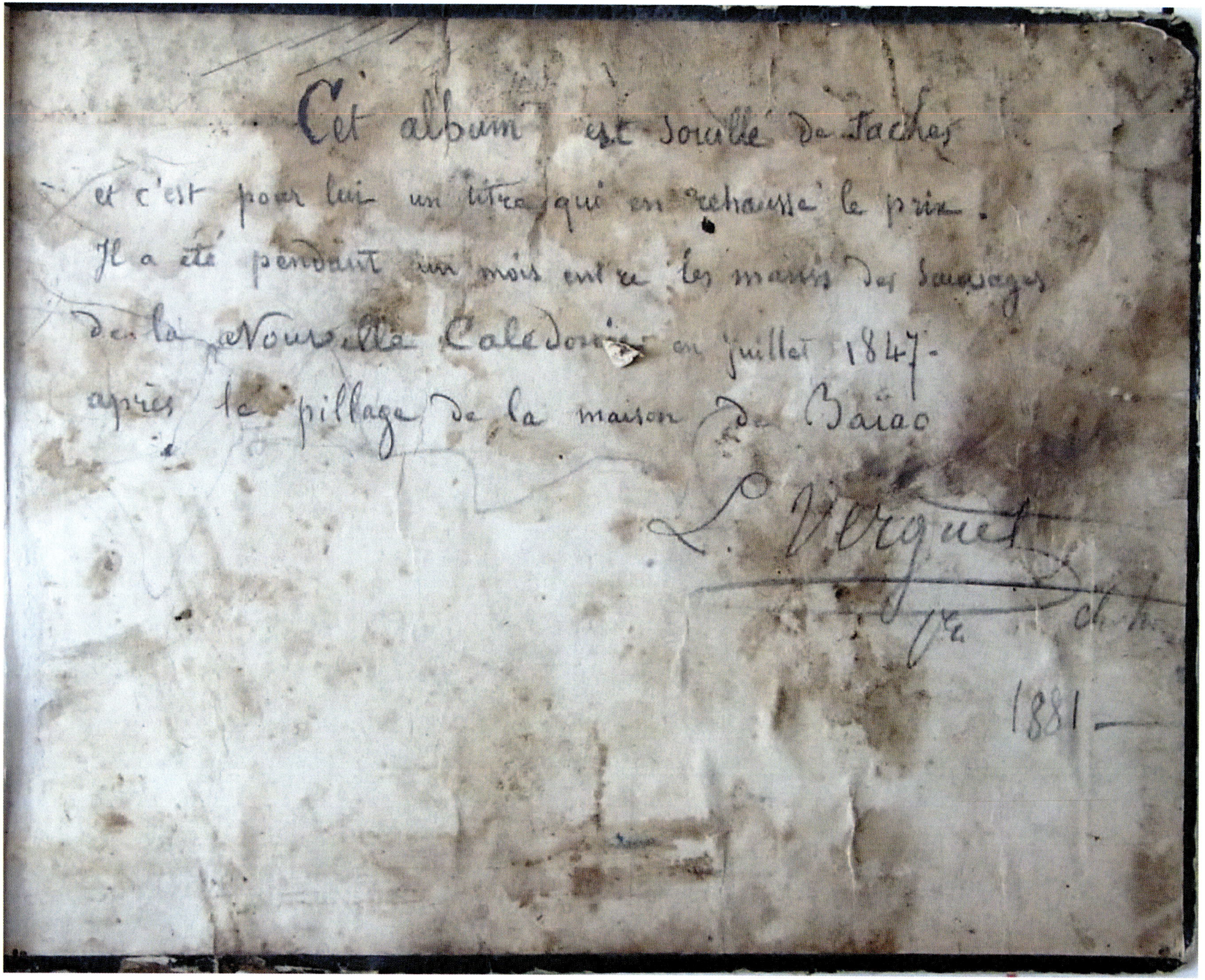

Cet album est souillé de taches
et c'est pour lui un titre qui en rehausse le prix.
Il a été pendant un mois entre les mains des sauvages
de la Nouvelle Calédonie en juillet 1847.
après le pillage de la maison de Baïao

L. Verguet

1881

Back cover
of the sketchbook

"This album is battered by use and its value increased thereby. It spent a month in the hands of the savages of New Caledonia in July 1847 after the looting of the Baïao house.

L. Verguet
1881"

Introduction

On 19 January 1914 in the town of Carcassonne in the South of France a priest died. His demise was not unexpected; Fr Clair Marie Léopold Verguet was ninety-seven years of age. He left a curious collection of spears, clubs, masks, photos, papers, and artworks, of which most were sold to an antiquarian, and some kept by his diocese and family. Fifty years later, in 1964, a Monsieur J. Podevigne, handed Verguet's sketchbook to the archivist at the General House of the Society of Mary in Rome. The note he left with it says that he had found it a decade before in Lyon in a basket of papers about to be thrown out. He had asked of two priests whether it ought be disposed of and was told that it was all right, 'they weren't great sketches'. Instead, he acquired it and kept it until he had the opportunity to offer it to the Marists. The archivist accepted it gratefully and added it to the Verguet file, where it joined a trove of correspondence and some other sketches.

In the fifty years since then, the sketchbook has been cherished and shown off as a treasure, especially to visitors from the South Pacific. A few scholars have seen it and designs within it have been reproduced. It travelled to Sydney to the Museum of Australia and was photographed. Advice was given as to how to conserve it,

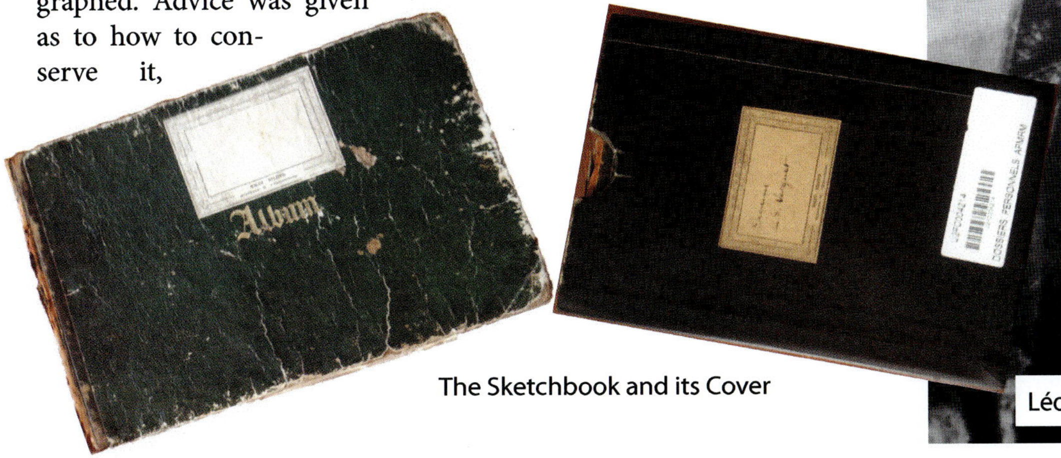

The Sketchbook and its Cover

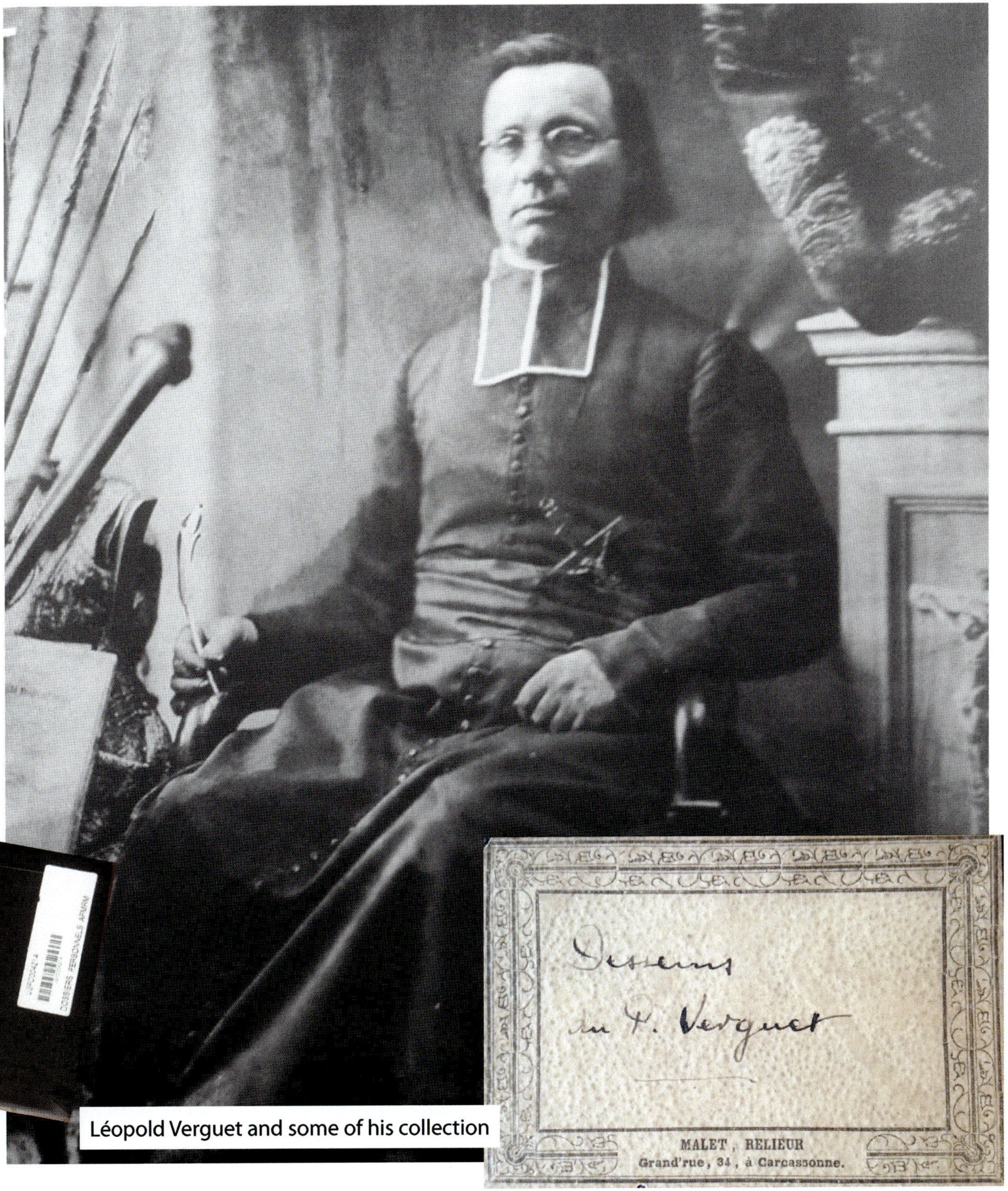

Léopold Verguet and some of his collection

and interest expressed in acquiring it.

In 1995 Solomon Islands issued a special series of four stamps to celebrate one hundred and fifty years of Christianity. The designs on those stamps incorporated images from Verguet's sketchbook.

Now, in 2014, a century after the death of Verguet, we wish to draw on the sources in the Archives of the Marist General Administration to show this remarkable sketchbook to a wider audience, and to tell the story of the priest-artist and of the extraordinary adventure he was engaged in.

Mervyn Duffy SM
Alois Greiler SM

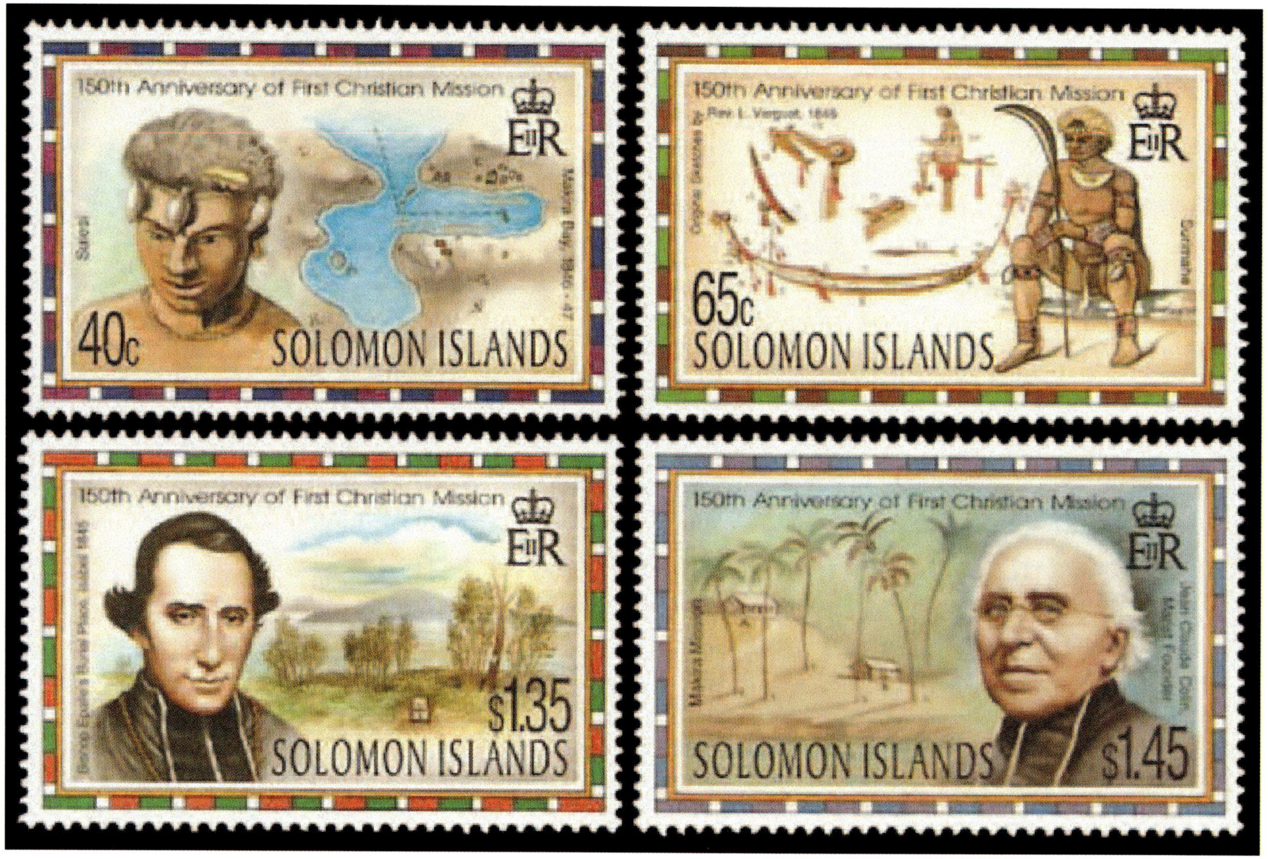

Solomon Islands stamps commemorating the 150th Anniversary of the First Christian Mission
40c has Verguet's portrait of Souiessi and his map of Makira Bay
65c has Verguet's portrait of Sourimahe and of a pirogue and its details. Verguet's name appears.
$1.35 has a portrait of Bishop Epalle and a sketch of where his grave was
$1.45 has Fr Jean Claude Colin, the founder of the Society of Mary, and a sketch of the Makira Mission

Verguet in Europe

Preparation for Mission

Carcassonne

The nineteenth century was a time of a great revival of missionary activity by the Catholic Church. As a youth and seminarian Léopold Verguet was inspired by the letters of missionaries which he had read in the *Annales de la Propagation de la Foi (Annals of the Propagation of the Faith)*, a French missionary journal. The lay organisation, *Propagation de la Foi,* not only published the *Annales* it also collected donations to fund the missions it publicized. In 1842 they asked Fr Jean-Claude Colin, superior general of the Marists, for a preacher to promote the foreign missions and he assigned Fr Antoine Dubreul. From the autumn of 1842 until spring 1844 Dubreul toured many dioceses in the south of France, including Carcassonne and Montpellier.

In addition to preaching about the missions to encourage donations, Fr Colin had asked him to look for priests who were keen to be missionaries. On 15 December 1843, Dubreul sent a report on candidates from various dioceses: from the diocese of Montpellier he mentioned Montrouzier, a pious and zealous deacon with talents; from the diocese of Carcassonne he identified Verguet, 'vicar at the cathedral, 26 years old, who did his theology at Toulouse and then Saint Sulpice (Paris) so as to enter more easily the seminary for the foreign missions.' Verguet was someone with a desire to be a missionary and now a congregation that was looking for missionaries had established contact with him.

Lyon

Verguet visited the Marist head house in Lyon and was pleased by what he saw. He wanted to go either to China or Oceania. Initially, both his father and his bishop refused permission. In 1844, the bishop and his father relented and allowed him to join the newly established Society of Mary, one year after his ordination. From February 1844 Verguet was a novice in Lyon, together with Thomassin and Montrouzier who would be part of the same mission group.

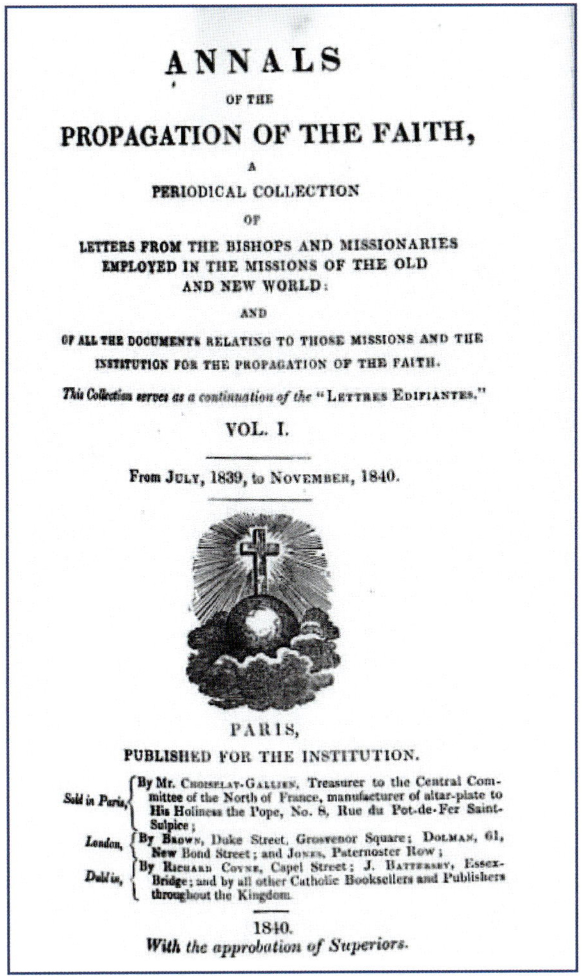

ANNALS

OF THE

PROPAGATION OF THE FAITH,

A

PERIODICAL COLLECTION

OF

LETTERS FROM THE BISHOPS AND MISSIONARIES EMPLOYED IN THE MISSIONS OF THE OLD AND NEW WORLD:

AND

OF ALL THE DOCUMENTS RELATING TO THOSE MISSIONS AND THE INSTITUTION FOR THE PROPAGATION OF THE FAITH.

This Collection serves as a continuation of the "LETTRES EDIFIANTES."

VOL. I.

From JULY, 1839, to NOVEMBER, 1840.

PARIS,

PUBLISHED FOR THE INSTITUTION.

Sold in Paris, By Mr. CHOISELAT-GALLIEN, Treasurer to the Central Committee of the North of France, manufacturer of altar-plate to His Holiness the Pope, No. 8, Rue du Pot-de-Fer Saint-Sulpice;

London, By BROWN, Duke Street, Grosvenor Square; DOLMAN, 61, New Bond Street; and JONES, Paternoster Row;

Dublin, By RICHARD COYNE, Capel Street; J. BATTERSBY, Essex-Bridge; and by all other Catholic Booksellers and Publishers throughout the Kingdom.

1840.

With the approbation of Superiors.

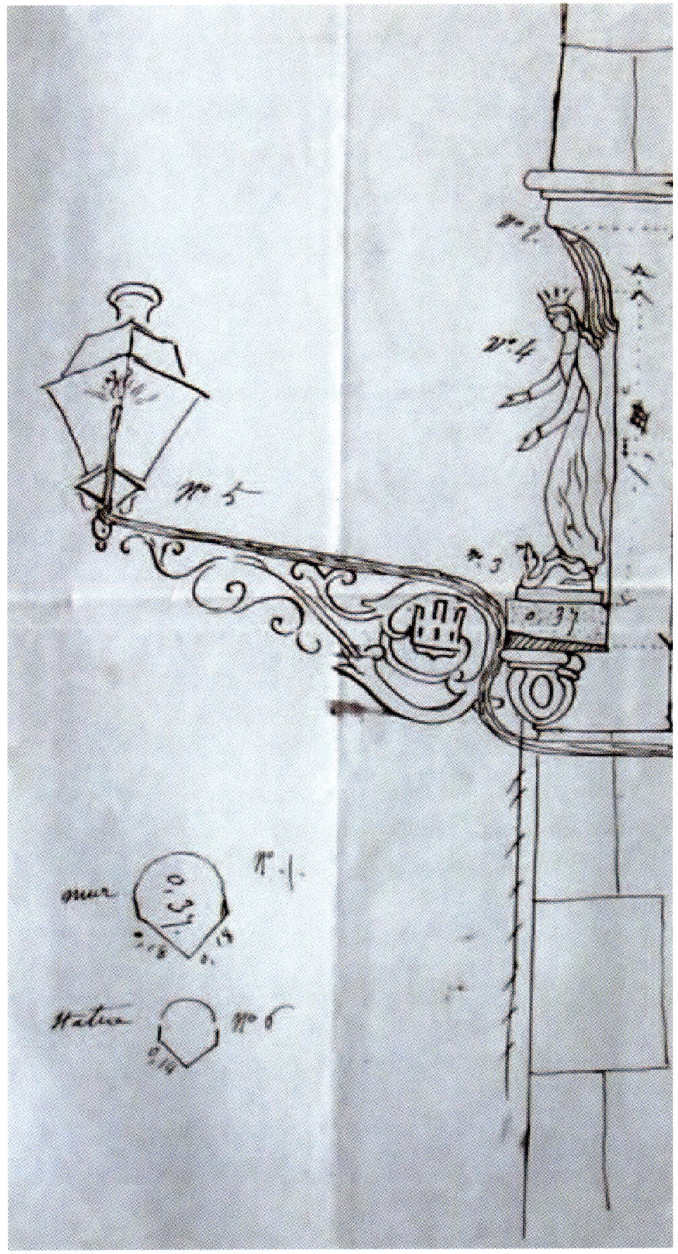

This sheet with the design for a lamp post with crown motif and statue of the Vigin Mary is among Verguet's papers but the whereabouts of the statue, if it exists, is unknown

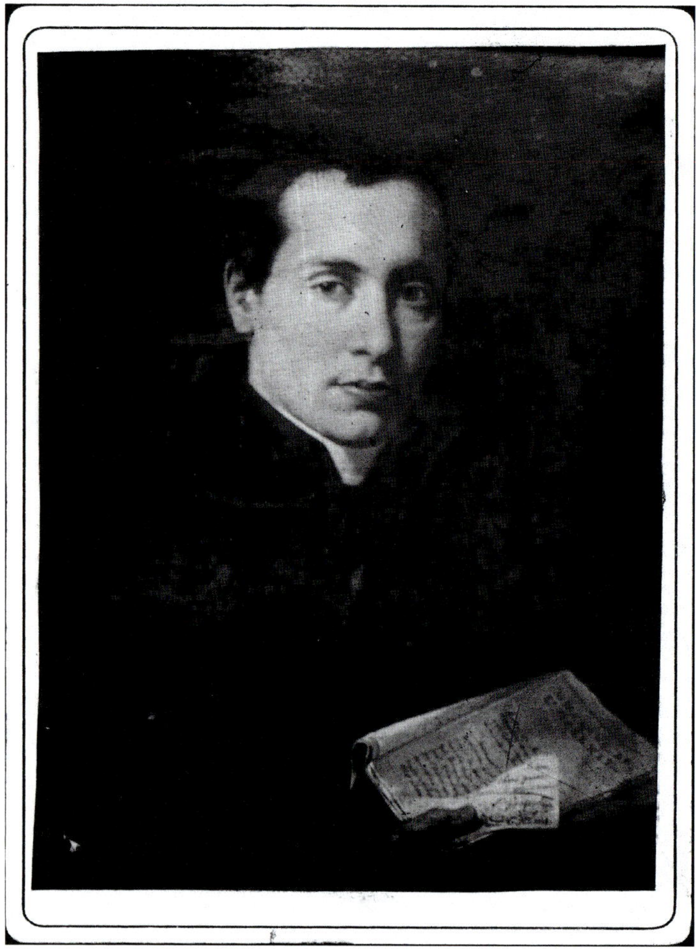

While in Rome in 1844, Verguet had his portrait painted, and photographs of it made, which he sent to family and friends as a souvenir

He is shown holding a text about Oceania

2 January 1845 - Bishop Jean-Baptiste Epalle
to the Central Committee of the Propagation of the Faith at Lyon

The huge land masses that [Melanesia] comprises are separated, so to speak, only by straits. From Cristobal which is on the south-east point as far as Guilolo on the nor'west point, that is to say an area of 8.5 leagues the biggest stretch from one island to another would not be more than 26 to 27 leagues. So, although the vicariate of Melanesia includes a lot of seas, the land masses are still quite numerous, huge enough when combined to create a small continent. The mission is centred in New Guinea because of its position. It alone has an area of 40,000 square leagues, in other words it is a third larger than France.

Rome

In May, Colin sent Epalle, Dubreul and Verguet to Rome to prepare for the Melanesia mission 'to learn the true apostolic spirit' and to negotiate with the Roman Congregation *Propaganda Fide*, the headquarters of Catholic missionary work. From the beginning the Marist general had wanted to form his missionaries in Rome before despatch, but financial problems and the urgency with which they were required meant this had not happened. Epalle, Dubreul and Verguet were the first for whom it was a reality, albeit brief. They arrived 14 May and stayed until the end of July 1844.

In its planning of mission, *Propaganda Fide* notionally allocates vast areas of the globe to a 'vicar apostolic' who then leads a mission into one part of that territory. Areas that have not been contacted are then able to be carved off as new vicariates. Acting on this basis the Holy See sub-divided the existing Vicariate of Western Oceania whose vicar apostolic was Bishop Pompallier working in New Zealand, to create the new vicariates of Melanesia and Micronesia. The latter was to be held in reserve for Bishop Pompallier in case he should be expelled from New Zealand now that Britain had claimed that country as a colony.

On 21 July 1844, Cardinal Fransoni, head of *Propaganda Fide,* consecrated Epalle as bishop for the vicariates of Melanesia and Micronesia. He was expected to establish a mission territory that would eventually become a diocese. As this diocese was not yet established he was ordained as Bishop of Sion, a 'titular see'; a diocese that once existed but no longer functioned as such. Verguet and Dubreul attended the ceremony in the chapel of *Propaganda Fide*. The next day the three of them had an audience with Pope Gregory XVI who referred to them as '*tutte tre giovinotti*' – all three youngsters. Epalle was thirty-three, Dubreul thirty and Verguet twenty-seven years of age. Fransoni, on behalf of *Propaganda Fide*, gave some funds for the mission. By far the bulk of their funding came, however, from the French lay organisation with the similar name: *Propagation de la Foi.*

Verguet used his time in Rome to improve his artistic skills in the Roman schools of painting. Bishop Epalle drew up various plans for his vicariates. In fact, the Marists never entered the vicariate of Micronesia which consisted of the Gilbert, Marshall and Caroline Islands. As the name suggests they are small island groups scattered across an enormous area of the Pacific Ocean.

Lyon (again)

On 8 August the three Marists were back in Lyon. At the beginning of September 1844, Dubreul visited the *Société orientale* at Paris and was together with Montrouzier and Verguet inscribed as 'corresponding members'. The Oriental Society was particularly interested in the Orient, Algeria and the French Colonies, but also discussed and published material on 'the geography, the history, the literature, the sciences, the religions, the mores and the customs of the peoples of diverse regions.' A parallel would be the later American organisation: the National Geographic Society.

In September the Marists held their annual retreat in Lyon. During this retreat, Verguet, Montrouzier, Thomassin and Brother Prosper made their religious profession as members of the Society of Mary. Their time of initiation was complete and they were now members of the congregation. The ceremony ended with a lengthy sermon, which was given by Montrouzier. The Retreat concluded in a similar fashion and it was Verguet who gave the final address. It was the custom that these talks were given by the younger fathers.

Paris

In November, Verguet and Montrouzier went to Paris to prepare for their expedition. Verguet visited the church of *Notre-Dame des Victoires*, a Marian shrine, to pray and called at the Rothschild Bank to get money. He visited Saint Sulpice, the seminary where he had studied, and gave a talk to the students about the missions. The Marist group called on various government officials seeking backing for the mission to the Solomons. Montrouzier and Verguet visited Édouard Dulaurier, a famous Orientalist. Their mission was perceived as being of scientific and national import as well as of importance to the Church. Montrouzier spent the time preaching on Sundays on the missions and visited many 'savants' where he got useful advice for his work as naturalist. They enquired about a ship leaving Le Havre for Australia but found none available.

Bishop Epalle joined them in Paris. He wrote to the Council of *Propagation de la Foi* about his plans for the mission. Maps of the Solomon Islands did exist, though often inaccurate and incomplete. Epalle went across to London, from where he wrote that he had found a suitable ship, the *Bussorah Merchant* of 600 tons.

London

The mission band assembled in London. Claude Jacquet had left the archdiocese of Lyon without permission from his bishop. Epalle, busy with preparations, assumed that everyone had the necessary clearances. This lack of proper process was to understandably upset Jacquet's bishop who communicated this to Colin, the Marist General. However before any of the consequences of this jurisdictional dispute could be applied to either Epalle or Jacquet they had both been killed.

This was the eleventh band of missionaries to be sent to Oceania by the Marists. It numbered 14 men, one of the largest groups to go. Epalle was thirty-six years of age as they set out.

With the Bishop were seven priests and six brothers:

Fathers (age at departure):

- Etienne Chaurain (25)
- Jean-Pierre Frémont (24)
- Claude Jacquet (22)
- Xavier Montrouzier (24)
- Jean-Marie Paget (26)
- Joseph Thomassin (26)
- Léopold Verguet (27)

Brothers (religious name in brackets):

- Claude (Bertrand) Besselles (30)
- Jean (Aristide) Brun (23)
- Joseph (Hyacinth) Châtelet (27)
- Jean-Pierre (Gennade) Rolland (27)
- Augustin-Prosper (Prosper) Rouesné (28)
- Charles (Charles) Vincent (41)

The brothers had been trained as catechists and helpers for manual work. They were lay religious, belonging to the Marist Brothers of the Schools, a group founded by Marist priest Marcellin Champagnat. The priests were better educated than the brothers, thanks to their years of seminary training. Montrouzier was a Sorbonne-trained naturalist, and before they left, Colin had asked him to send scientific reports on the islands. Epalle had worked as a Marist priest-missionary for four years among the

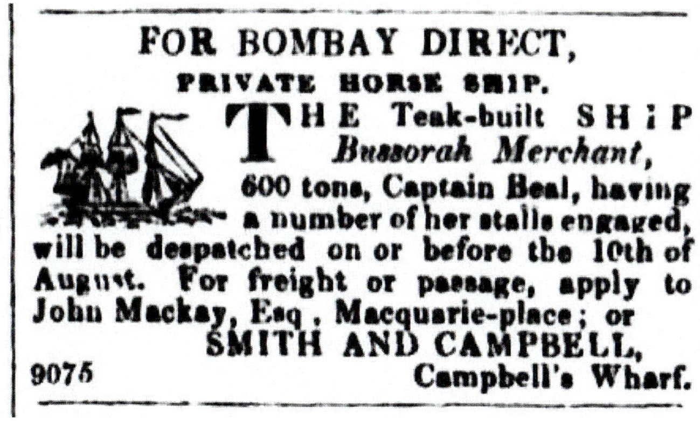

Advertisement placed in the *Sydney Morning Herald* 26 June 1845

Maori in New Zealand before returning to France to report and to raise funds. He was the only one of the group with mission experience, though the Polynesian Maori with whom he had worked are an entirely different culture from the Melanesian Solomon Islanders. Verguet was a talented artist and set out equipped with art-supplies including his sketchbook. He was tasked to record what he saw and send back pictures.

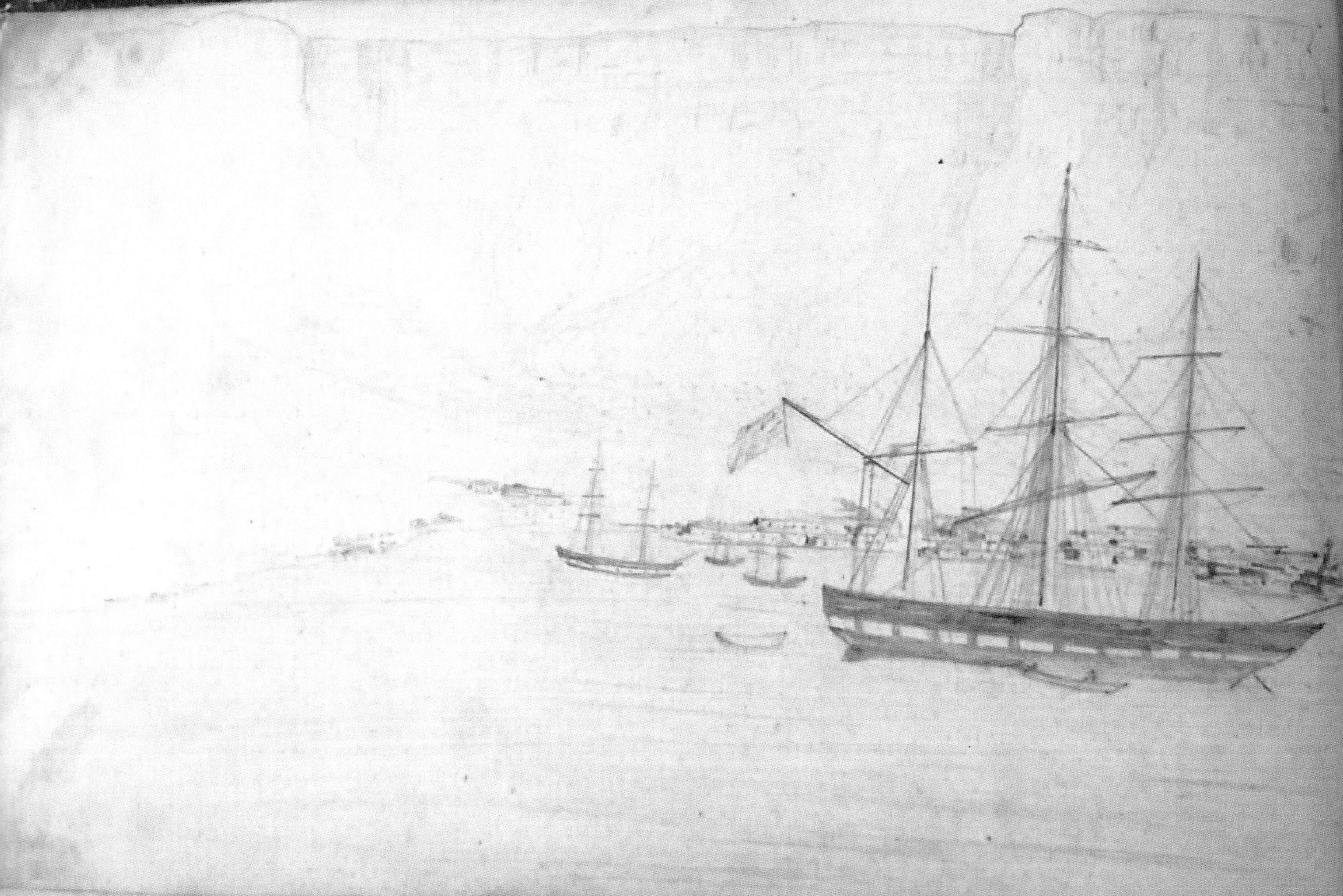

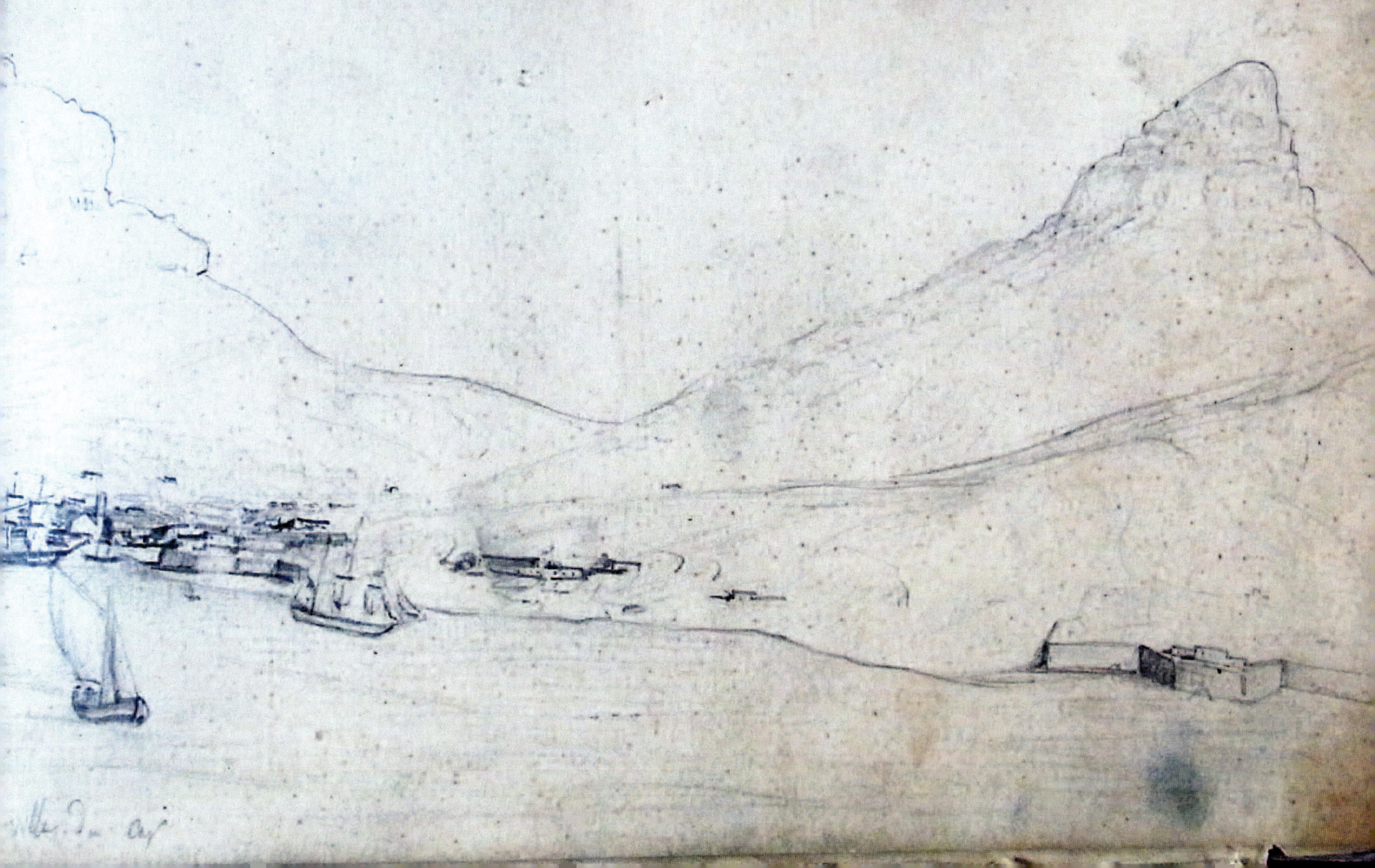

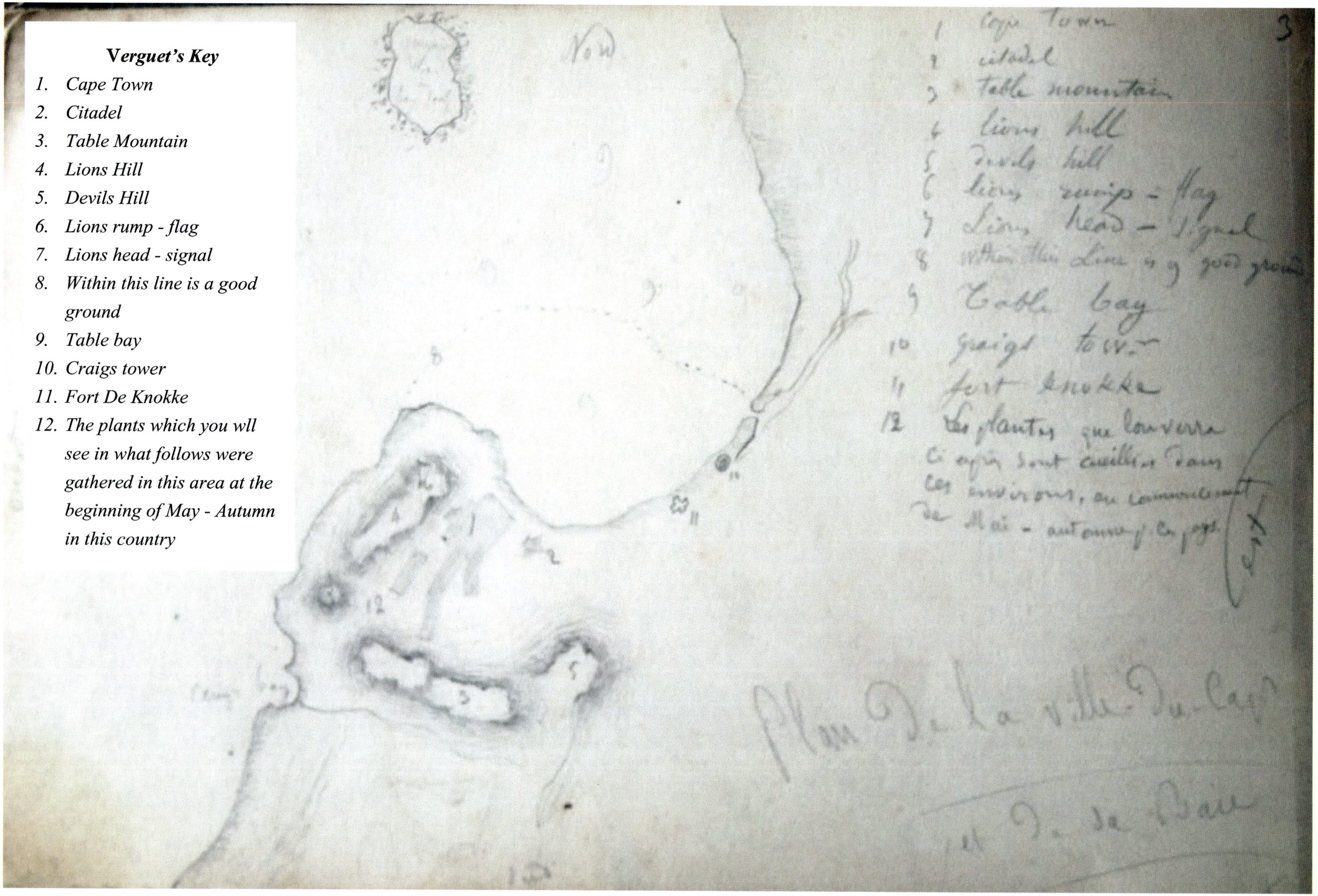

Verguet's Key

1. *Cape Town*
2. *Citadel*
3. *Table Mountain*
4. *Lions Hill*
5. *Devils Hill*
6. *Lions rump - flag*
7. *Lions head - signal*
8. *Within this line is a good ground*
9. *Table bay*
10. *Craigs tower*
11. *Fort De Knokke*
12. *The plants which you wll see in what follows were gathered in this area at the beginning of May - Autumn in this country*

The Journey London – Cape Town

February-May 1845

The voyage from London to Cape Town took three months. They departed London on 2 February 1845 and arrived at the Cape on 1 May. Their arrival was duly reported by the *Annales de la Propagation de la Foi*. Their comments in letters give us an idea of life on board. Verguet considered Captain Beal to be anti-Catholic, to the extent that even other non-Catholic passengers began to defend the Marists from his jibes. Frémont reported to the Superior General that they had followed their religious rule of life while on board; reciting the Office, doing their spiritual reading and continuing the other practises and, in addition, had classes each day in either theology, liturgical rubrics or English. Without going into detail he mentioned problems with Brother Prosper. Writing later, after they had arrived in the Solomons, Montrouzier, contrasted the latter part of their travels with this first leg. 'What a pleasure to travel on the *Arche d'Alliance* with

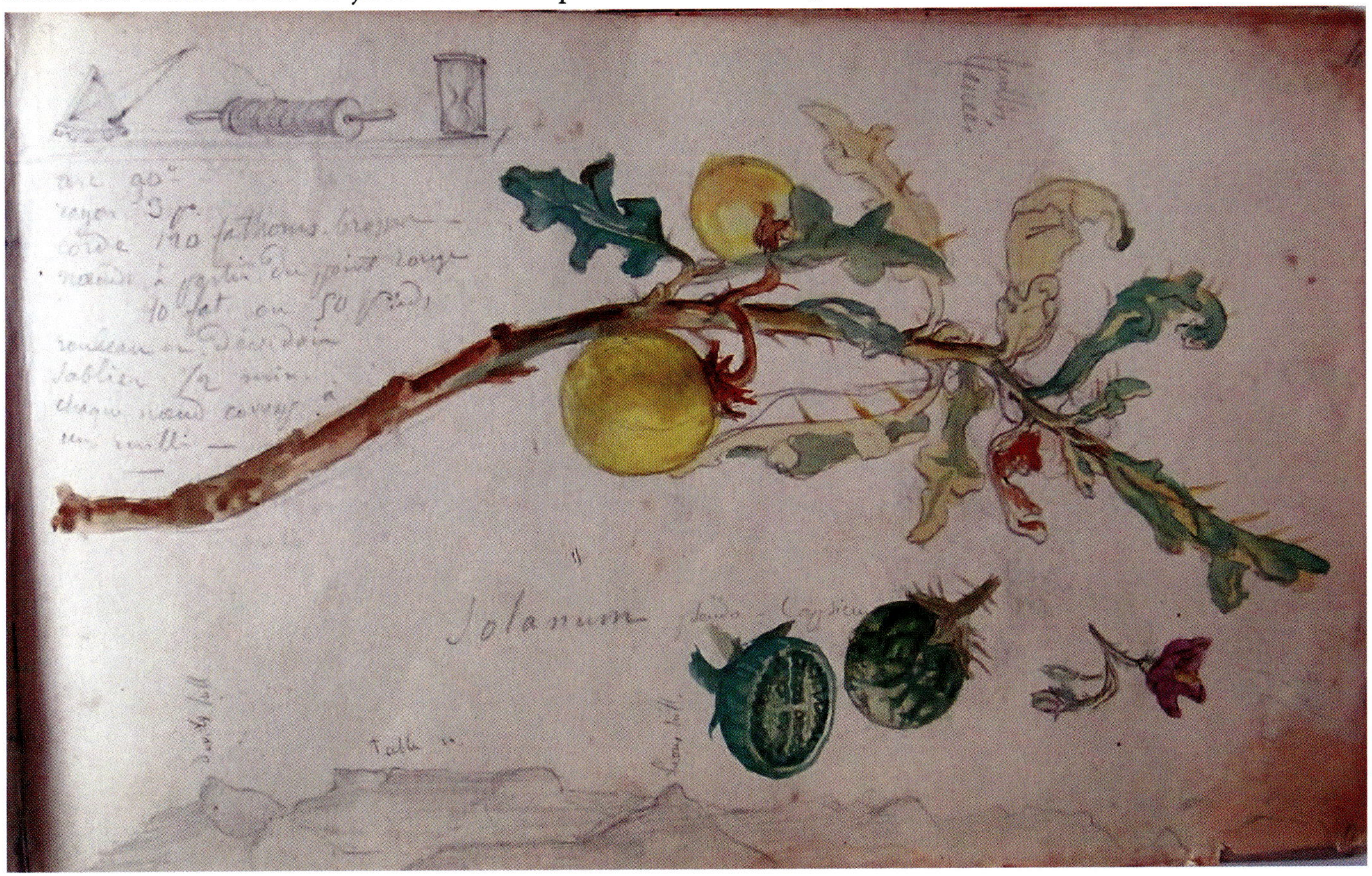

Verguet's varied interests: How to do depth soundings; Table Mountain from the sea; a plant which he identified as *Solanum Pseudocapsicum*. The purple flower suggests it is *Solanum Mauritianum*.

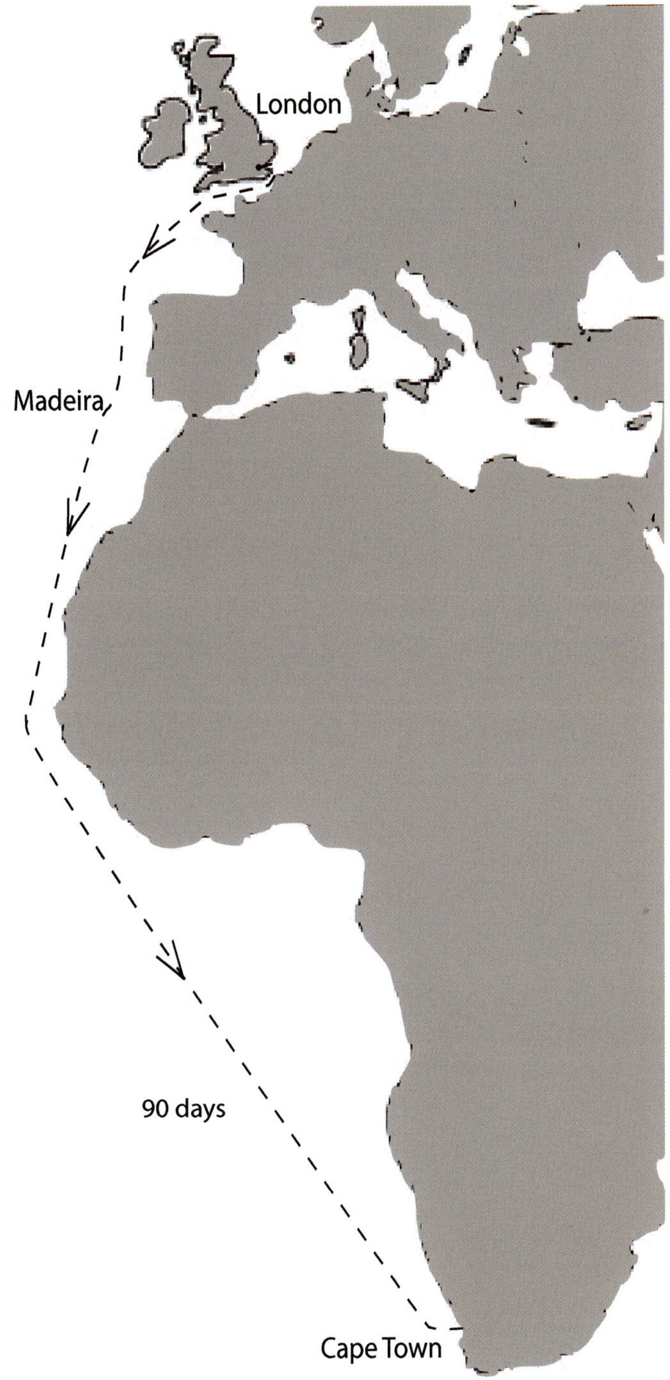

Auguste Marceau, with mass and prayers and peaceful conversations compared to the disputes and difficulties on the English ship from London to Sydney.'

The difficulties that the missionaries experienced in sea travel were not restricted to English ships. In 1843, Fathers Moreau, Bernard, and Chouvet travelled on board a French navy ship, the *Rhin* (Captain Auguste Bérard) from France to Australia. Moreau described for Colin the difficulties they suffered from the crew, officers and pupils of the *Ecole de Marine*, their ridicule against church, clergy and religious, especially Jesuits, and their language and behaviour much of which he found abominable. For that reason he would not like to have brothers travel on such a ship in order to protect their moral life or priests who do not have a very good education – otherwise 'they will have themselves eaten' by the officers. On the other hand, Moreau details the advantages: the journey is free, the ship is big and well-directed which softens the danger of sea sickness, and the provisions are good: French food and drink and doctors on board.

The *Bussorah Merchant* with Epalle's party called in at Madeira enabling mail to be put ashore for another ship to take back to Europe. Montrouzier began working on a 'natural history' and in the letter to his parents discusses books on the Bible and on Protestantism that might be useful in debate with the missionaries of other churches.

From the first to the fourth of May 1845 the group stayed in Cape Town, South Africa. We have descriptions and drawings from Montrouzier and Verguet. They climbed the Cape peninsula and collected samples of the vegetation. It was their first experience of being outside Europe, with people of a different race and culture, but only a stopover on their long journey to the Pacific.

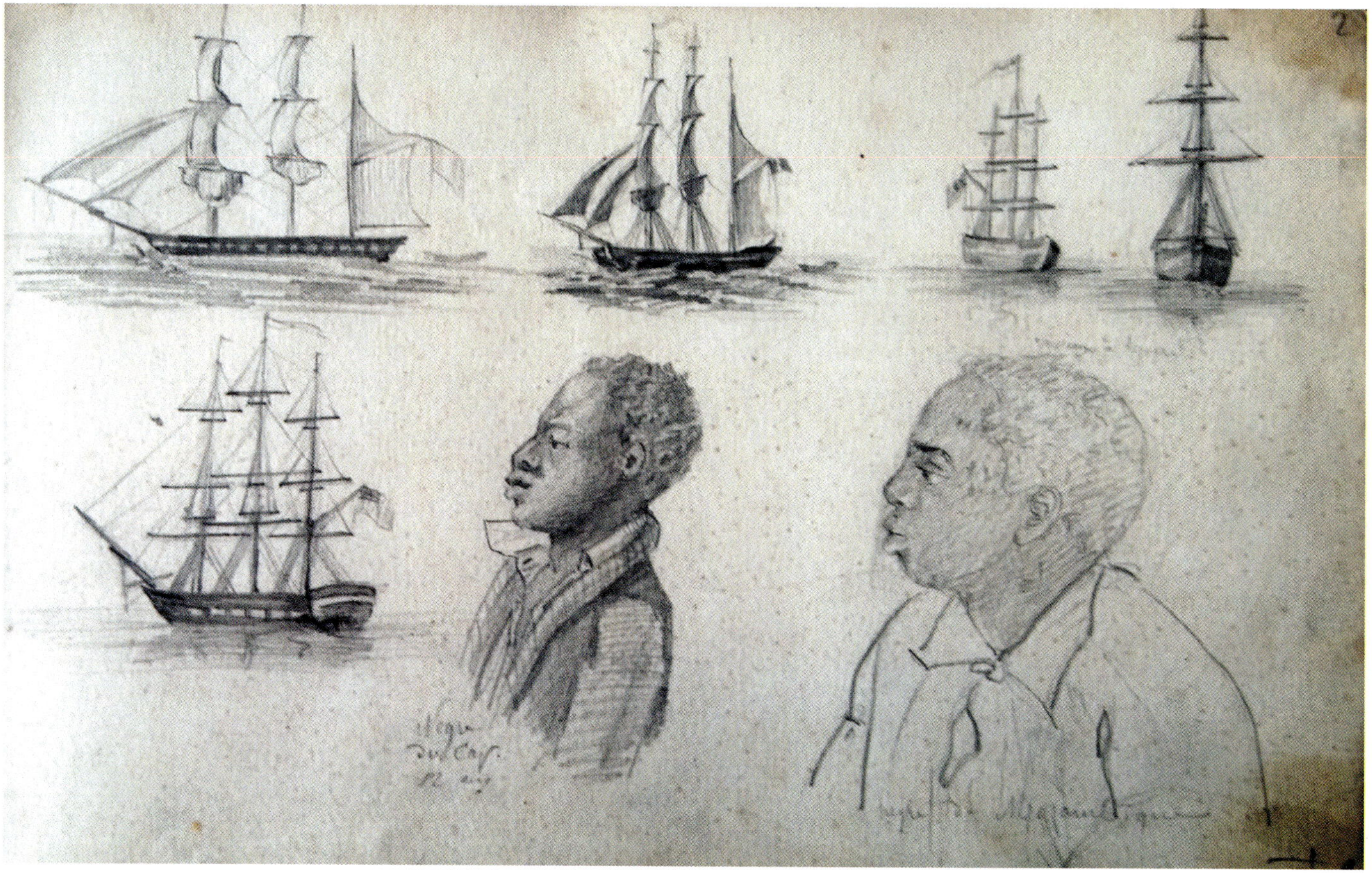

Verguet sketches ships (perhaps different views of the *Bussorah Merchant*) and draws a portrait entitled 'Negre du Cap' putting alongside for comparison purposes a sketch of a 'Negre du Mozambique'

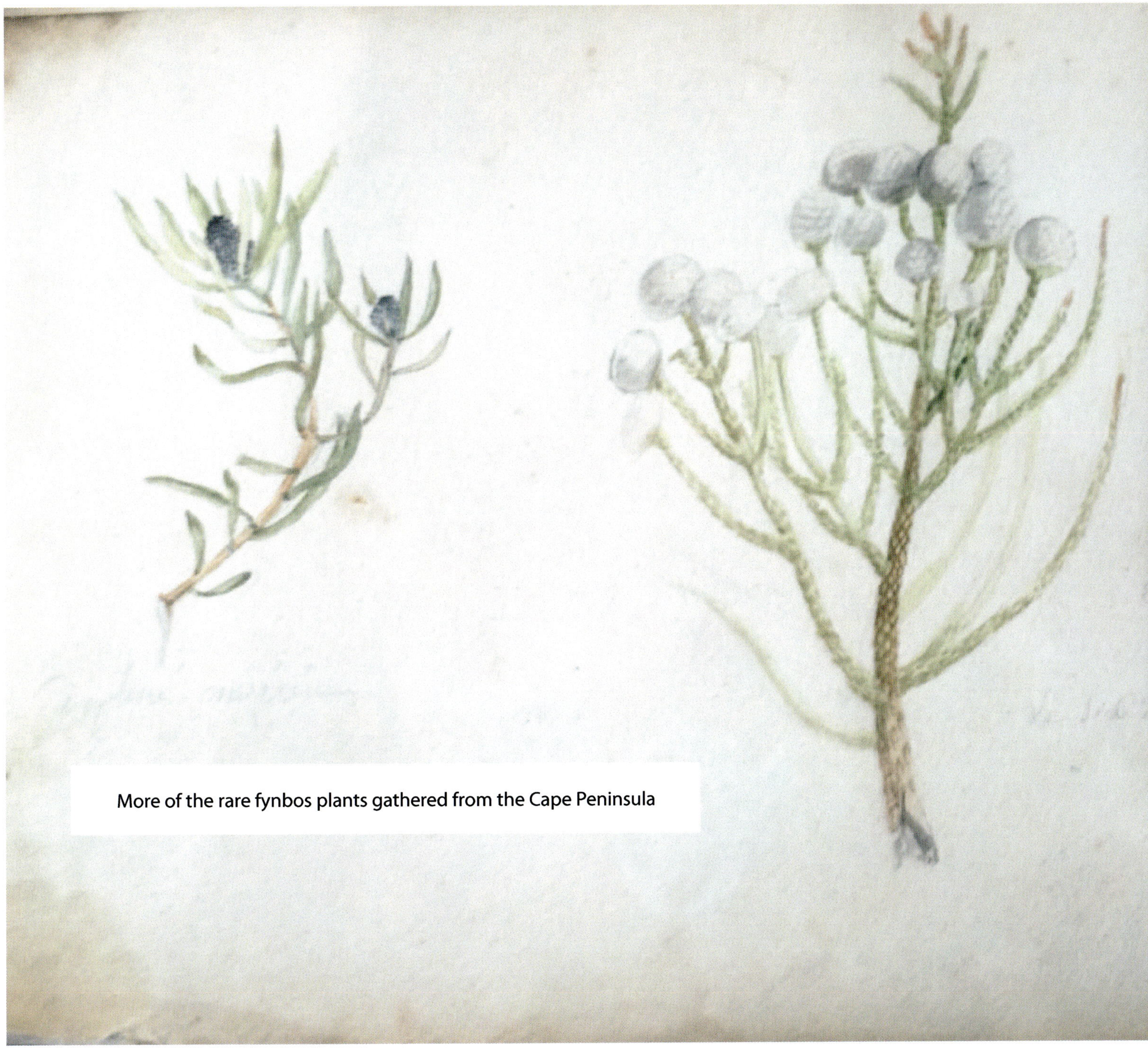

More of the rare fynbos plants gathered from the Cape Peninsula

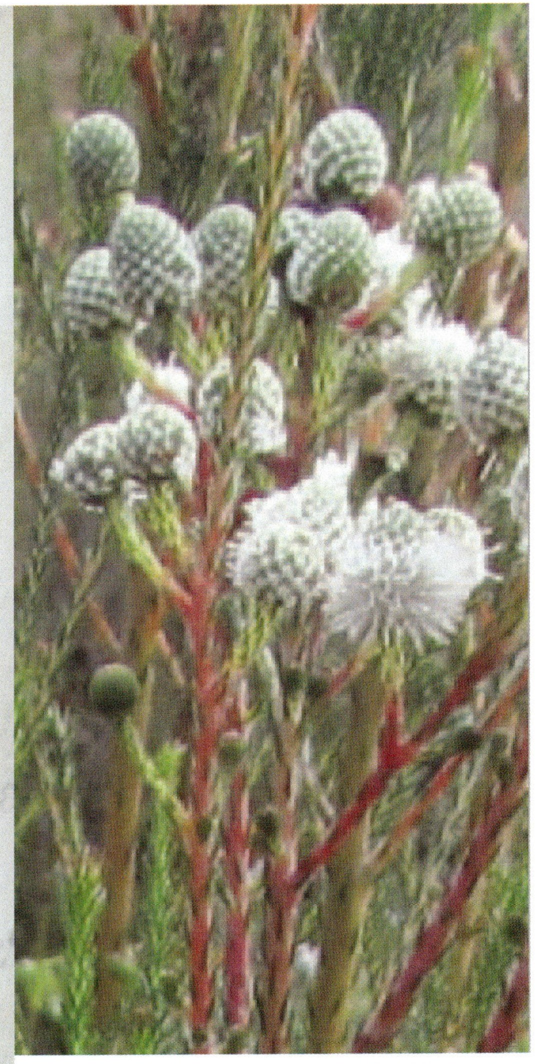

White Fynbos photographed by Dr Evelyn Mervine

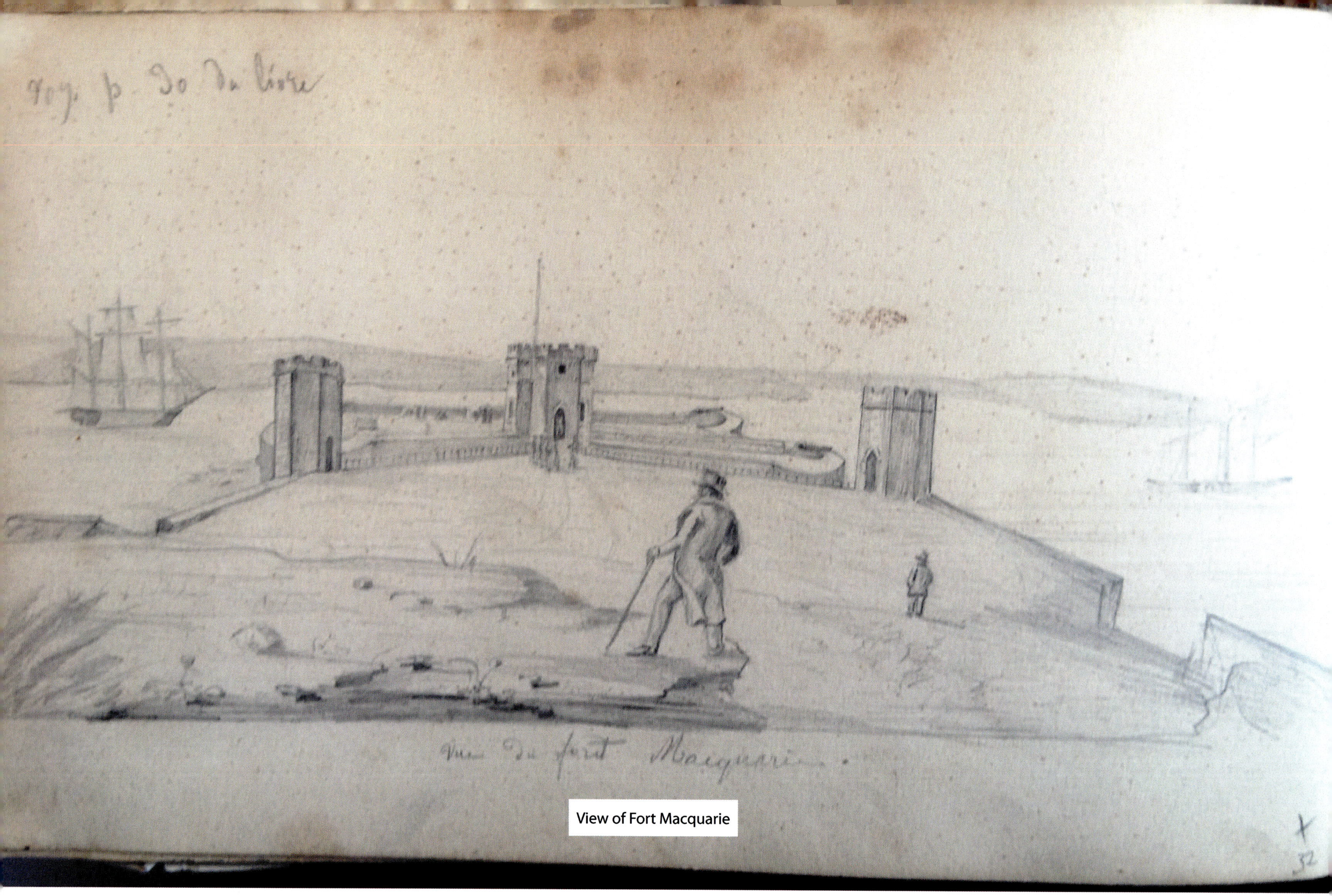

View of Fort Macquarie

Surviving the Storm

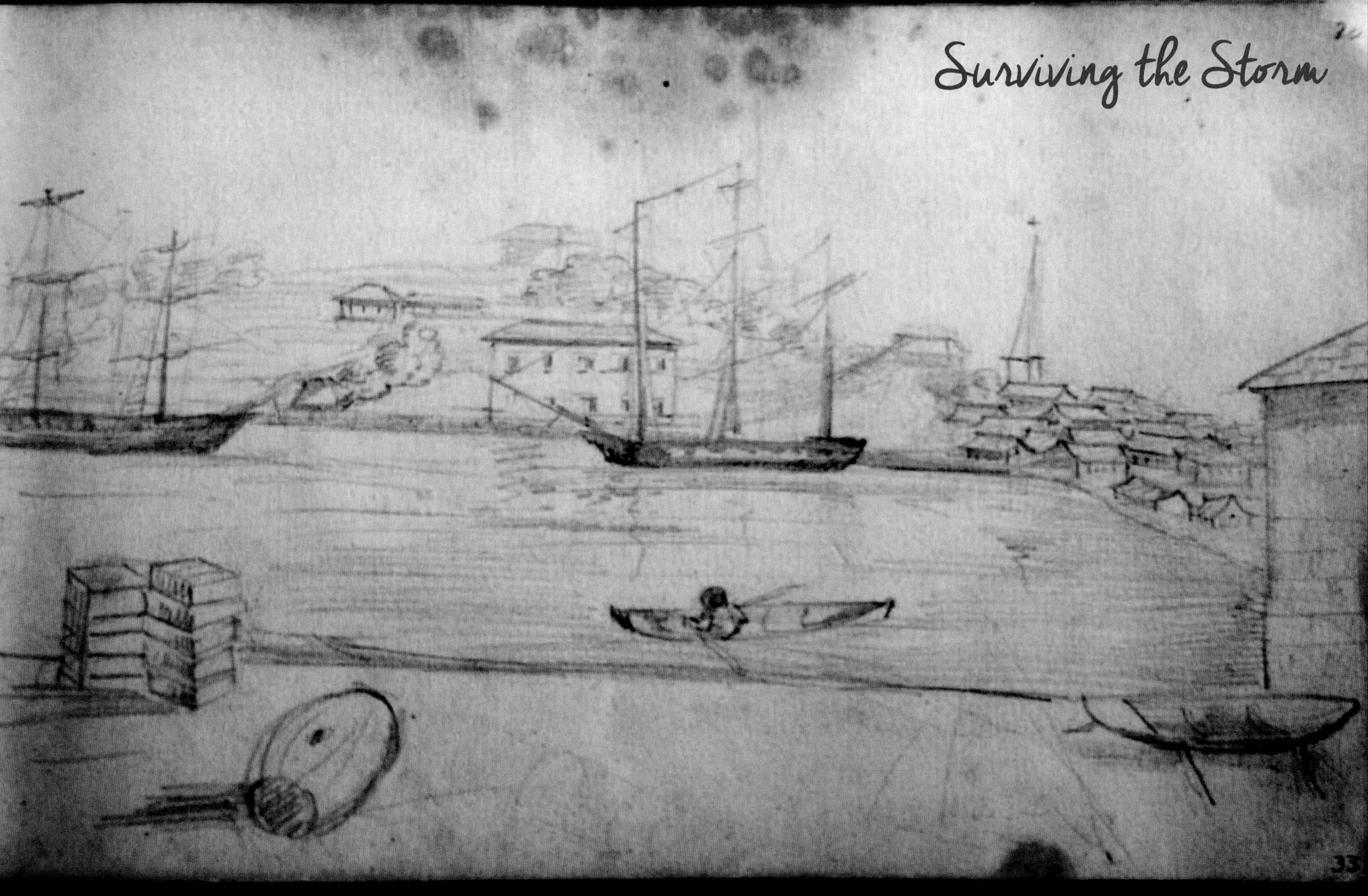

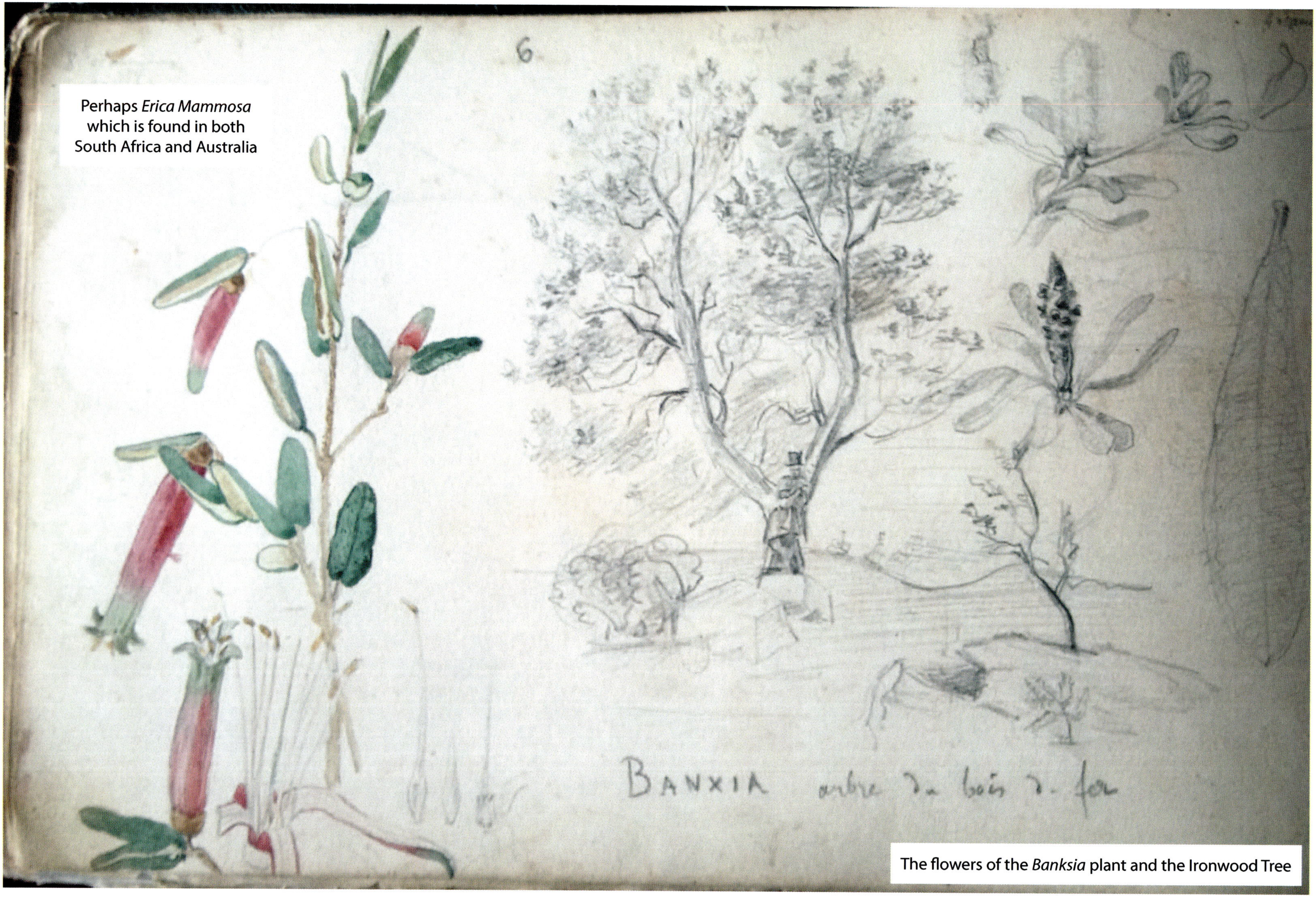

Perhaps *Erica Mammosa* which is found in both South Africa and Australia

The flowers of the *Banksia* plant and the Ironwood Tree

The Journey Cape Town - Sydney

May-June 1845

On 4 May 1845 the *Bussorah Merchant* set sail for Sydney with its band of missionaries aboard. The trip around the Cape was tranquil and they thanked God for the good weather. Unfortunately it did not last. The next stretch of their journey was dogged by a series of heavy storms. Epalle and others were badly seasick and the trip took longer than expected. Finally, as they were behind time and somewhat off course, the Captain decided to sail through Bass Strait between Australia and Tasmania rather than go via the longer route further south. This was a dangerous option; while they were in Sydney they heard the news of the migrant vessel the *Cataraqui* going down in Bass Strait with the loss of 414 lives.

June-October 1845: Long stay in Sydney

Finally, on 22 June, they reached Port Jackson the harbor of Sydney. The Marists wrote back to Lyon about their arrival. Epalle described the journey as pleasant except for the bad weather between the Cape and Sydney. They needed a good rest now. Fr Antoine Dubreul, who had arrived in Sydney earlier that year to be the Mission Procurator, mentioned that Epalle had been sick during the voyage but now felt better. He, Fr Jean-Louis Rocher, and Br Auguste were in Sydney looking to set up a supply base, a Procure, for the Oceania missions. According to Rocher, at that time Sydney was a town of 42,000 inhabitants, a third of whom were Catholic. There were three Catholic churches with a fourth under construction. The Marists stayed initially with Bishop Polding, the bishop of Sydney, but then shifted into their own house; a rented property next to the newly erected Procure in the pleasant suburb of Woolloomooloo.

Verguet sketched various monuments and views of Sydney. He visited and painted some of the Aborigines who came into the town. His description and drawings are very valuable in view of the paucity of firsthand accounts for the 1840s. After initial conflicts between natives and settlers, the aborigines withdrew to the interior. When Verguet was there some still lived nearby and ventured into the town. They slept in caves or in the bush, some living near the house in Woolloomooloo. They made a

ARRIVAL OF THE RIGHT REV. DR. EPAILLE.

ON Sunday last, the Right Rev. Dr. Epaille, Vicar Apostolic of North-western Oceanica, accompanied by seven clergymen and six lay brothers arrived in Sydney by the *Bussorah Merchant*. His Lordship and suite we are happy to say, have all arrived in good health, although the voyage was a somewhat tedious one; the *Bussorah Merchant* having met with a succession of heavy gales after having left the Cape of Good Hope on the 4th May. It is not yet known at which of the islands his Lordship will fix his residence, and it may probably be some few weeks before he takes his departure from Sydney.

Bishop Epaille previous to his elevation to the episcopacy, was for some time engaged on the mission at New Zealand, having filled the office of Vicar General to the Right Rev. Dr. Pompallier.

Sydney *Morning Chronicle* - 25 June 1845

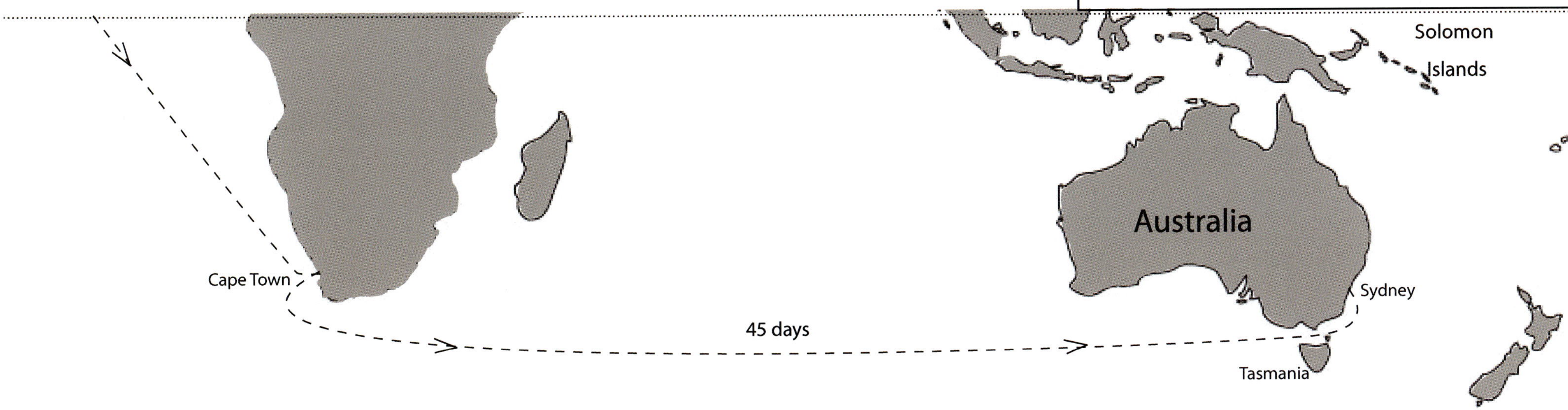

Aborigines

During my stay in Sydney, I made several pastel drawings of Australian natives. I am leaving them with Father Dubreul; he will send them to you at the first opportunity. The box of colours which I bought in Paris for the mission has not been found. It was lost on the ship, the Bussorah Merchant, or it may have been forgotten in London. - 18 October 1845

little money by selling gum to the settlers, of which, according to Verguet, most was then spent on alcohol. He writes that the natives took over many vices from the Europeans and he discerns a recurring pattern: The Europeans bring vices and give bad example; the Protestant missionaries teach heresy; only the Catholic missionaries bring the true Christian culture, virtuous behavior and the true religion.

Verguet visited the tribe of Chief Tamara who camped near Double Bay. He found the aborigines to be timid but generally easy to approach. They allowed him to draw some portraits: Tamara himself, Belé, and a woman with a child. He sent the portraits back to Europe. Paget talked with Tamara about their religious beliefs. They were shy about Verguet painting them but enjoyed seeing the result.

The Marists stayed in Sydney longer than they expected to because of their need for rest and problems with their luggage as well as uncertainty about where to go and how to get there. Epalle's first plan was to start on Ponape in the Caroline Islands, while in Sydney his plans changed to the much larger islands to the north. Epalle wrote to Colin "all agree on New Guinea as the field of battle." A Captain Blaxland recommended San Cristobal where he had called several times and found the inhabitants less ferocious than elsewhere. Blaxland had proposed this to Protestant missionaries as well but they were afraid of the malaria on these islands. Since his time in Rome, Epalle had been considering the idea of New Guinea, in particular Waigeo, near Vogelkop, in western New Guinea. He had maps from Dumont d'Urville of Thousand Ships Bay on Santa Isabel. Plus, he wanted to open a station on Ponape so that the vicariate of Micronesia was not neglected.

In August Epalle reported to Colin and addressed the question of why they were still in Sydney: Firstly, the

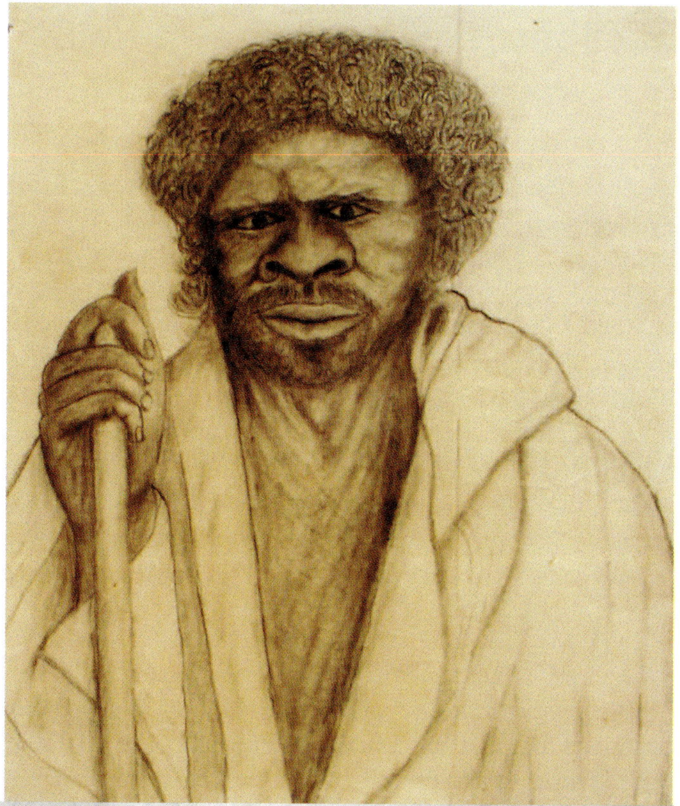

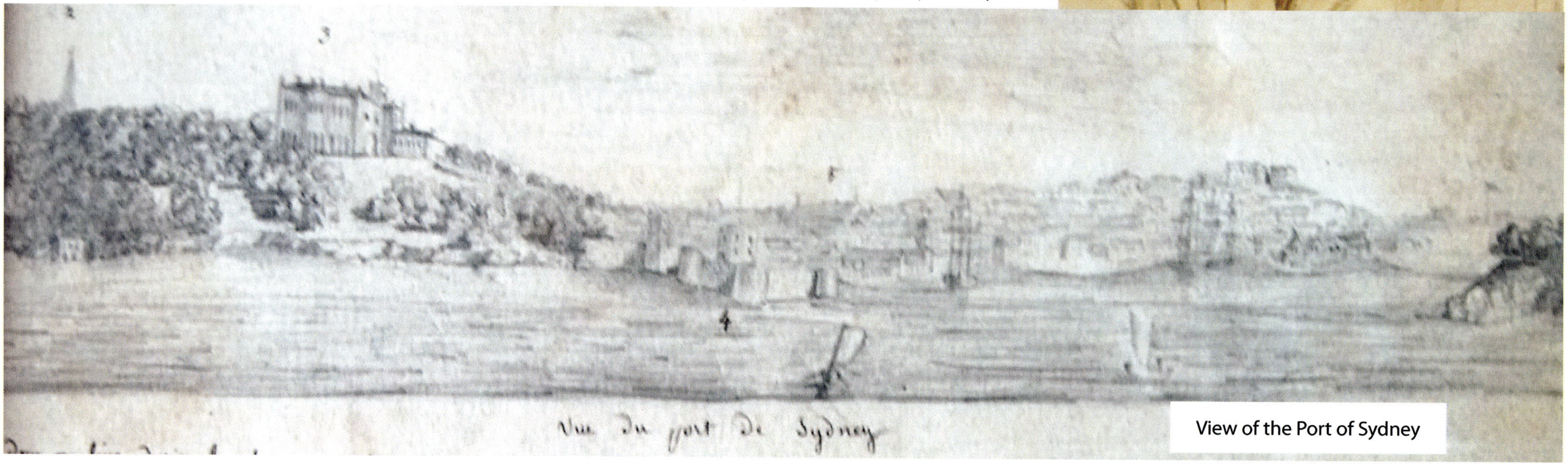

View of the Port of Sydney

Aborigines

...In a letter of 15 August 1845, I wrote to M. Gary, my brother-in-law, 'it is not rare to see near the entrance to Port Jackson gatherings of natives. The rocks of the coast provide many caves there, where they can pass the night sheltered from bad weather. Furthermore these semi-naked people are not fastidious about their choice of a sleeping quarter. In good weather the first place they come to will do. I have often noticed two who come to pass the night in a forest beside our house, opposite our windows. They light a little fire and then lie down, smoking a pipe to put them to sleep; when the man has smoked enough, he passes the 'tongue-burner' to his wife. Soon they are asleep and the fire is out... Those of them who decided to remain among the Europeans have become quite inoffensive people, but retain the distinctive characteristic of Australian natives. They are easy to approach and I have been able to study them at my ease. I have even drawn several of them, whose portraits I have sent to Europe... While I was drawing the portrait of a woman one of my confreres, Father Paget, who had joined me, questioned Tamara about his religious beliefs. The chief made himself understood in a kind of English jargon which the natives learn easily. He showed much good sense in his words; he was not embarrassed like the other natives; his eye was lively and sharp; he was conscious of this superiority. We learned from him that the savages of these parts believed in a being who created the sea, fishes, trees, axes, fire, in fact, everything. 'Where will you go, Tamara, if you are good', my confrere asked him. 'I will go to Heaven', he replied. 'And if you were wicked, where would you go?' 'I would go into the fire', he said. I have not changed his answers in any way. We spent all the morning there talking to these people and teaching them the catechism. They did not seem to me to be as deprived of intelligence as I had expected from reading the accounts of certain travellers...

luggage was damaged and took a long time to sort out. Secondly, Bishop Polding of Sydney was causing difficulties with respect to their supply base, the Marist Procure, because he wanted only Benedictine priests in his diocese. Finally, Bishop Pompallier of New Zealand was in town. Pompallier, Polding, Epalle and Dubreul had discussed the tensions between Pompallier and the Marists in New Zealand over the resourcing and manning of the Mission Stations. Colin and the Marists wanted viable religious communities, Pompallier wanted to spread his men as widely as he could. Epalle was deeply involved in this having spent four years in New Zealand, having worked as assistant to Pompallier, and having met with

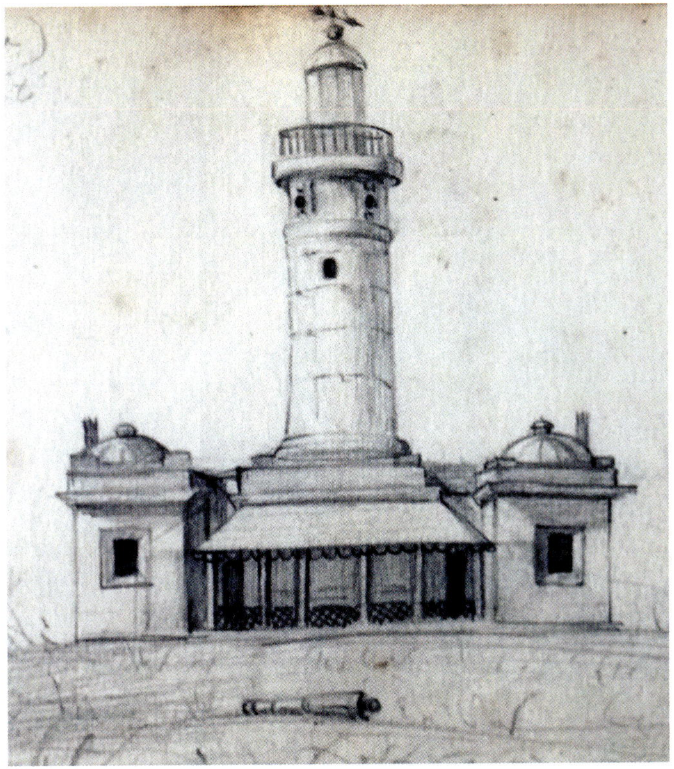

The Macquarie Lighthouse seen from Sydney
It was built in 1818 and replaced in 1893
Verguet's sketch is of the original
Australia's first lighthouse

New Zealand Wars

...The war in New Zealand is not to the advantage of the English; they have always been beaten by the natives. The governor has made some criticism of Bishop Pompallier for contributing a little to rousing the natives through his publications and books written in the Maori language. It is a calumny which will become a disadvantage to the one who has shamelessly put forward that suggestion without their being any proof. - 28 September 1845

Colin in France and Cardinal Fransoni in Rome. These discussions were intense and did not achieve their intent of healing the rift between the Bishop of New Zealand and the priests working in his diocese. Epalle informed Pompallier of the creation of the two vicariates of Melanesia and Micronesia and how they were intended to provide him and his priests a territory in which to work in the event of the English expelling them from New Zealand. Epalle mentioned that the long stay in Sydney had eaten into their funds so that he had decided to skip the planned visit to the Marist mission on the island of Wallis. Instead, they would go to the Solomons via the mission on New Caledonia which was rarely visited by ships.

Bishop Pompallier

...Bishop Pompallier is not well; yet from his voice we know that his chest is a little tired; if I can draw his portrait before leaving, I shall send it to you. Father Montrouzier is very busy with Natural History; he proposes to send you a rather large collection of plants from this country. We are going from time to time to collect specimens together. I have copied the plan of the intended store house; Father Dubreul will send it to you as well as that of Maryville which I have copied from off a government plan. The hot weather is beginning to be noticeable; we often go bathing. If we knew how to swim a bit that would help us a great deal in the case of a shipwreck. - 28 September 1845

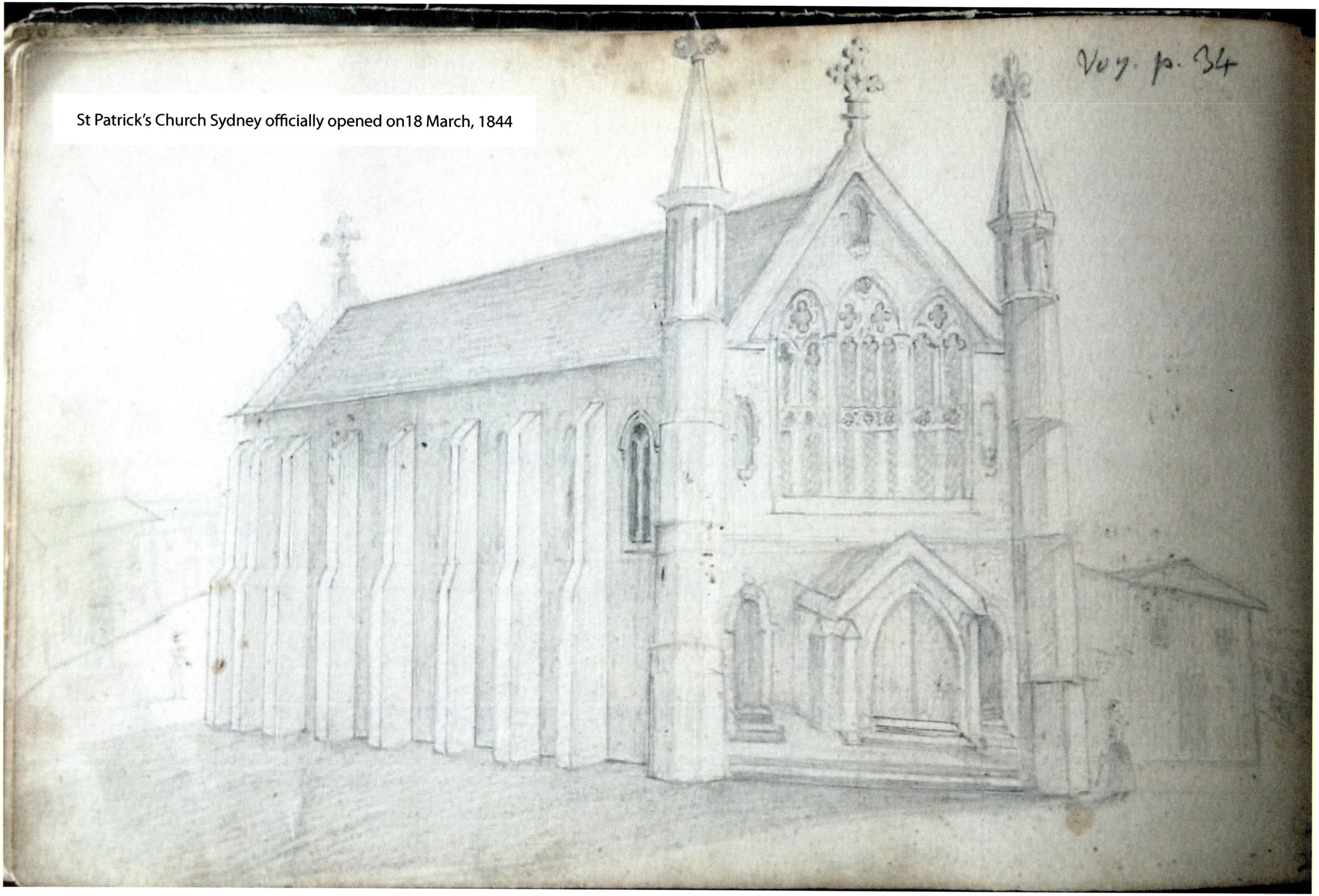

St Patrick's Church Sydney officially opened on18 March, 1844

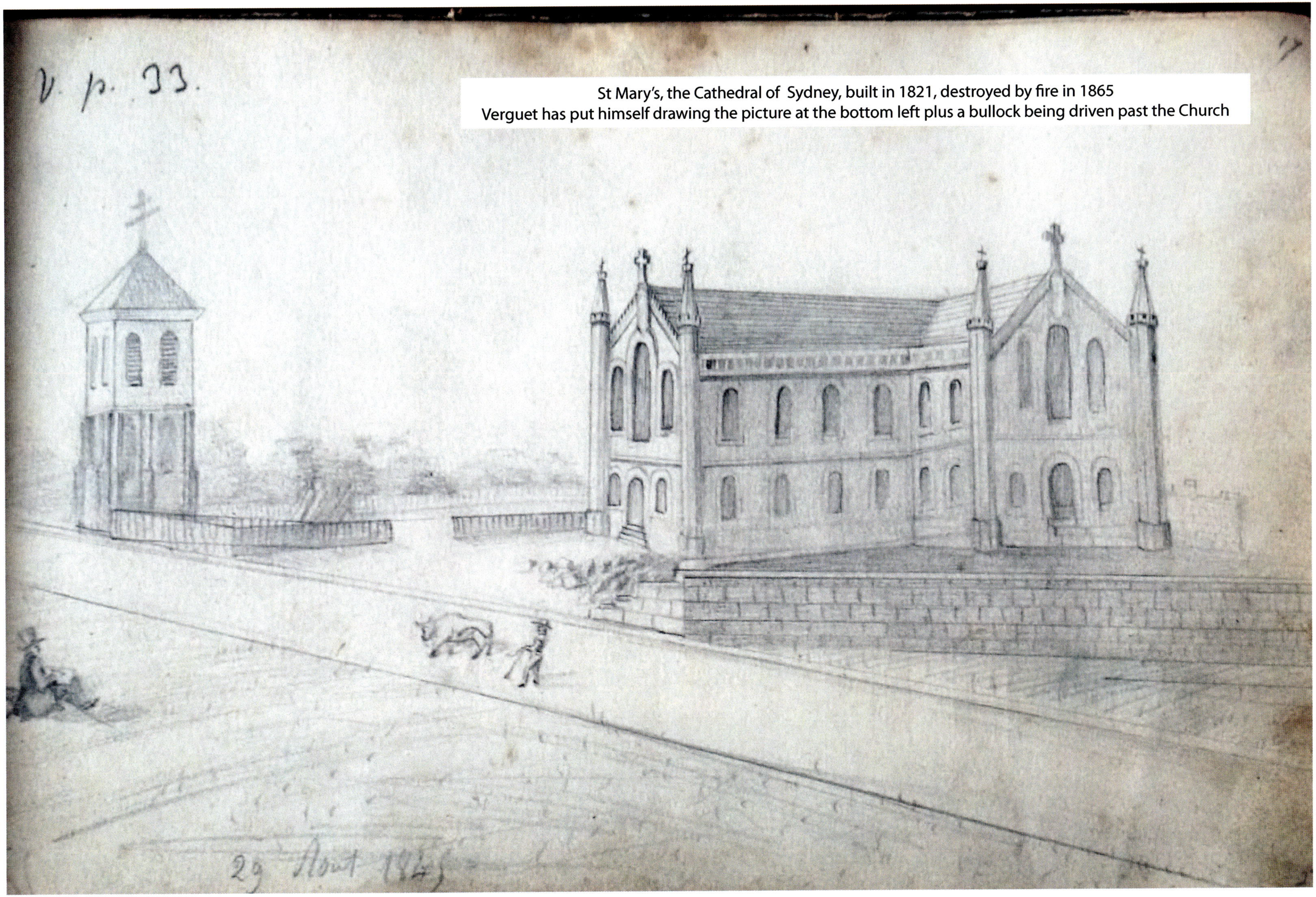

St Mary's, the Cathedral of Sydney, built in 1821, destroyed by fire in 1865
Verguet has put himself drawing the picture at the bottom left plus a bullock being driven past the Church

Pompallier & Hone Heke

Very reverend Fr Colin,

Bishop Epalle was afraid that in our letters to our parents or to our friends we might write about New Zealand or about Bishop Pompallier some things which it would be better not to say because of the hostilities which occur between the New Zealand natives and the English. Accordingly, Bishop Epalle recommended that we should not speak in our letters about Bishop Pompallier or about New Zealand. Already two letters had been written, one to my father and the other to a respectable priest of our region. Since the details which I give them seem to me to be interesting and since Bishop Pompallier says nothing about that in his letter about the attacks on Kororareka, I am sending this information to you, reverend father, so that you may become aware of them, and then you will do what you wish with my letters.

Allow me to add here some new details which Bishop Pomapllier gave us about Hone Heke. Bishop Pompallier knew this chief for a long time before these last victories of the New Zealand natives made him famous. Hone Heke was considered a very valiant man. He was reputed to like slaughtering people; after the victory he massacred those whom he defeated and pillaged those who had sold them arms and munitions. The first conversation of Bishop Pompallier with Hone Heke took place under these circumstances. The bishop was visiting a new tribe. A crowd of natives surrounded him and he spoke to them with goodness. He was often interrupted by those who spoke about Hone Heke. Heke was going to come, Heke was going to answer for them, Heke had many questions to ask. "That is good," said the bishop, "when Heke comes, I will speak with him. While waiting, listen to me."

John Heke arrived. He came forward calmly, full of reserve. He greeted the bishop (Ten-eracocohé); the bishop accorded him the same civility, and continued to talk about religion. The New Zealanders had led the bishop into a large building somewhat like a barn where they could all be together. Hone Heke went to sit on one of the highest beams in the building. He listened for a moment, then he attracted everyone's attention by these words which he addressed to Bishop Pompallier: "Hey, say now, stranger! You come to preach another religion to us, but do you know that many things are said against this religion? People say this, they say that, they say something else and again something else, etc." And there followed all the objections of the Protestants against penance, the church, celibacy, images, the honor given to saints, etc. While he was speaking, the bishop noticed that Heke had made a good choice for his position; from up there he dominated the assembly, and more than once he caused them to laugh at the expense of the Catholics. So as to have a position that would be just as advantageous, the bishop climbed up next to him and kept on smiling.

When Heke had finished speaking, the bishop took up his objections and refuted them one by one. He insisted on the unity of the church, the need for an infallible authority. He noted how recent Protestantism was and compared it to a cut and faded branch which still dared, despite its dryness, to pretend to be the tree from which it had been separated. Hone Heke listened attentively. The New Zealander never disputes just for the pleasure of disputing, but rather in order to find the truth. If he sees the truth, he cannot help but saying "that is true" and he does not bring up again a proposition which he has thus conceded. The conference of the bishop with Hone Heke had lasted about two hours. At the end, Hone Heke showed that he was very happy. He said to the bishop: "You are right, your religion is the only true one. What were you doing in your country, and why had you not come here twenty years ago? Today, we would all be for you." Then he addressed his own people: "The religion that this bishop preaches seems good to me. We should all practice it. The other religion is mere fantasy; this one is solid, it does not change.

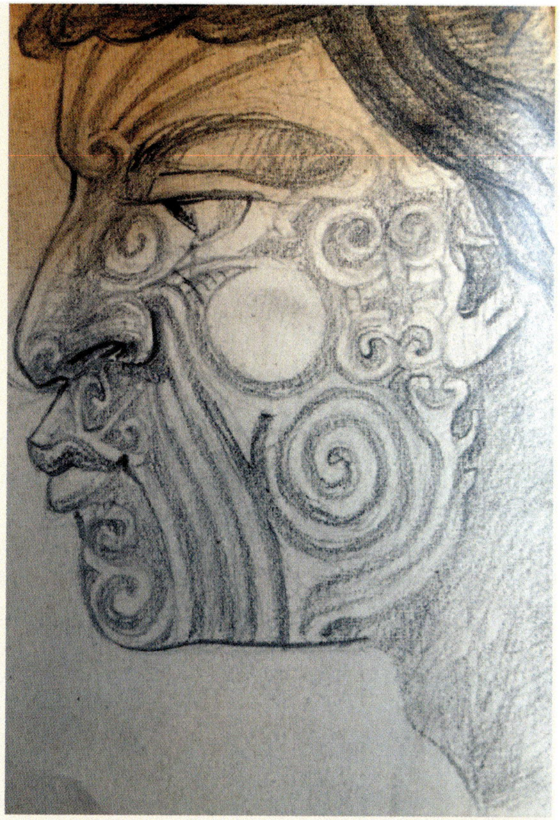

"The first conversation of Bishop Pompallier with Hone Heke took place under these circumstances.

From that moment on, Hone Heke never stopped having much respect for Bishop Pompallier and his missionaries while he showed only contempt for the Protestant missionaries and their bishop. Here are some examples. – The Protestant missionaries, before these last disturbances, thought they had the upper hand on the minds of the New Zealanders. They boasted that they led them with the greatest of ease and that they not only uprooted vices from their hearts but that they had removed even the most minor imperfections. In their eyes, smoking was a bad thing; when the Protestant bishop saw a New Zealander smoking, even if he were the chief of a tribe, he simply went and snatched the pipe from the man's mouth and smashed it against the earth. Hone Heke heard about this and was patient for a while, but finally, bursting with anger, he went and found the Protestant bishop. He had decided to do everything to give the Protestant bishop a good lesson. He went before him with a pipe in his mouth, sat down before him without saying anything and without taking off his hat. His terrible eyes said everything. The reformed bishop did not dare to do anything. Heke, seeing his cowardice, puffed big clouds of smoke in his face. The bishop did not have a word to say. Finally, Hone Heke spoke up: "There was a time," he said to him, "when you used to break the pipe of New Zealand chiefs who smoked in front of you. Take care not to do so again, this is the lesson I am teaching you now."

Another time, the Protestant missionaries went duck hunting in a pond that was taboo. They were warned to withdraw, but they despised these orders. The warnings were repeated, but they continued to hunt. Hone Heke ordered his people to fire bullets near their ears, and they made off very quickly. Heke was not satisfied with that; he went and found the bishop and asked for compensation.

"What do you want?"
"Horses."
"I don't have any."
"Well then, I'm going to extract payment."

And he turned to his men:
"You, take that belt; you, that carpet; you, these knives, etc."

The objects which suited him he had his men carry away, and warned the bishop to observe taboos better in the future.

One day, that same bishop, a sower of troubles and largely the cause of the war which has just broken out (that is the opinion of a Sydney newspaper. That newspaper, the Chronicle of the 4th of October, said that the English authorities in New Zealand took offense when the Protestant missionaries led the natives to shake off the yoke to become sole masters of the country. But God caused things to turn out differently. They have become embroiled in the ruin of their fellow citizens, and it could happen that the Catholic religion might come out of these struggles more triumphant than ever!) That bishop, I say, was speaking to Hone Heke in these terms when he saw that the war was not having the outcome he desired: "Why are you waging war? Haven't you signed the treaty in which you recognized the English as masters of the country?" Hone Heke answered him: "I read in Saint Paul that when he was a child he thought, he spoke and he acted like a child, and when he had grown up, he thought, spoke, and acted as an adult. I am doing the same thing. Then I acted as a child, today I am acting as a man."

I have the honour of being, very reverend father,
Your very humble and very affectionate servant

Léopold Verguet,
apostolic missionary

Sydney, 10 October 1845

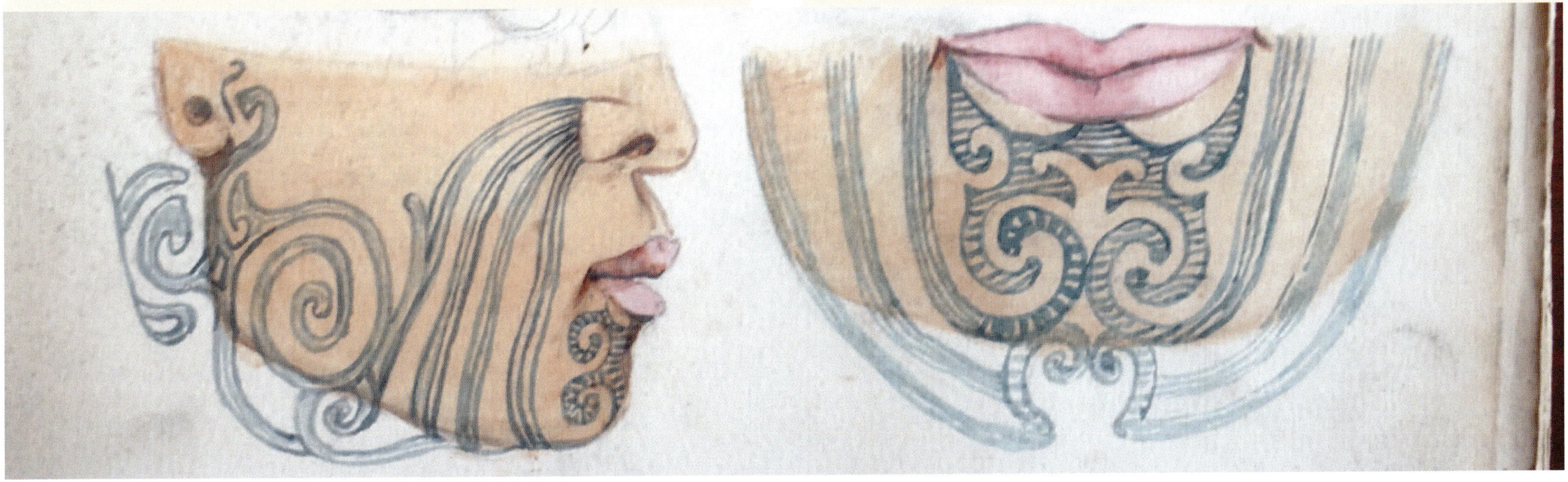

Verguet, first personal crisis:

28 September 1845

Jesus Mary Joseph

Very reverend Father Colin,

I am having some difficulty in telling you about what is on my mind because I feel it is not praiseworthy. Yet it is really necessary that I should talk to you about it. You yourself have asked me to write frequently, besides I am convinced that you will feel for me in my misery.

I feel so to speak an aversion in renewing my vows. On the ship, towards the end of the passage, I was of a mind not to renew them. At Sydney I was sent from one festival to another and it has been more than three months that we have been here without my being able to decide to make another step towards my final vows. Religious obedience frightens me now that I have experienced a little of it. I can't put an end to my own wishes. I do not think that I have done anything visible that can give my colleagues some doubts about the state in which I find myself. I speak about it only to my chaplain. I can't decide to talk about it to the bishop. If I listened to my own inclinations I would immediately leave the Marist Society because the bishop wants with him only those priests who are completely involved, but when I think of the confidence which you have shown you had in me in letting me leave before the end of my novitiate I would always reproach myself for not having responded to it. After a lot of hesitation I have finally decided to write back to you about it. I still love the missions a great deal; I am looking forward to being among the natives; dying there as a martyr would be for me the crowning joy. On the other hand I cannot cope with the idea of not seeing my parents again. I would like to return to my country in eight or nine years, if I am still alive. I would make the passage at my own expense and on arriving in France I would beg you to dispense me of my vows. I am of the firm opinion now that if this present state of worry persists, you will have no difficulty in dispensing me from my vows, when I beg you to do so. My wanting to respond at least in some small way to the trust that you have shown in me behooves me to renew my vows at the same time as my colleagues. I will pronounce them with the intention of committing myself in a limitless way on the sole proviso that you will be able to dispense me from them.

I have the honour, very reverend father, of being your very affectionate servant and unworthy son in Jesus and Mary,

Léopold Verguet
Society of Mary

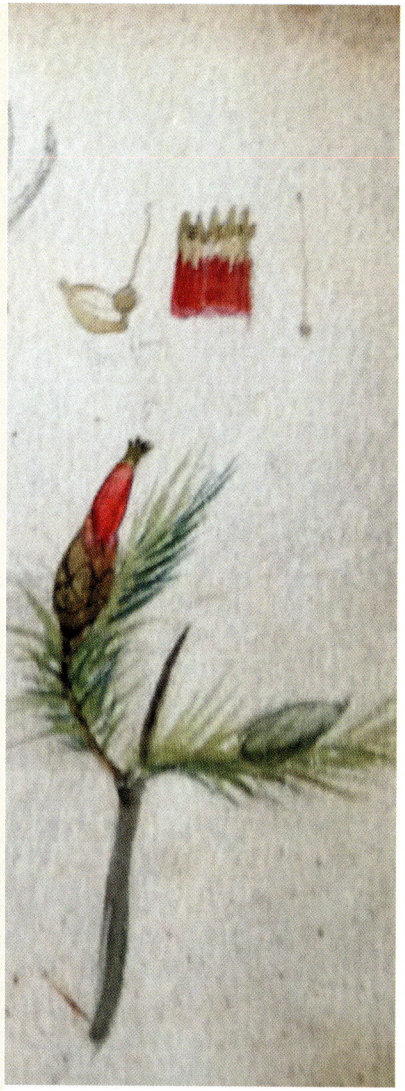

Apart from the problems of travel, language, church authorities and uncertainty about their final destination, the group was also experiencing internal difficulties. Verguet wrote to Colin with doubts about his religious vocation. Montrouzier wrote that, despite Epalle making him pro-vicar, he and the others criticize his administration and Montrouzier wanted to resign from the responsibility. There were other tensions in the group which were to emerge later. Thomassin did not see Epalle as a good leader and administrator but as a man 'building castles in Spain'. Thomassin and Montrouzier did not like each other. Verguet was critical of Epalle as leader. There were different concepts of how to conduct their mission: Epalle, influenced by Colin, wanted a religious convent; a big group living together. Frémont and others favoured a more dispersed outreach; groups of two or three missionaries who would be more dependent on the locals.

Before they left, Montrouzier sent back to France a parcel with plants and curios and Verguet posted plans of the Procure and drawings of the town and of aborigines.

23 October: Departure

Rocher had negotiated about a ship with Didier Numa Joubert a French merchant and ship owner. On 23 October 1845 at 3pm they set sail on board the *Marian Wat-*

EXPORTS.

October 23.—*Marian Watson*, schooner, Captain Richards, for the South Sea Islands: 15 casks and 7 bags biscuit, 1 cask lemon syrup, 5 barrels flour, 2 horses, 1 bull, 1 cow, 6 barrels beer, 2 quarter-casks wine, 10 cases and 1 hogshead wine, 2 c- ses olives, 1 cask sugar, 1 case plums, 1 bag coffee, 1 case drugs, 5 cases tools, 1 half-chest tea, 1 case linseed oil, 2 cases bells, 2 cases seeds, 1 case soap, 1 case plants, 1 cask nails, 4 baskets wine, 1 case snuff, 1 hogshead Geneva, A. Wilson; 1 quarter-cask brandy, W. R. Scott; 6 tierces tobacco, G. Thornton.

Sydney Morning Herald 23 October 1845

son, under Captain Richards, an Englishman. Their vessel was likened to Noah's Ark because of all the livestock and provisions they took. It was a spacious ship of 140 tons, described as one of the best-built ships in Sydney. Epalle had hired it for 110 pound sterling (2750 francs) per month. In addition he had to cover the daily food costs and the cost of the ship's return to Sydney. Colin was to consider the expense extravagant but, for what they wanted to do, there was no cheaper alternative in Sydney. Montrouzier described their departure to his brother Henri. In the morning, they received a blessing in the cathedral. Bishop Polding, Bishop Pompallier and many priests and lay people accompanied them to the ship. They were viewed as likely martyrs.

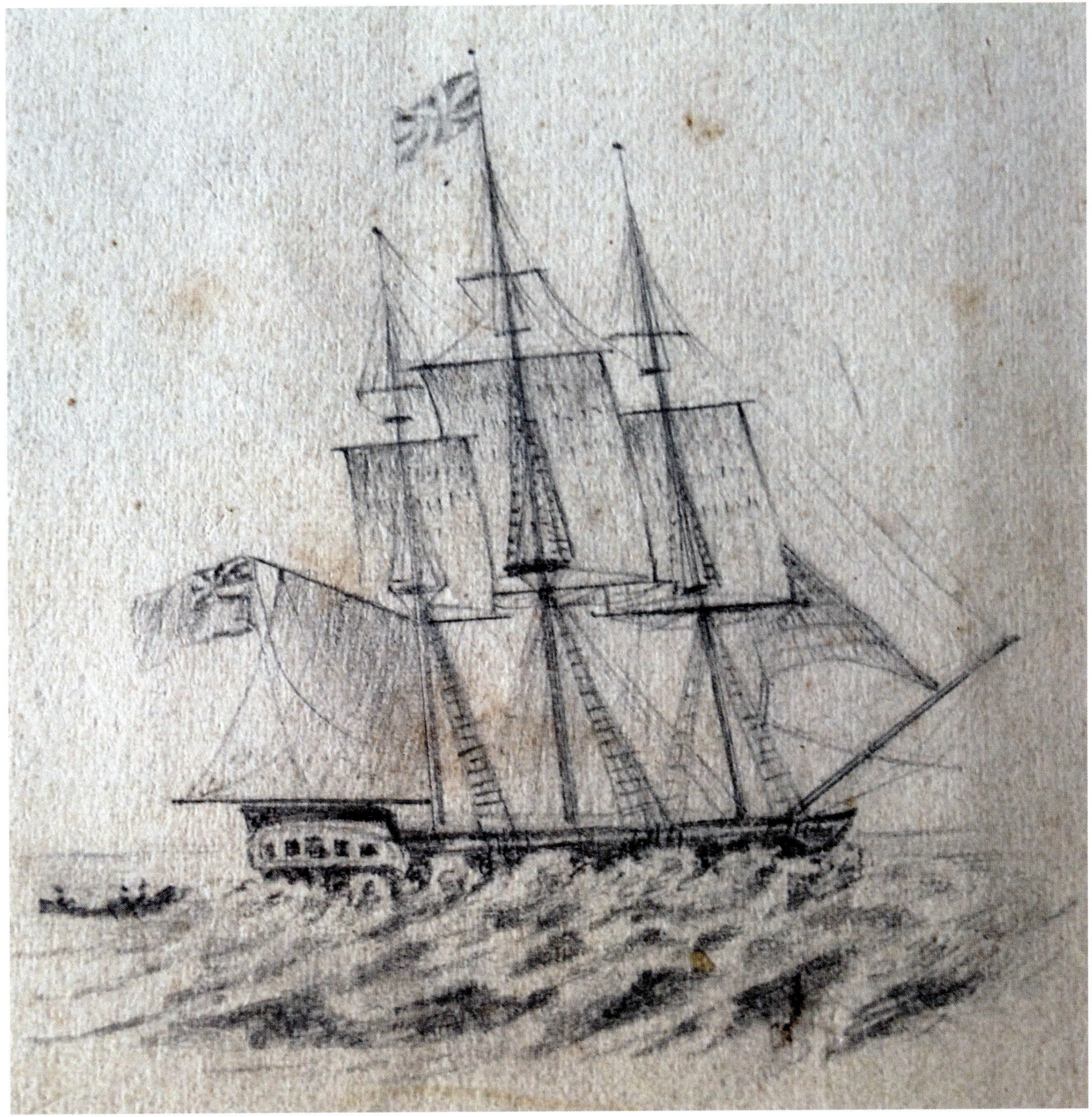

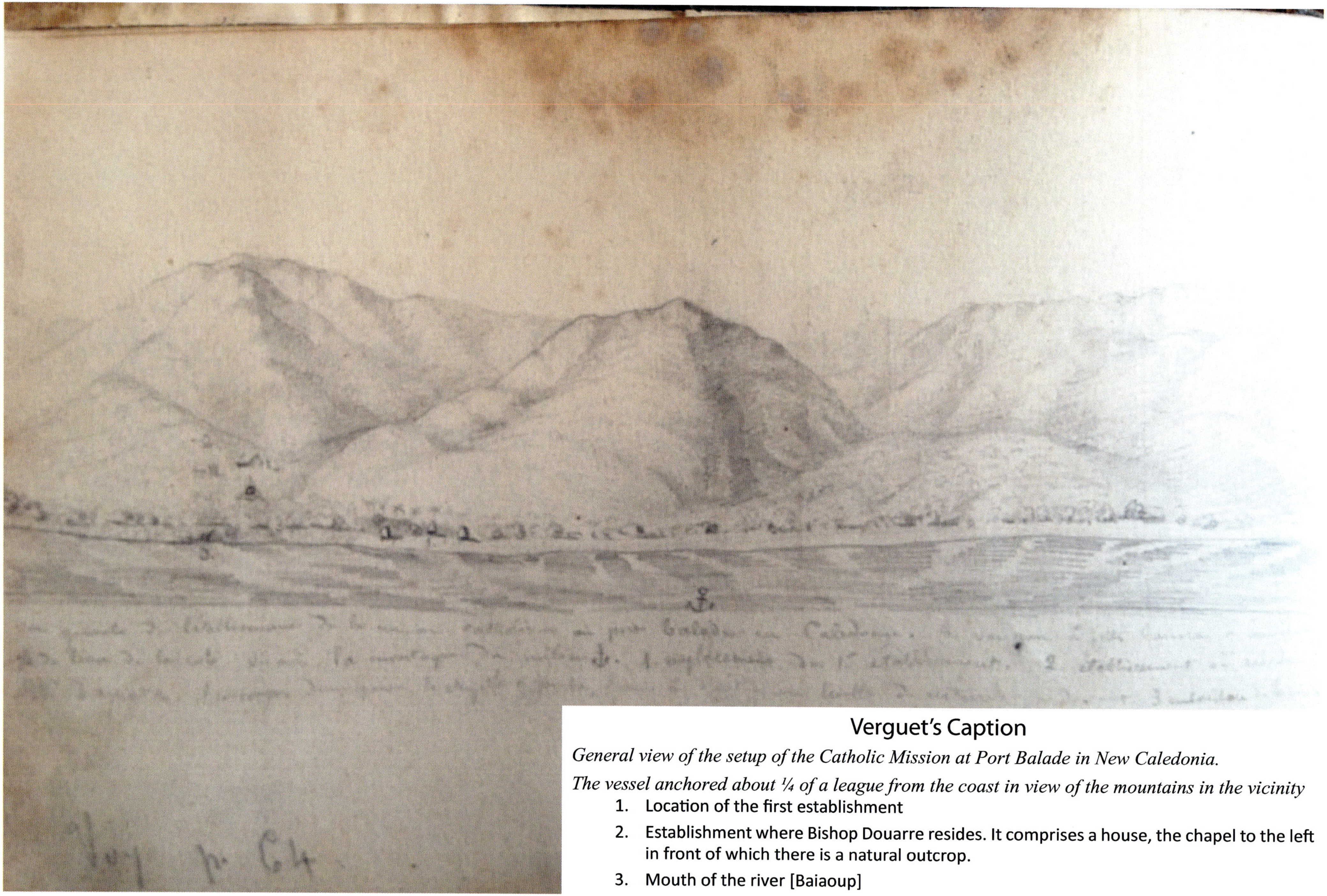

Verguet's Caption

General view of the setup of the Catholic Mission at Port Balade in New Caledonia.

The vessel anchored about ¼ of a league from the coast in view of the mountains in the vicinity

1. Location of the first establishment
2. Establishment where Bishop Douarre resides. It comprises a house, the chapel to the left in front of which there is a natural outcrop.
3. Mouth of the river [Baiaoup]

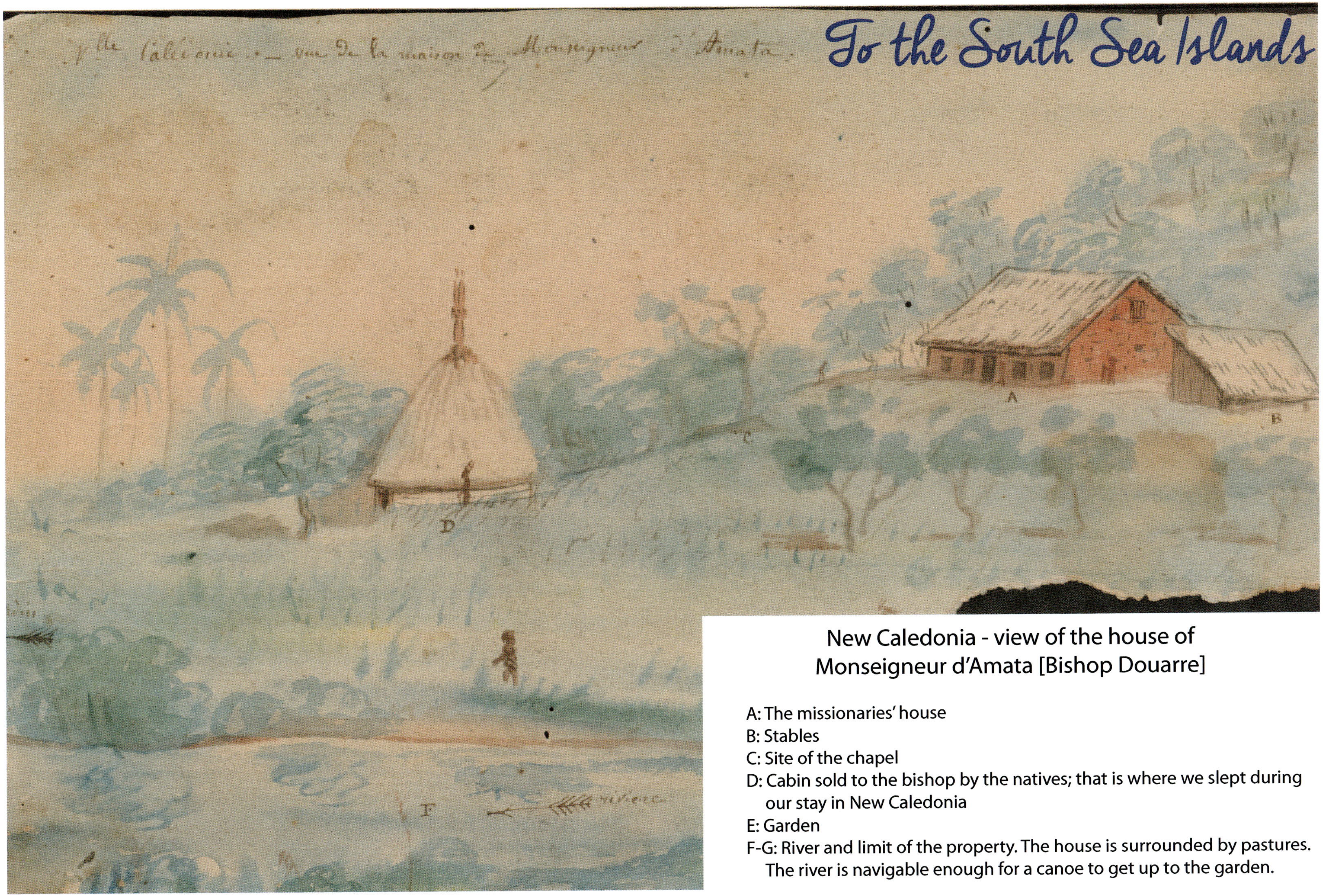

New Caledonia - view of the house of Monseigneur d'Amata [Bishop Douarre]

A: The missionaries' house
B: Stables
C: Site of the chapel
D: Cabin sold to the bishop by the natives; that is where we slept during our stay in New Caledonia
E: Garden
F-G: River and limit of the property. The house is surrounded by pastures. The river is navigable enough for a canoe to get up to the garden.

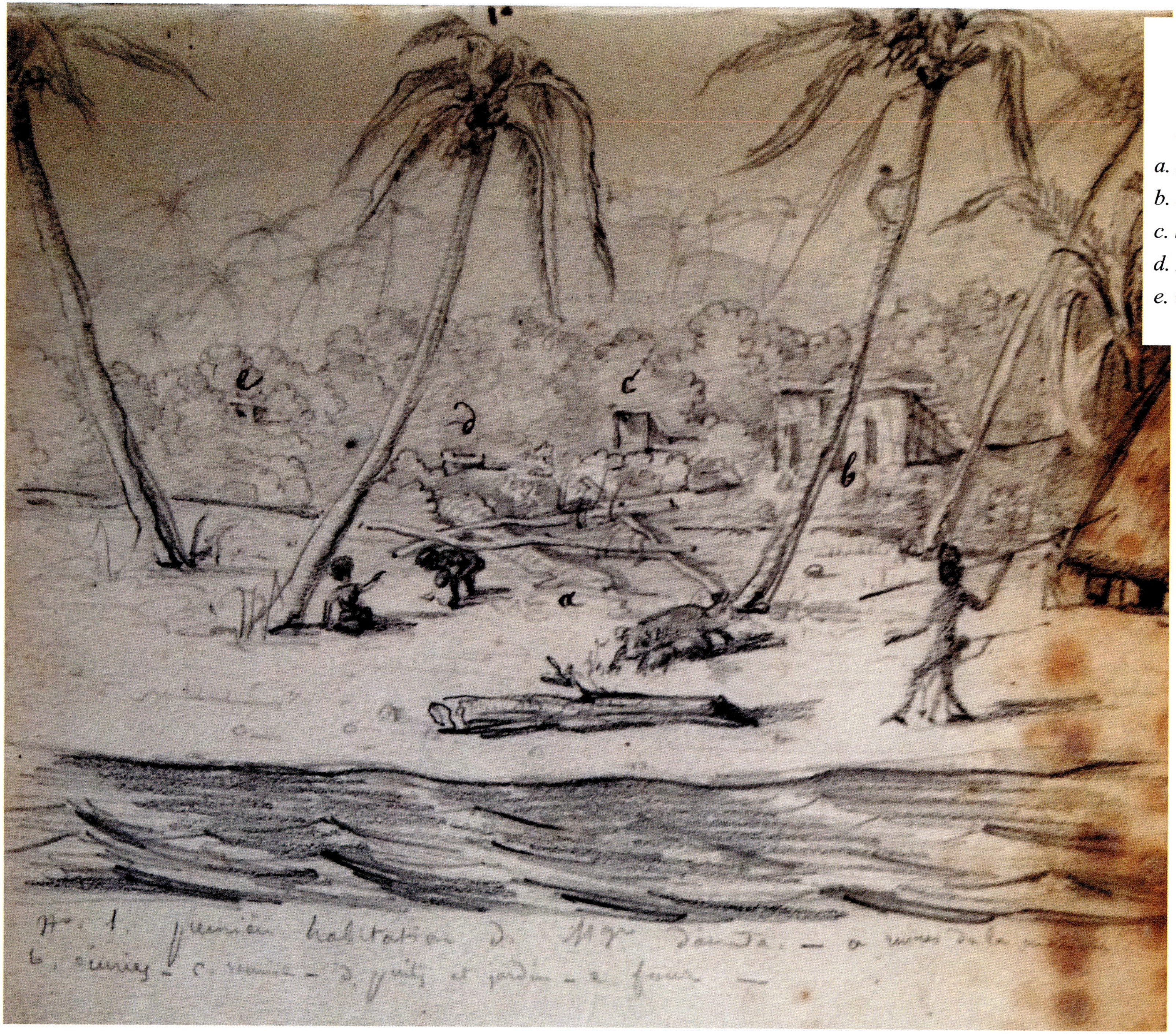

Verguet's Key

The first dwelling of Bishop Douarre

a. Ruins of the House
b. Stables
c. Shed
d. Fruits and Garden
e. Oven

The Journey Sydney - New Caledonia

Xavier Montrouzier to his brother Henri Montrouzier, SJ., January 1846

We left Sydney on the 23 October on the Marian Watson, a fine craft expressly built to take passengers, with a light breeze which soon sped us to the open sea. That morning in the Cathedral, the blessing of the Most Holy Sacrament had been given to draw down on our heads graces from on high, and at the time of departure, Bishop Polding, Bishop Pompallier, Doctor Gregory, vicar general, a number of priests and simple laity affectionately shook our hands and asked Heaven to protect us. Above on the mast was fastened a standard on which shone a cross, of the kind that in this case had a hint of religion, of Catholicism.

Seasickness did not delay to make itself felt. Bishop Epalle especially suffered very much. Now, at the end of a week all are up on their feet. We were heading for New Caledonia which we had to visit to help the missionaries. The wind has been propitious from the start, but then it has been so directly contrary, that it was necessary to tack for two weeks, which, given the difficulty of finding the entrance of port Balade, lost in the midst of banks of coral, only permitted us to anchor on the 17 November.

We did not have an entirely tranquil spirit at the time of boarding. We were told things hardly reassuring according to the account of Bishop Douarre and his companions and these rumours, vague it is true, but to which the reputation of the ferocity of the New Caledonians gave at least some probability, really inspired some fears in us. They did not last long. Hardly had the boat reached the coasts than we saw coming and heard the natives cry out. They were few in number and offered some coconuts.

November 1845: New Caledonia

The *Marian Watson* was sighted by the Marists on New Caledonia on 12 November 1845, but unfavourable winds prevented them making landfall until November 17. New Caledonia is 1500 km from Australia, about 400 km long and averages 50 km wide. Europeans discovered it fairly late; James Cook first sighted it in 1774 and it was he who gave it the name because the landscape reminded him of Scotland. Beachcombers and traders in sandalwood and in sea cucumbers lived there before the missionaries came. From 1842 there was trade between Sydney and New Caledonia and New Caledonians had visited Australia. Balade was on early French maps and hence a target for missionaries.

Verguet came during Bishop Douarre's first attempt to establish a mission and was to be present again when the Marists had to withdraw in August 1847. Their first station was opened on Christmas 1843 in the village of Mahamate, at the north-western end of the bay of Balade. One of the first missionaries was Father Philippe Viard, later bishop of Wellington in New Zealand. In July 1845 the Marists built their station (house, chapel, and fence) at the foot of the mountain, the other side of the river from the village of Baïao; often called the 'mission of Balade'.

That November Verguet's group stayed for a week with Douarre. The local chief Goa welcomed them. Four hundred children were baptized, adult catechumens were being prepared for baptism, and two locals became catechists. In general the work was extremely difficult and dangerous. Epalle left Brother Bertrand behind to support Douarre's

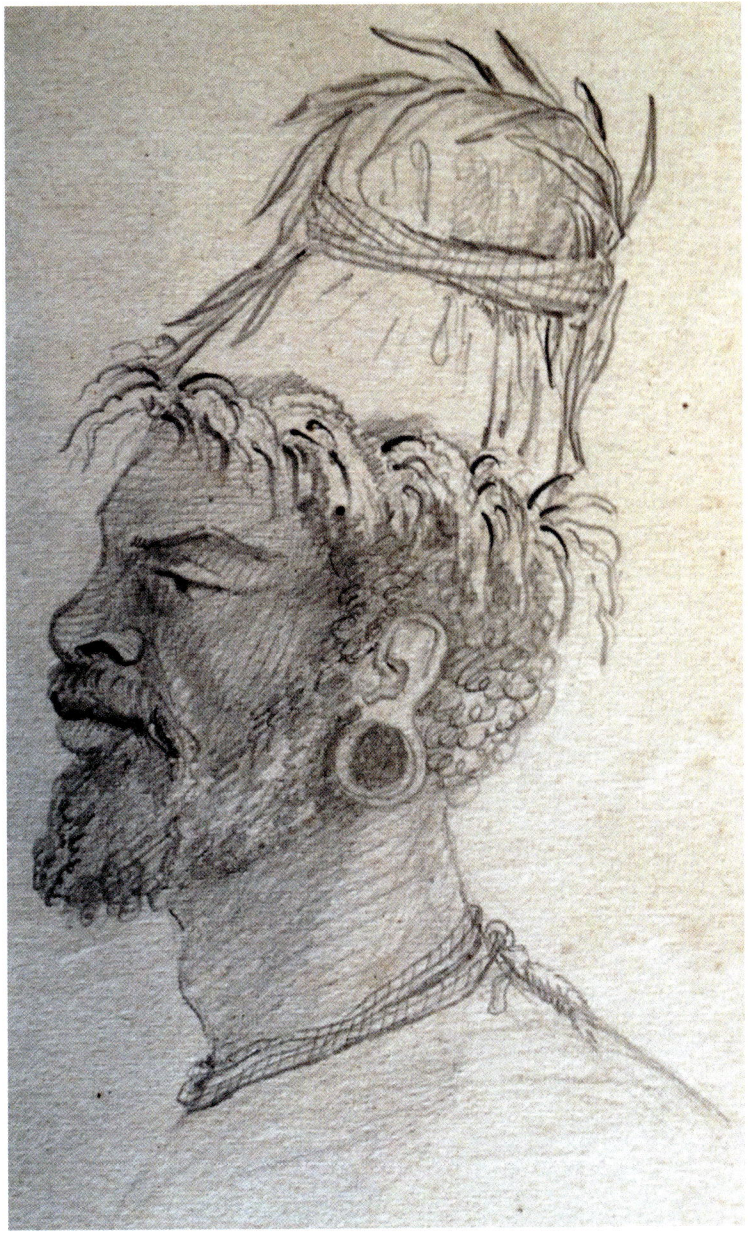

Aliki-Goa, Chief of the tribe of Goa, New Caledonia

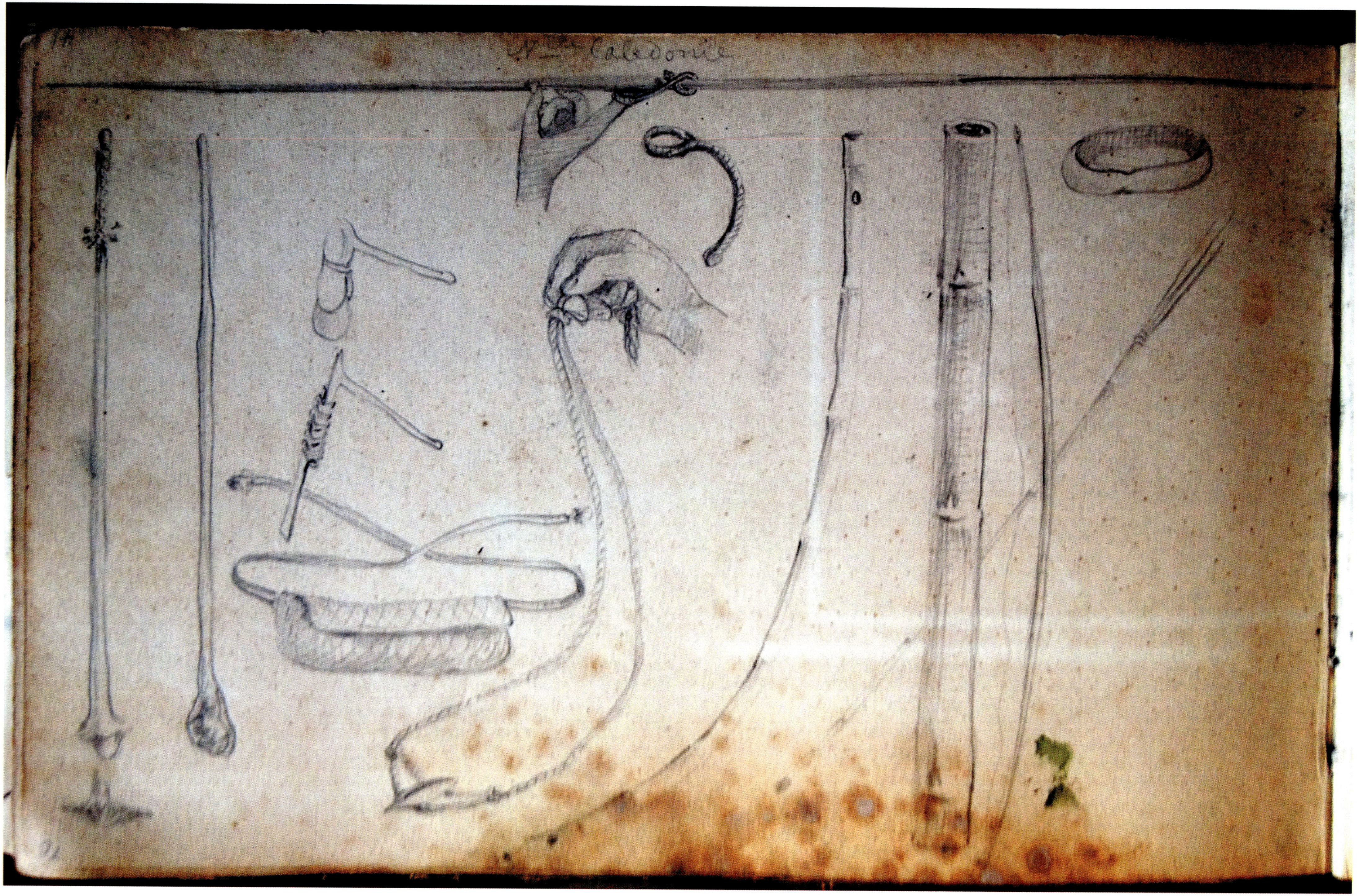

A variety of implements from New Caledonia, note the mechanism and technique for launching a light spear using a string looped around the index finger.

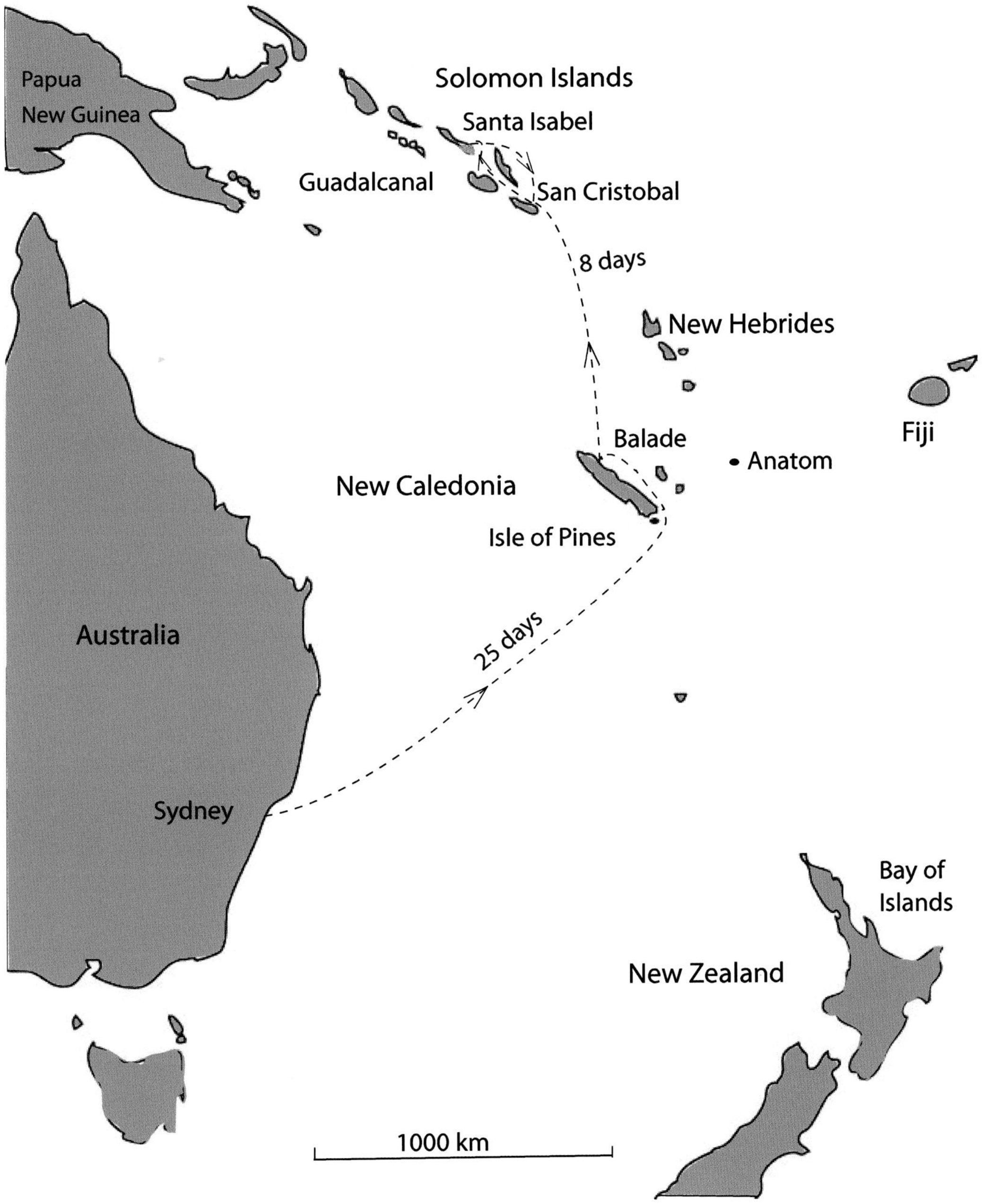

group.At Balade lived the Pouma tribe. Verguet, in his first experience of life on a Pacific Island, described the local people on their canoes, their weapons, music, huts, and their way of life. Verguet concluded: These people are friends of Bishop Douarre and there is a good hope of them becoming Christians.

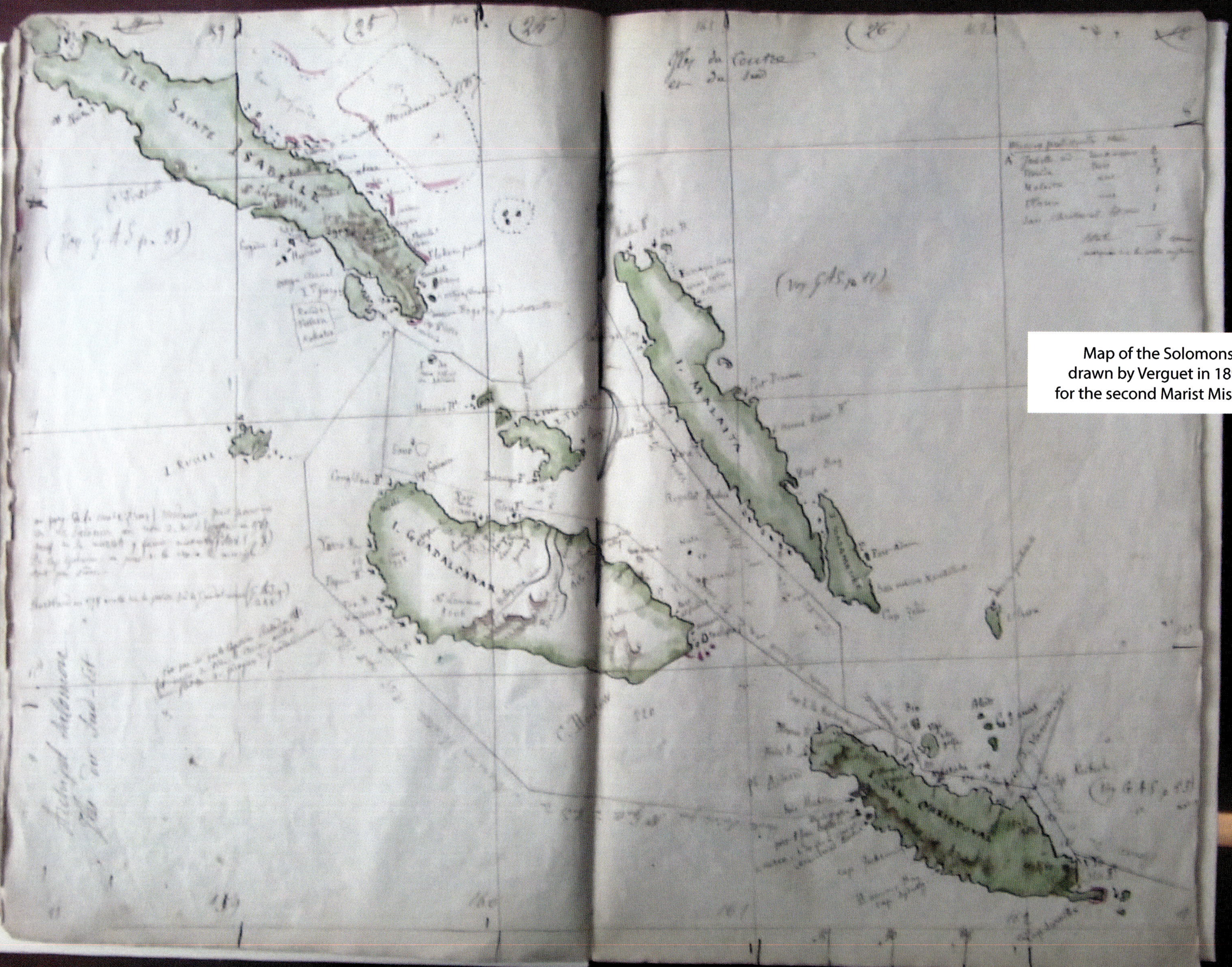

Map of the Solomons
drawn by Verguet in 1893
for the second Marist Mission

The Killing of a Bishop

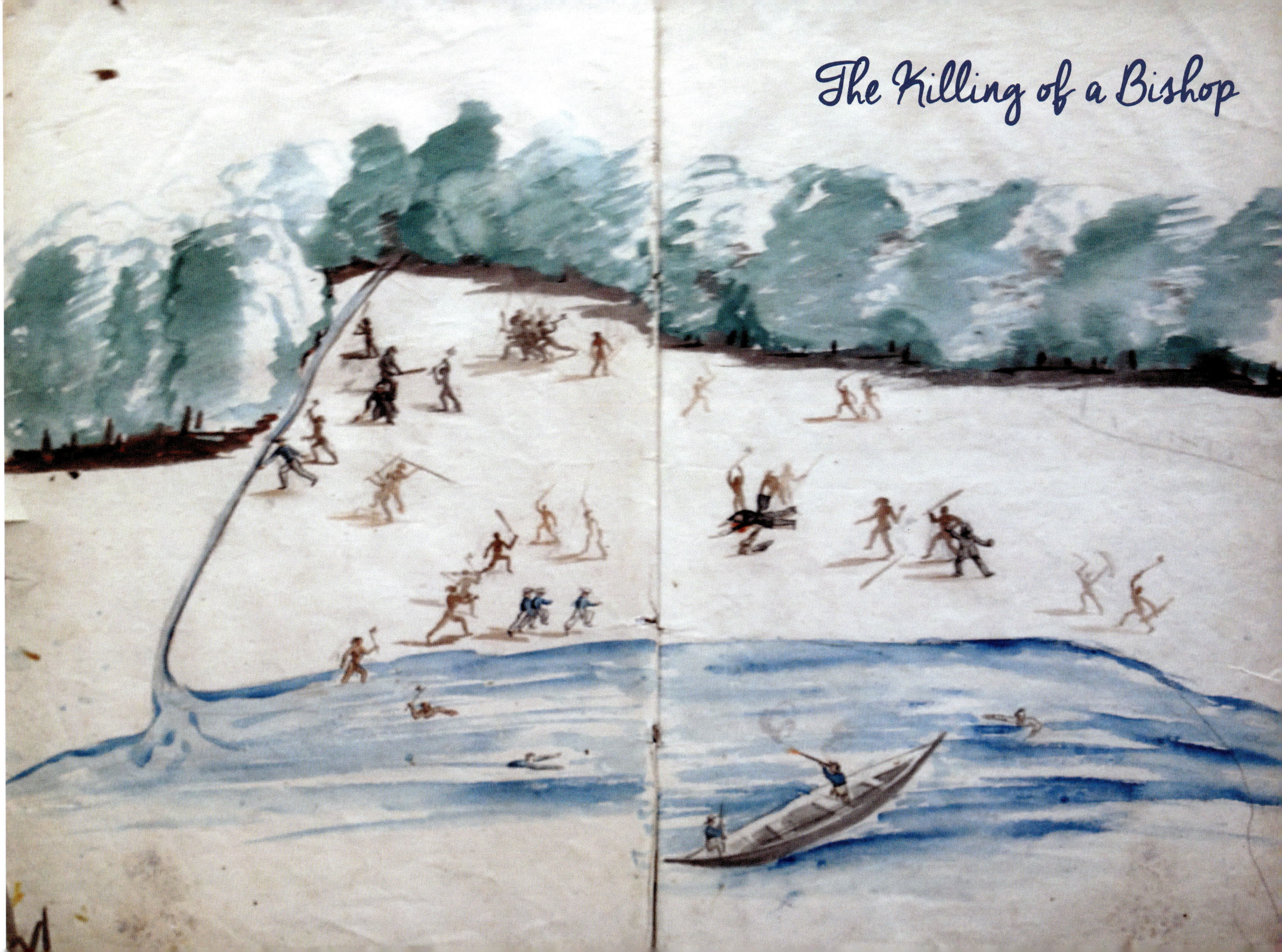

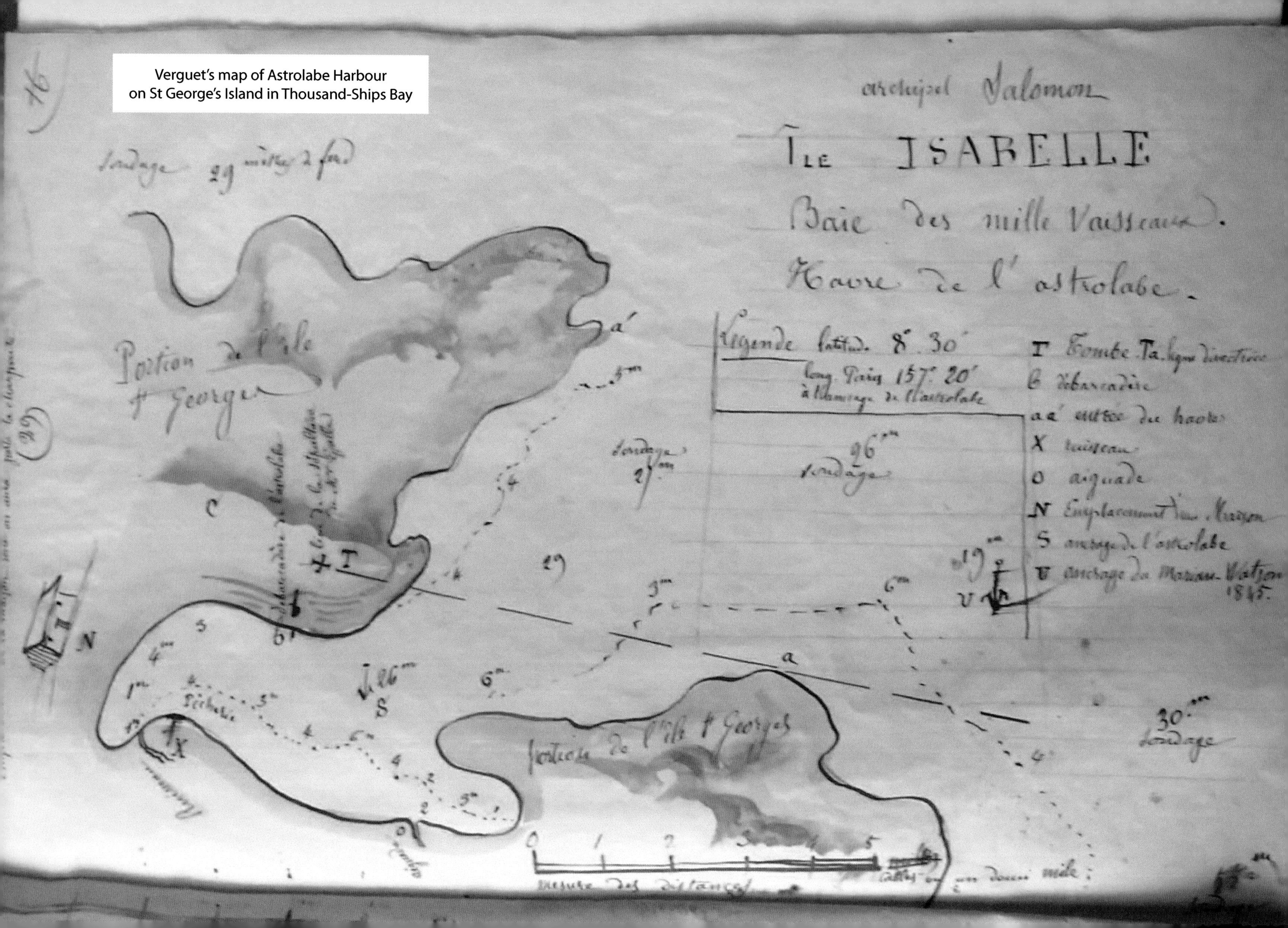

Verguet's map of Astrolabe Harbour on St George's Island in Thousand-Ships Bay

In the Solomons 1845-1846

New Caledonia to the Solomons

On 23 November 1845, Epalle's group left New Caledonia and made an eight-day voyage to the island of San Cristobal, now called Makira. Two days out they narrowly avoided shipwreck on a reef. On 1 December they sighted 'Arossi Island' as Verguet called Makira. Epalle entered his vicariate for the first time and, to mark the event, dropped overboard a medal of the Immaculate Conception to indicate that "Mary is in charge of this mission." The next day they anchored at a bay they were later to call Port Saint Jean-Baptiste in honour of Jean-Baptiste Epalle. They went ashore and took three days to survey the area, looking for a suitable place to establish a mission. The locals were reasonably friendly but they decided to move to Santa Isabel, the main island in the centre of the Solomons, bigger than San Cristobal despite the latter having better ports for which they had maps.

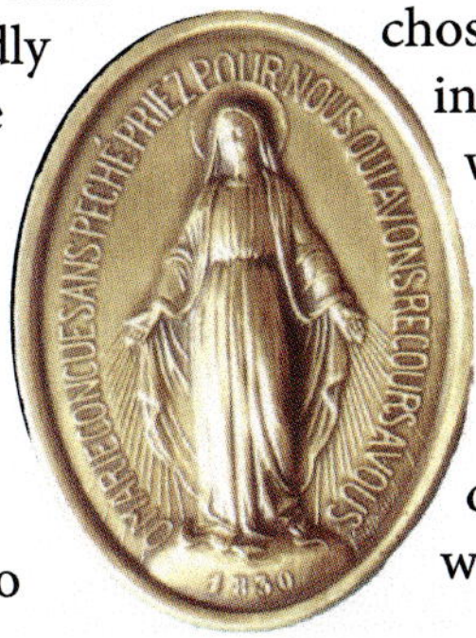

From 7 to 12 December the *Marian Watson* travelled along the south coast of Guadalcanal. On at least one occasion they made contact with local people who came out on their pirogues to trade with them. Verguet described the trip as slow but pleasant.

Arrival on Santa Isabel

Isabel is a large landmass - 225 km long, 25 km wide and 5,525 square kilometres in area. On 12 December they reached *Baie des Mille-Vaisseaux* (Thousand Ships Bay) which they knew from d'Urville's map from when he was there on the *Astrolabe*. They anchored in Astrolabe Harbour, which is sheltered by St George's Island, and were immediately surrounded by canoes. After consultation, they chose their shore party, with Epalle leading it. First contact was made and gifts were exchanged. Three days passed in this fashion with Epalle and a party going ashore each day and returning later to the vessel. They detected hostilities between different groups of the local people, but Epalle still wanted to establish the mission there.

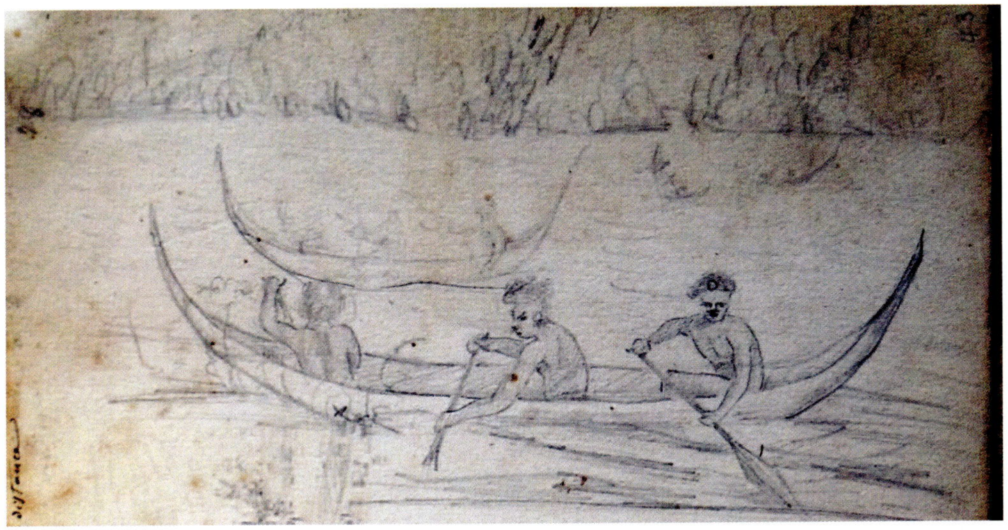

Pirogues off the coast of San Cristobal

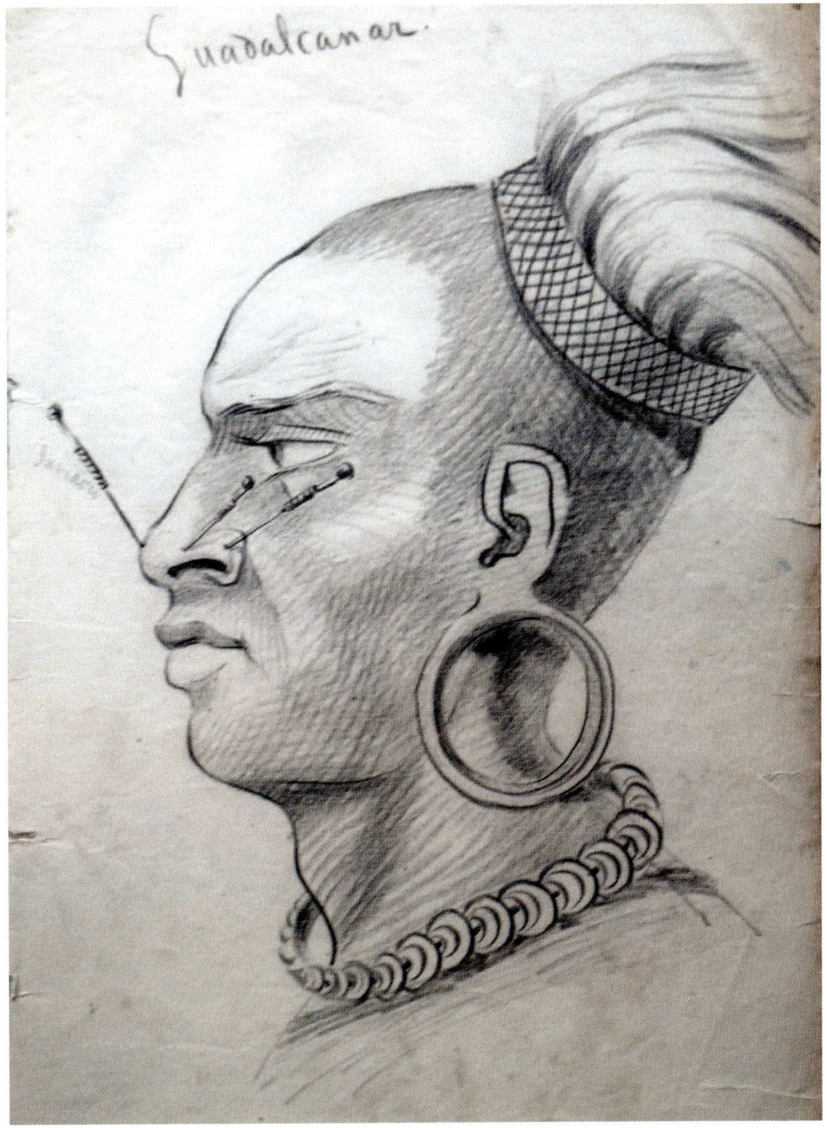

Man of Guadalcanal

Attack on Santa Isabel

On 16 December, a Tuesday, Epalle got up earlier than usual, prayed quietly before reciting the office with the other Marists and went ashore despite being very tired. He said, 'If I would allow nature to rule I would not go today … I will come back earlier than usual…' He was right, they left at 8 am and he was carried back on board by 11 am. Epalle was wearing black and white trousers (a detail faithfully recorded by Verguet). With him went Chaurain, Frémont, Prosper, and Blemy, second officer of the *Marian Watson*. Some sailors stayed behind in the boat which had taken them ashore. They landed and realized the people were angry. The sailors going ashore had left their weapons in the boat – normally they took pistols and rifles with them. Epalle still went ahead. There were about forty to sixty locals, all armed with clubs and spears.

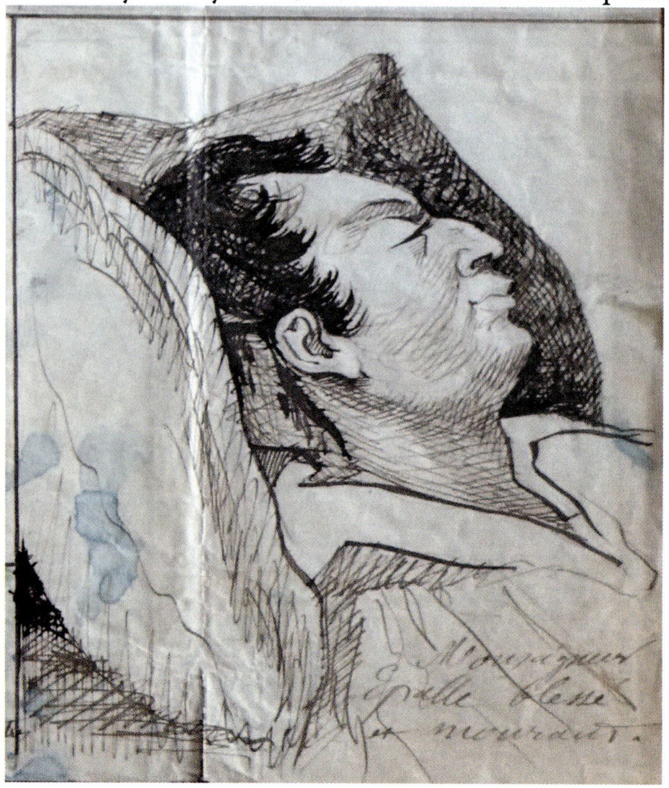

The dying Bishop

Gifts were offered but the chief was not pleased. Brother Prosper noted the weapons and said: 'they are ready to fight!' One group tried to overturn the boat and splash water on the guns, which suggests prior planning and familiarity with firearms. Three attacked and plundered Epalle. He received five axe wounds and two stab wounds from spears. Chaurain, also wounded, returned from the boat to rescue Epalle. The sailors shot from the boat and the locals fled. Chaurain carried Epalle, helped by Frémont and Prosper both of whom had also been injured. The doctor on board examined Epalle and declared him mortally wounded. Father Jacquet anointed the Bishop. Over the next two days the missionaries discouraged the Captain's proposal for a punitive expedition: 'Not blood for blood.'

In the afternoon of 19 December Epalle finally died without having recovered consciousness. The news spread over the next months to Australia, New Zealand and eventually France. Captain Richards gave a report on the death Epalle when the *Marian Watson* returned to Sydney on April 23, but already by 3 February the news had been published in the *Cork Examiner* in Ireland. Montrouzier wrote an account on 31 December in a letter to his brother.

On 20 December at 4 o'clock in the morning they celebrated the funeral on board and buried the bishop on St George Island. To avoid the body being desecrated they kept the grave inconspicuous but Verguet prepared a precise map of the location. He considered Epalle to be a martyr and saint and wanted his remains to be appropriately honoured rather than left in an unmarked grave.

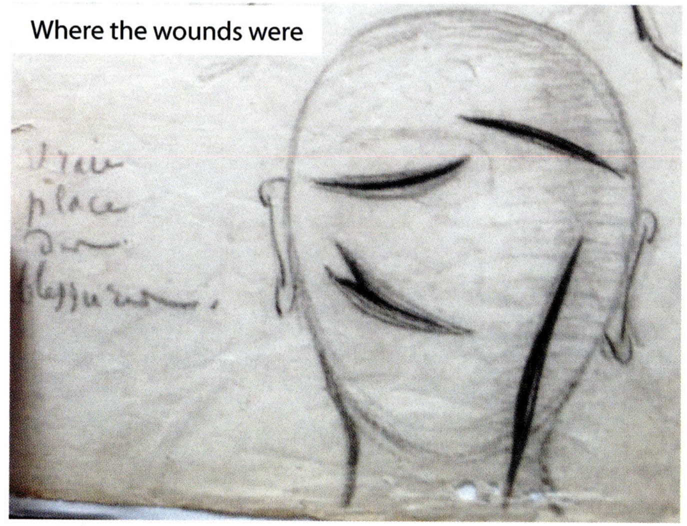

Where the wounds were

Frémont was now in charge of the group of missionaries and discussed with them what to do. They tried again to make contact on Santa Isabel without success. On 23 December they returned to Arossi. On 28 December they visited the north of San Cristobal, the tribe of a man called Loukou. Loukou and two others of the tribe had been to Sydney and spoke some English and were able to act as interpreters for them. The missionaries decided to set up their base in Loukou's area where they felt safe and welcome. The mission to the Solomons was begun but in very low spirits. 'But how few we priests are! Our chief has fallen in the field of honour. Our provincial has been wounded. All that does not increase our numbers. Then, what a lot of expense we incur to establish ourselves here.'

Traumatised

5 September 1846 — Fr Étienne Chaurain to Fr Jean-Claude Colin

Since the terrible day when I saw with my very eyes and a couple of feet away, natives massacring and mutilating the body of my bishop in such a barbaric way and at the same time as much to defend myself and to rescue at least the remains of our martyr, I had to struggle with wretches who wanted to kill us for no other reason than to have our clothes. Never, I told you, never have I been able to find in my heart a single feeling of love for the natives. That involuntary feeling is even more now; it is an insurmountable dislike which rises up in me every time I notice a native.

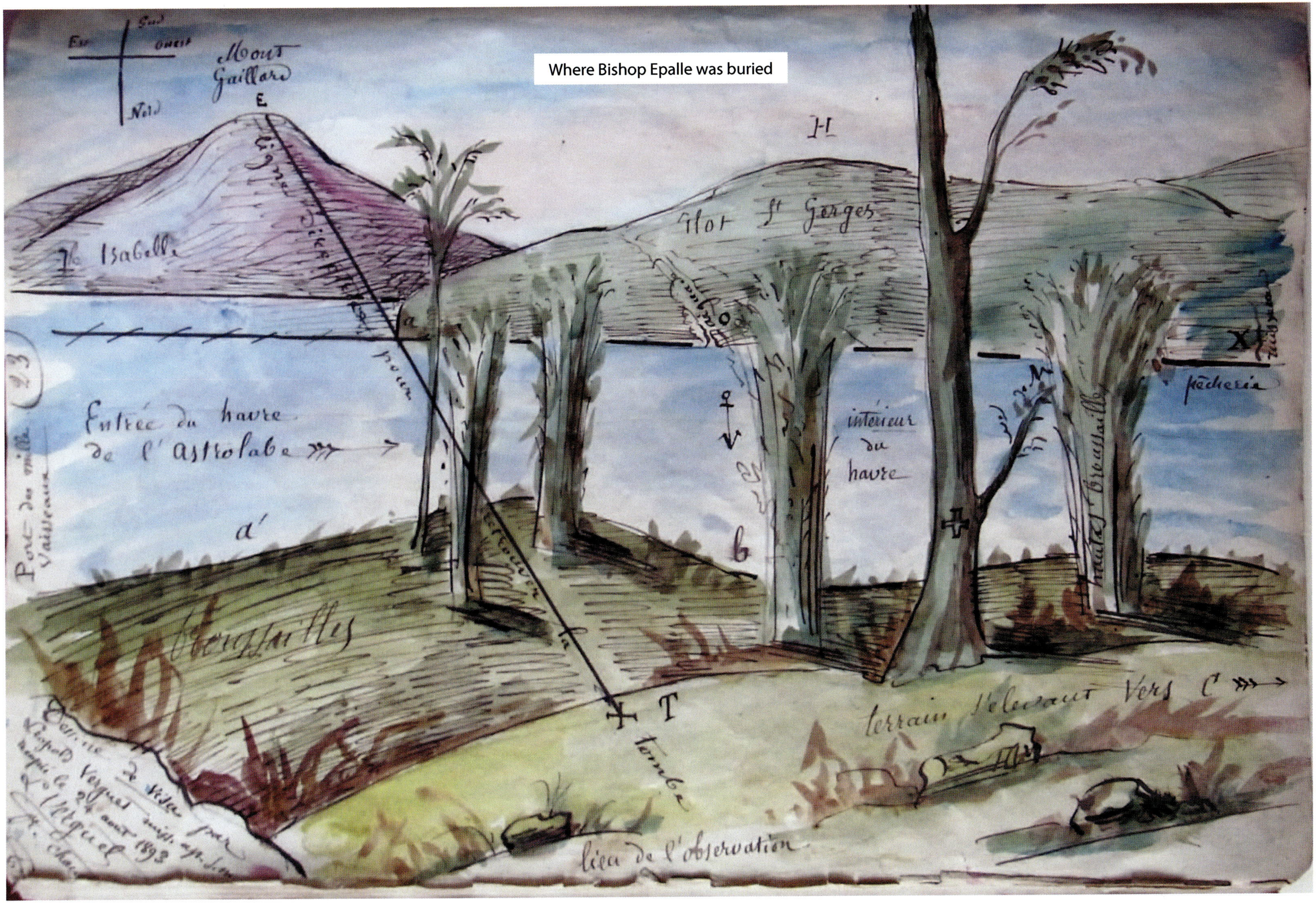

Where Bishop Epalle was buried

31 December 1845, Father Montrouzier to his brother Gabriel

My dear brother,

There is no point hiding from you a piece of news which the Annals of the Propagation of the Faith won't be slow in publishing. After all, if at first you feel that it is upsetting, I am sure that reflecting on it for a short time it will become comforting. Bishop Epalle has been taken away from us by his death, but that was only to go and intercede for us in heaven. He was the first apostle of the Solomon Islands and also the first martyr. Here are the details of the incident and what happened previously to it.

Having left New Caledonia on 24 October and having escaped on the evening of 25 October the extreme danger of being shipwrecked, we arrived on 1 December off the coast of San Cristobal. It is the first island in the Solomon archipelago and we dropped anchor on 3 December. The people, the terrain, everything would have been quite suitable for us. But there was not sufficient there to occupy eight missionaries. ... The bishop wanted to establish a mission station at Isabelle, the centre of the archipelago. We got there on 12 December and straightaway we were surrounded by canoes whose paddlers invited us to go to their place. They pointed out to us a spot which we thought was dangerous and they kept on saying the word mate-mate which in all the languages of Oceania means something ominous. We ignored that warning, thinking that they were probably enemies of the tribe they were pointing to or else even that perhaps they wanted to warn us against an unhealthy climate. We dropped anchor opposite a spot about two leagues away, near Astrolabe Harbour, in Thousand Ships Bay.

The bishop immediately called us together to appoint a committee of two priests and a brother to go and reconnoitre the island. He wanted to go with them. Reverend Fathers Frémont and Chaurain were appointed with Brother Prosper. They all set off immediately, whereas we had been told to give a friendly welcome to the natives who were coming on board and to learn as many words as possible and to make plenty of observations. That is how the committee acted in its expeditions. It took with it the second officer of the ship and four sailors. It went unarmed, but that did not prevent the captain from getting his men to take some rifles and some swords. It left between eight and nine o'clock in the morning and returned rather late in the evening. On Friday and Saturday we noticed several aspects which gave little satisfaction. There were no villages and pretty well no chance of building a small cabin with a garden because the jungle was too thick and the land too mountainous. On Sunday we rested. On Monday we started searching again and we were rather lucky to find a river and a favourable spot. Yet we noticed straightaway several things which were not encouraging. We saw several necklaces made of human teeth, and one of the natives wearing one showed us the spot where he had killed and cut up his enemy. We

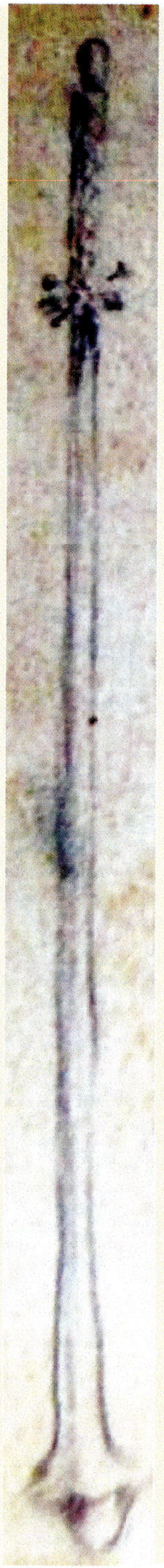

were also offered a child in exchange for an axe and several of us thought we understood that the offering was as a highly prized dish. On Monday evening all those details were brought back to a gathering we had; but nobody was scared. The bishop said, I see clearly that by starting with Isabelle Island, we are attacking the worst element; but that does not matter. ... On Tuesday they left at the usual time. The bishop felt tired. "If I listened to my body", he said," I would exempt myself from the heavy work." The weather had changed; he took his black hat instead of his straw hat, taking the precaution of removing the braid, no doubt he feared that it would excite greed among the natives. The night before he had torn his black trousers. He wore another pair in black and white checks. As he was leaving said, "I'll try not to be late." He was not mistaken. At eleven o'clock he was on the deck, bathed in blood, struck five times by an axe, pierced by two spears and bruised all over his body. Father Frémont received two blows of a club which cracked his skull and the third victim received one blow and we, in tears around our bishop, gave him the last sacraments and we asked heaven not to abandon us.

Here is how things occurred. The second officer asked the bishop where he was going. He said he was going to the enemy tribe. When they arrived the committee was surprised by the lack of enthusiasm of the natives approaching the longboat. Nevertheless the bishop and the others disembarked. Contrary to what they normally did, the sailors left their weapons on the boat. A native offered the third man some fruit. They gave him in exchange a piece if iron which he took to the chief who looked at it disdainfully. So the third man gave an axe. The chief took it, still disdainfully, and shook it fiercely and angrily. There were between 40 and 60 natives on the beach. Not one was smiling. They all had weapons, their clubs, their spears, their shields, their attitude was threatening. Brother Prosper then noticed an axe. He cried out: "Look, those people are ready to fight". The bishop said, "That's true". The sailors should have had their weapons. At that moment the bishop was struck from behind. He stayed still. He received a second blow. He fell down and everybody was attacked and fled. The second officer, seriously wounded was one of the first to get back to the boat and fired his rifle. The natives fled, except for three who stayed stubbornly around the bishop. They were busy, one in striking him and the other two tearing off his clothes and taking his hat, his snuffbox and a knife I had lent him. It was then that Father Chaurain on returning to the boat, without thinking of the danger, thought of nothing else but saving the body of the bishop. He jumped into the water, reached the shore and flew to the help of the bishop. He would have been killed had it not been for a second rifle being fired from the boat and sending all the wretched natives to flight.

" At that moment the Bishop was struck from behind

So he lifted up the body which he found dragged in the sand and covered in blood, and realizing that he was too weak to carry him called for help. Father Frémont and Brother Prosper went and helped him lift up the precious load and when all had come back to the longboat, they left hurriedly from that scene of treachery and cruelty.

I can't tell you, my dear brother, the impression I had seeing the longboat returning more than three hours after its departure. Mr Blemy, the third mate, had a blood-stained handkerchief around his head. Father Frémont also had around his head a rag red with blood. He bishop was lying down, immobile, on the knees of us priests and of our dear brother; his shirt was quite red; his head was nothing else but a wound but his face had not changed. The ship's doctor then examined the wounds; he said they were fatal and so we busied ourselves administering to this dear martyr the last rites. You could have no idea of the feelings we had what we felt at that time. As far as I am concerned, I can tell you that I have never felt my faith so roused as at that moment. I was overcome with the thought of our becoming orphans, without a guide, without support in the middle of unknown islands with the enormous task of founding a mission. But I was in a way proud of having a martyr in our midst, happy in being able to gather up his blood with towels and material which our good mother had given me.

The bishop remained suffering for several days. Constantly surrounded by priests and brothers, lying on the deck of the ship, deprived of so many things that he would not have lacked in France, he took his last breath on Friday 19 October at four in the afternoon a moment before I returned from St George Island where Father Verguet, some brothers and I had gone to wash some clothing---.

We gave the bishop's body all the honours which were deserved by his personality and the glory which he had just gained by shedding his blood for the cause of Jesus Christ. We dressed him in his pontifical robes; we put him on show and we shared with one another time to recite prayers around him. The following day, a Saturday, at four in the morning, we celebrated Holy Mass on the deck and we went to a solitary place on St George Island to lay the immortal remains of the first apostle-martyr of Melanesia, taking appropriate precautions to be able perhaps one day to recognize the place and recover his bones. While all this was happening, the crew showed tangible signs of their affection and we even had to use all our authority to stop them going and taking revenge on our behalf. [....]

Show this letter to the family; don't hide anything. But do explain to the members of the family that I am safe. Our good parents' imagination makes them see enemies always on my heels whereas I go in safety among my dear natives.

Goodbye, I embrace heart and soul and beg you to embrace our good parents for me.

Your good brother in Jesus and Mary,
Xavier Montrouzier,
Apostolic missionary

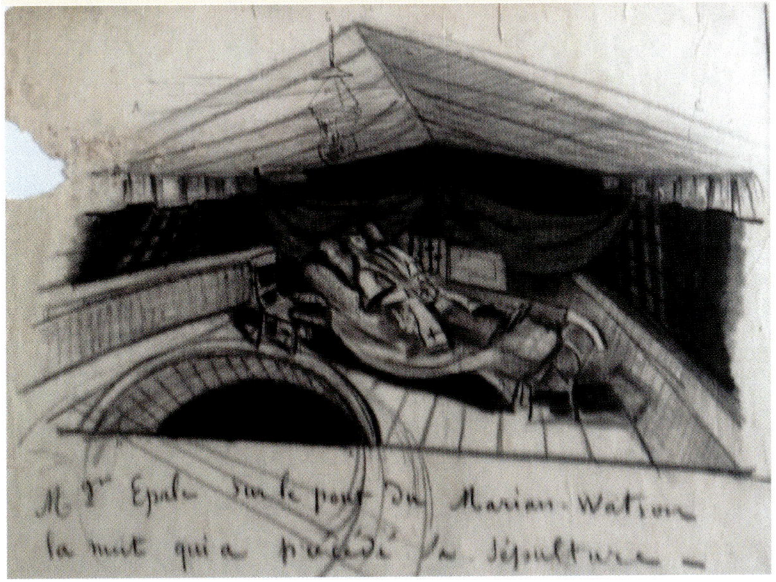

Bishop Epalle laid out on the bridge of the *Marian Watson* on the night before his burial

THE
MORNING CHRONICLE.

SATURDAY, APRIL 25, 1846.

DEATH OF THE RIGHT REV. DR. EPALLE.

By the arrival of the *Marian Watson*, on Thursday, from the islands of San Christoval and New Caledonia, we have received the melancholy intelligence of the death, by the hands of the savages, of the truly amiable and beloved Dr. Epalle, Vicar Apostolic of North Western Oceanica.

This event has cast a saddening gloom over the Catholics of Sydney, a gloom in which many of their Protestant friends also participate; as the mild, amiable, and gentlemanly deportment of the good Bishop, who resided amongst us for four months previous to his departure for the scene of his mission, endeared him to all who had the pleasure of forming an acquaintance with him.

It was hoped that the labours of this gentle and truly apostolic prelate would have produced much fruit in the islands of the Southern Seas, and that he would, in the hands of heaven, have been the instrument of bringing innumerable souls, who now sit in the darkness of the shadow of death, to a full knowledge of God's holy truths, as revealed by his only Son, and ever maintained and propagated by his one, only, and Catholic Church. He was a man well fitted for such a mission, for, though only in the prime of his life, he had long laboured, and with success, amongst the unenlightened heathens of the Southern hemisphere, having been for many years Vicar General to the New Zealand mission. Schooled as it were at the feet of such a master as the amiable and indefatigable Bishop Pompallier.

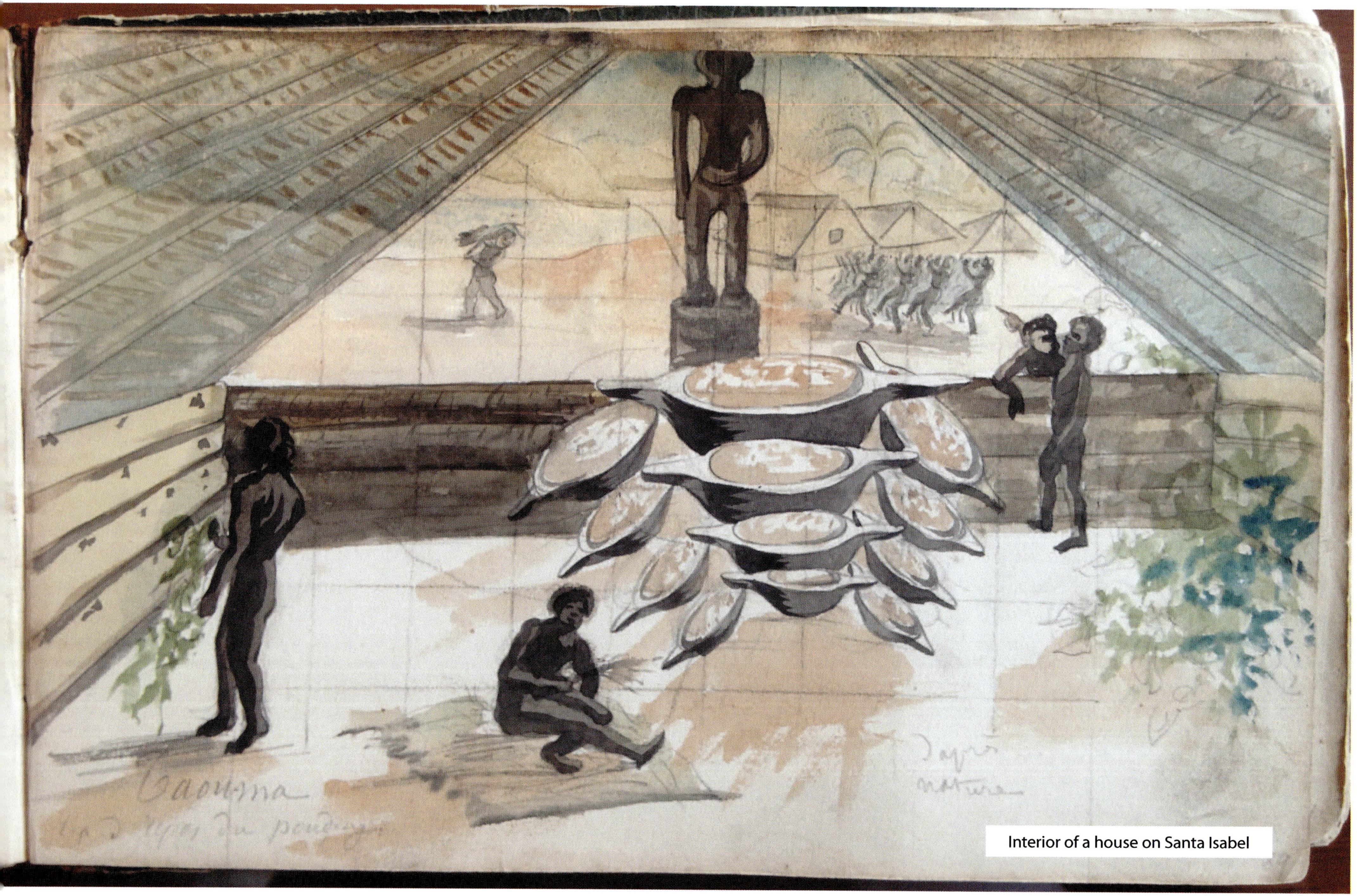

Interior of a house on Santa Isabel

Verguet, apostolic missionary

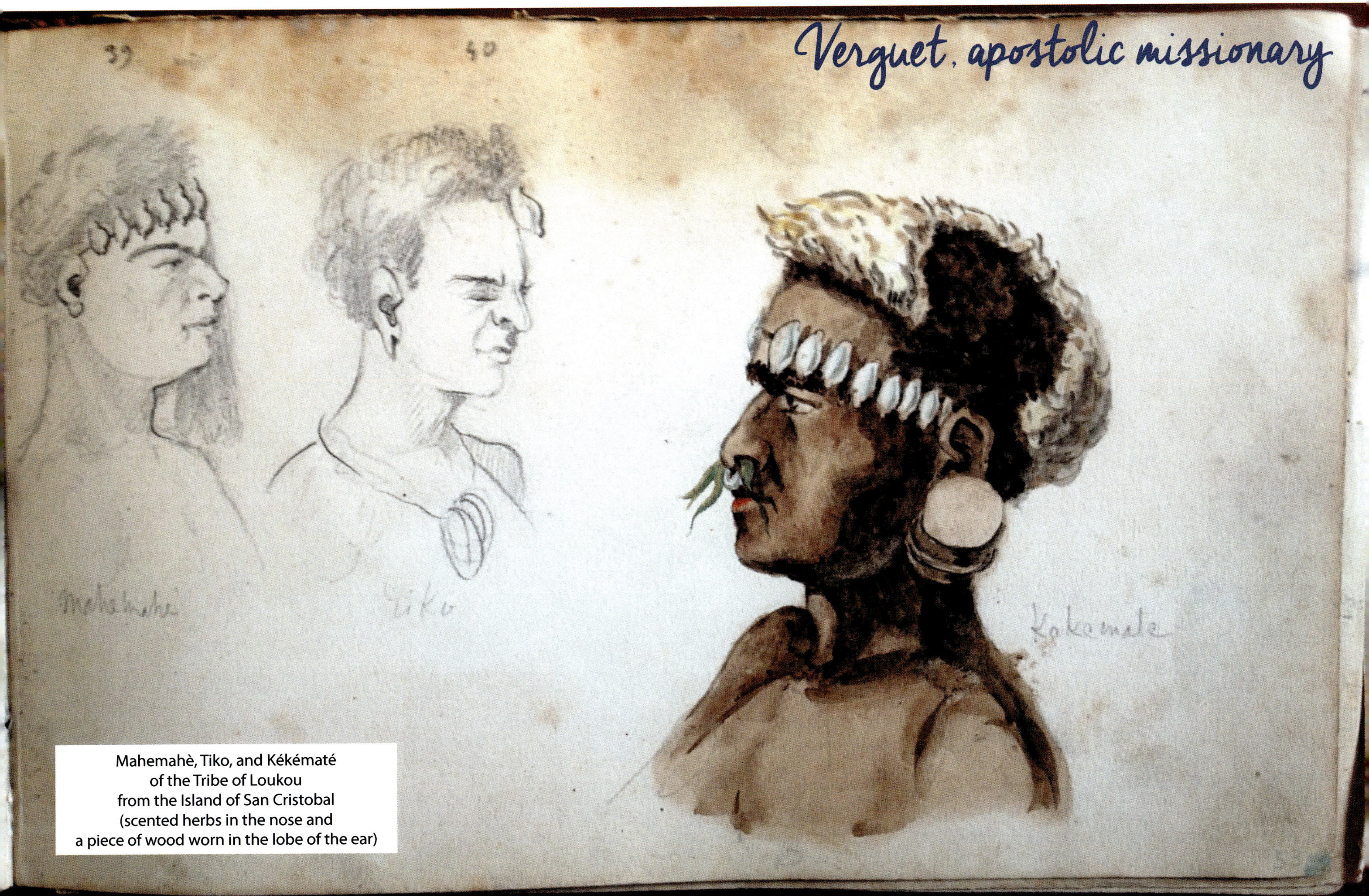

Mahemahè, Tiko, and Kékématé
of the Tribe of Loukou
from the Island of San Cristobal
(scented herbs in the nose and
a piece of wood worn in the lobe of the ear)

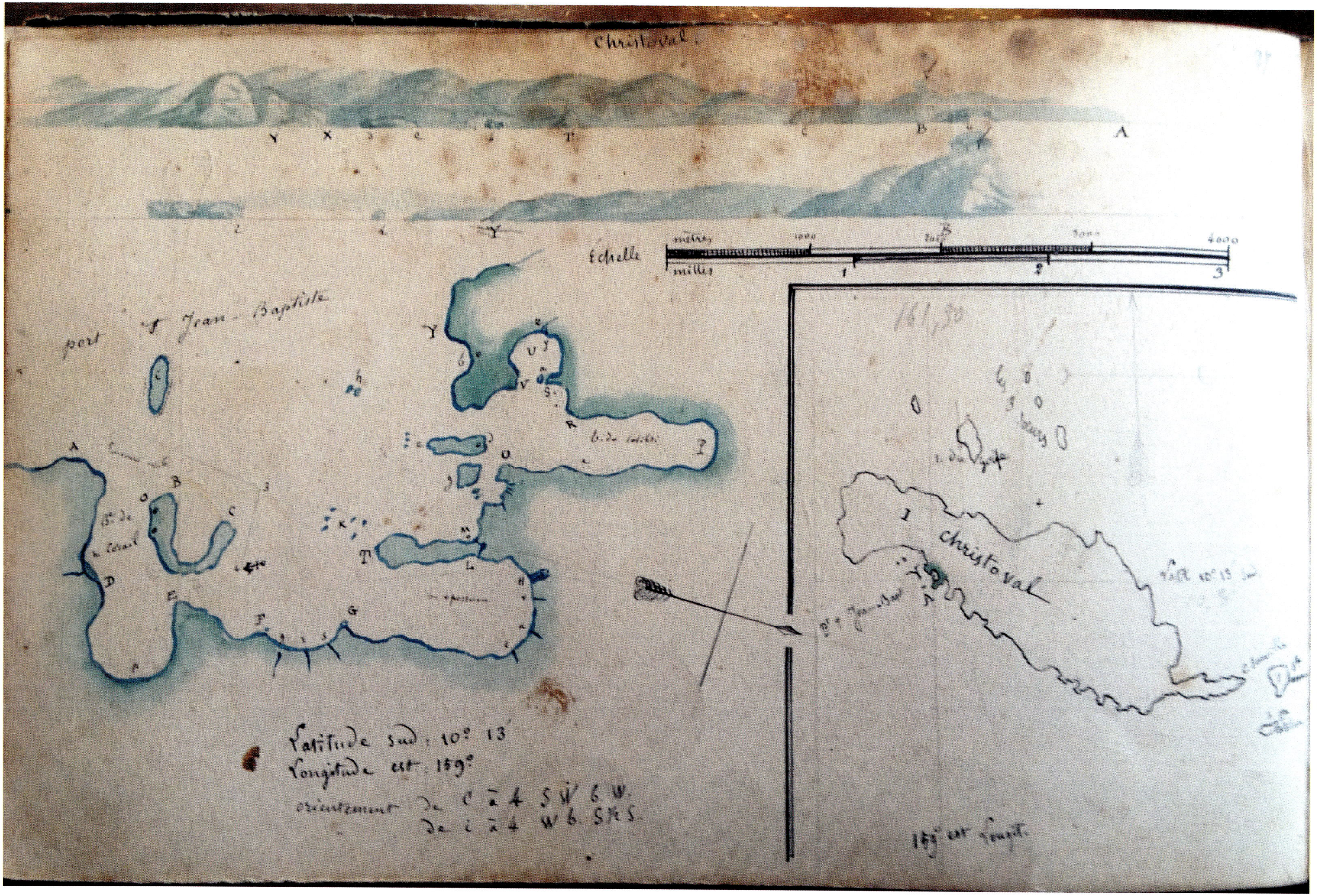
Christoval
Echelle
mètres
1000
2000
3000
4000
milles
1
2
3
port St Jean-Baptiste
Latitude sud: 10° 13'
Longitude est: 159°
Christoval
159° est Longit.

Verguet on San Cristobal

January 1846 – January 1847

On 3 January 1846 the Marists arrived back on San Cristobal. They established their little mission station at what they dubbed Port Sainte Marie in Makira Bay, close to many small villages; the Oné, Toro, Taroua, and Apahé were the tribes in this territory. Verguet describes and maps the area. The Arossi called him 'Perké' – their pronunciation of 'Verguet'. Verguet wanted to live in one of the villages. The group, fearful of the temptations of living with virtually naked people decided on a 'convent' style house some distance away. It was erected in timber with the help of the sailors before they departed. The Marists followed the daily routine of the motherhouse in Lyon. They put in a plantation of European plants. (Their vines died; the corn grew well; they had a bull and a cow.) Verguet spent some of his time shooting birds – he reports that it usually took him two shots to bring down one bird. He also made watercolour sketches of the birds and learnt the local names.

Narrative resumes on page 56

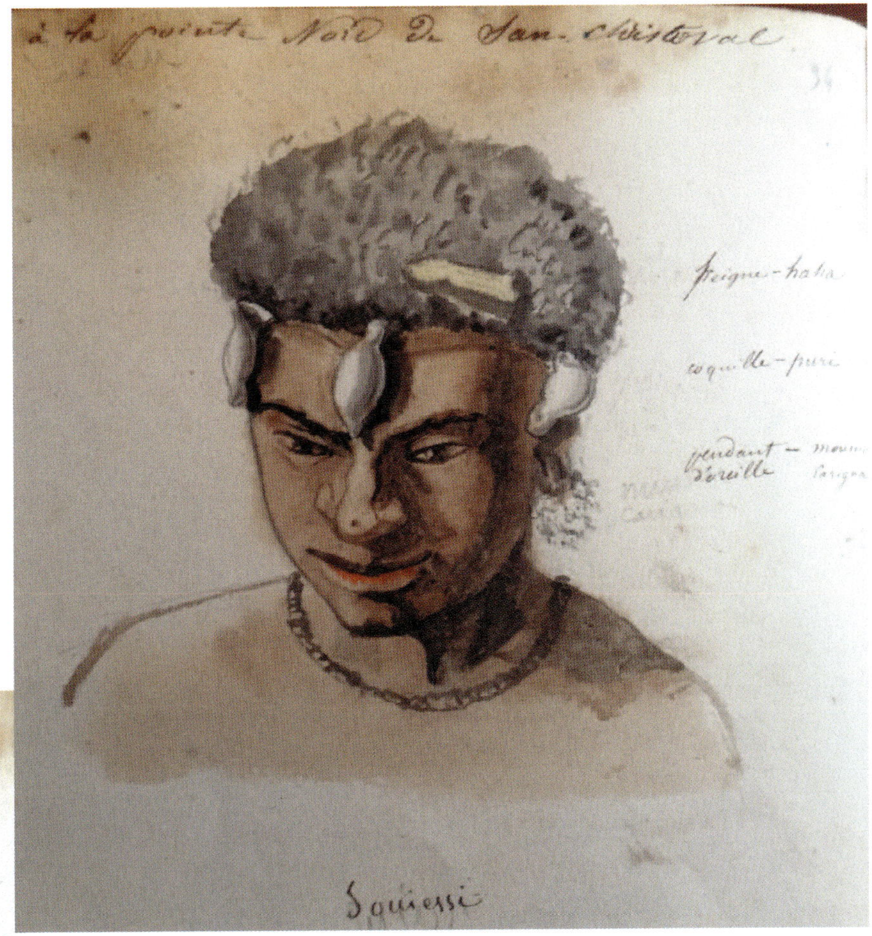

Souiessi of the Tribe of Loukou from the northern point of San Cristobal

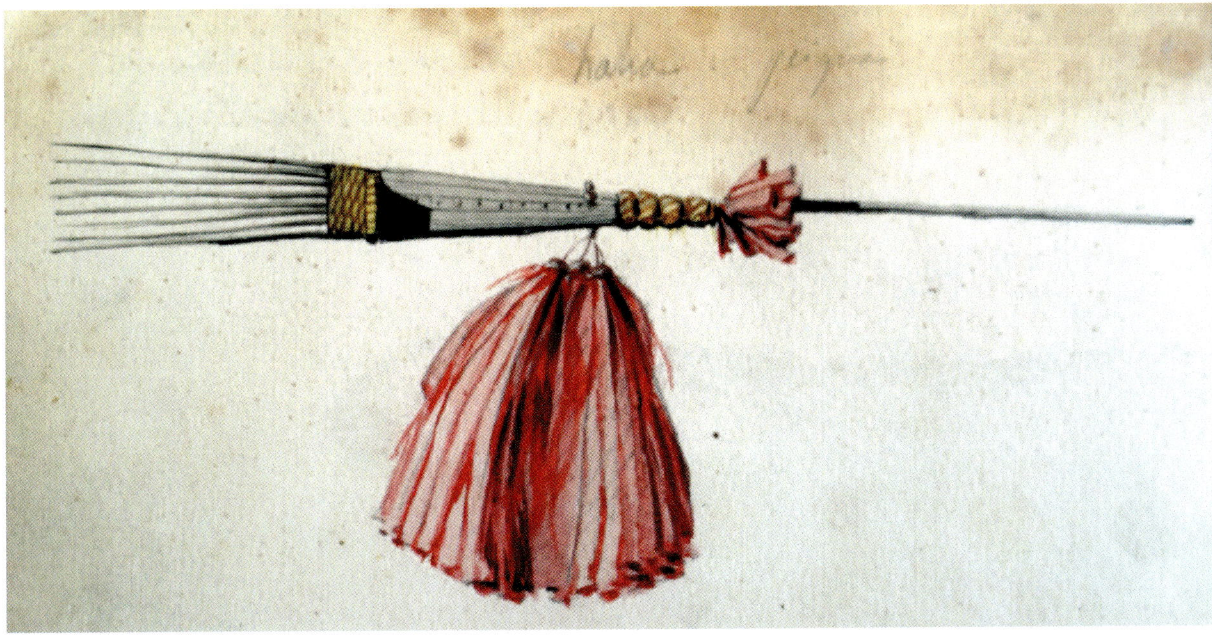

A comb for which the Arossi word is *haha*

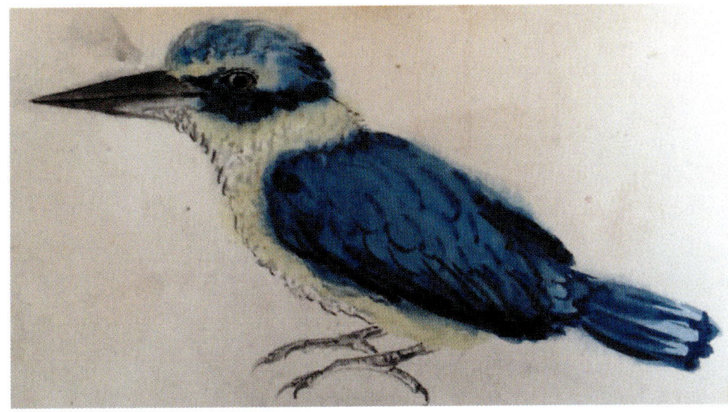

The bird the Arossi call *Uariagni*

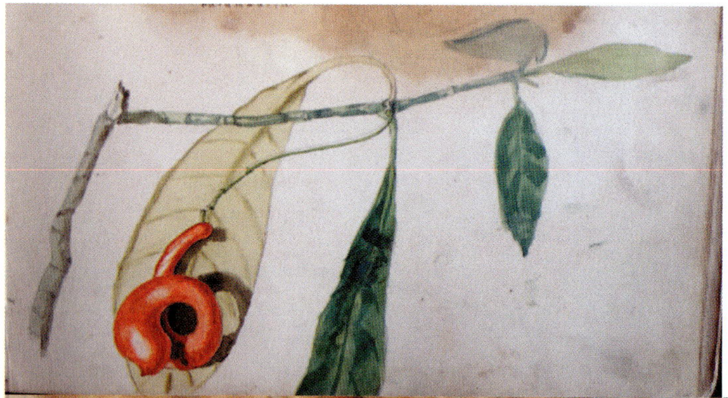

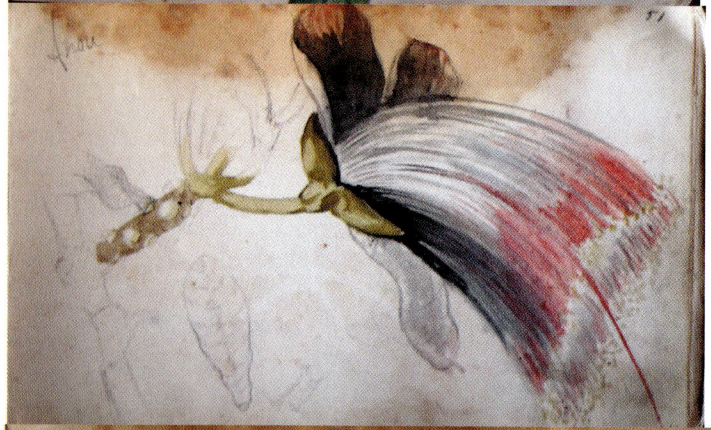

Guns and Stab-proof Vests
1846 - Fr Leopold Verguet to Fr Jean Claude Colin

I will not end this letter, very reverend Father, without saying a word about the accident which happened here just a few days ago. We built our house in the midst of continual fear. Every day we were under the threat of the coming of the Toro (the mountain people) who had, it was said, committed themselves not to allow a single white man to settle on Arosi, and who, after the ship left, were to attack us and put us to death. Several times strangers came in large numbers, and well-armed, to see us and to examine the work we were doing. Once they wanted to massacre us during dinner; we were eating at the place where we worked. The strangers were always around us; it would have been easy for them to do what they wanted. The Blessed Virgin protected us and we were aware of the danger only after we had escaped from it. From what our friends told us, these natives had chosen as their first victims Father Frémont and Brothers Genade and Prosper. Afterwards, so as to be safer, Frémont allowed those of us who wanted to bear arms. Since then I have always had a pistol in my belt.

One day, it was the 4th of February, around 5 o'clock in the evening, I happened to be on the terrace of the house. All of a sudden, I heard someone crying in the valley from the side of the stream: "I'm dead! Help! I have a lance through my body." I had no doubt that the Toros had come to attack us and I wanted to deliver Father Montrouzier, whose voice I recognized, and who I thought was in their hands, I fired the pistol and ran up to Father Montrouzier. He was on his knees, with his arms stretched out as on a cross, leaning against a fallen tree trunk which obstructed the way. He did not have the strength to get over it. In that position he was abandoning himself to God, he was offering the sacrifice of his own life. There was nothing more edifying than his words: "My God, I am happy! You are good, Jesus! Mary, you favour me! Yes, God, I give you my life... May your holy will be done," etc. He kept repeating the names of Jesus and Mary. Because he thought his life was about to end, he was asking for absolution. I gave it to him in the presence of my colleagues who had run from all over to be near him. We helped him to walk up to the house. When he saw me reload-

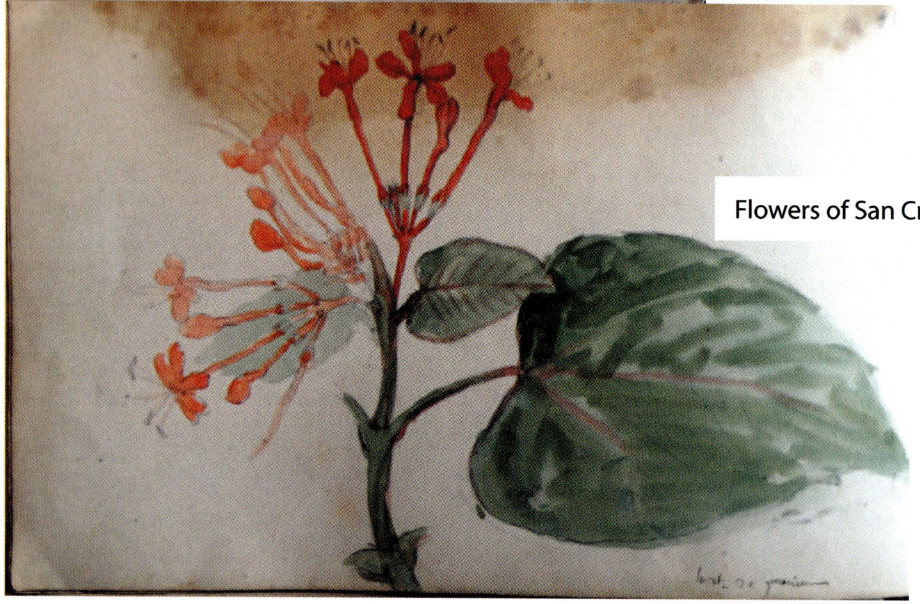

Flowers of San Cristobal

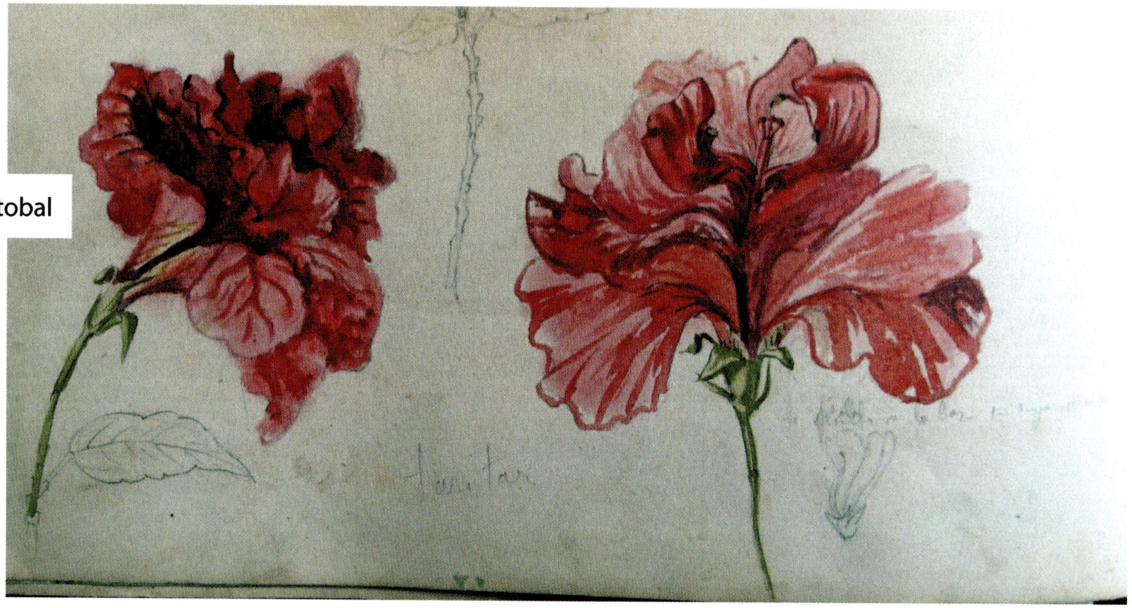

ing my pistol and heard the gunshots fired by the sailors, he begged us not to do any harm to the natives and particularly to the one who had wounded him. The name of that man is Orimanu. A sailor had taken too much liberty with his wife. Orimanu, who could not avenge himself against the sailor who was too well armed, chose his victim among us. With his lances in hand, he hid near the stream in the bush, hoping that someone would come and get some water before nightfall. Father Montrouzier, alone and unarmed, went to wash. He noticed the native and, seeing that he was coming toward him with the determination of doing him harm, he became frightened. He fled and was hit by the spear in his back. Never would the native have dared to strike him if he had been seen bearing arms. Father Montrouzier's wound was not serious. But the fright he experienced caused his heart to beat violently and he almost died from that. Father Paget gave him the sacrament of Extreme Unction on board the ship on 8 February. Since then, fortunately, Father Montrouzier has kept getting better and better. Today he has completely recovered.

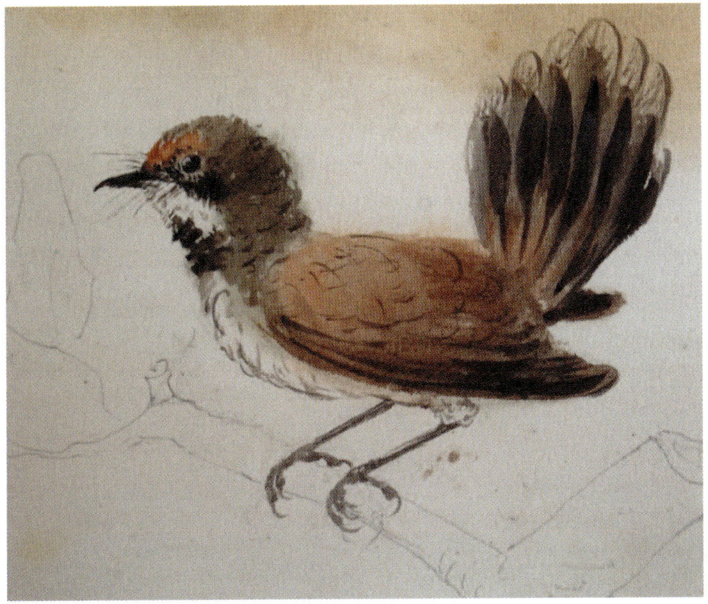

I wanted to report this to you, very reverend Father, as a proof of the usefulness of firearms in the archipelago of the Solomons. I am not talking about the sad day of the 16 December. Without the two gunshots the cannibals would never have let go of their prey. If Bishop Douarre has been successful in New Caledonia, he admits that, after God and our holy patrons, he owes this success to the firearms they had. I would consider it a good idea if in Melanesia the missionaries were to have firearms, not for killing men but so that they might be respected by the natives who would be seized with fright when they saw our men killing birds. I also think that they would be safer if they could put on a vest lined with zinc when they left the house.

Aside from these precautions, I would advise the superior of the missionaries who would go to found a station, to get from France or from Sydney a prefabricated house made of wood so that it might be set up upon arriving at the place of the mission. There would be much to be gained from that under several headings: 1. under the heading of the health of the missionaries who, upon arriving in a torrid climate, would otherwise be obliged to exhaust themselves in order to build a solid house. 2. It would avoid part of the disorders which the sailors indulge in... 3. The house built of dry wood would last longer. 4. It would cost less because we would not have to hold for such a long time a ship which would cost around 130 francs per day. The 4 walls of our house cost, according to this calculation, about 10,000 francs. Prosper says that if it had been made in Sydney it would have cost from 4000 to 6000 francs.

Please forgive me for making these observations, very reverend Father; I have in mind only the greater good of the missions. After the death of the bishop, we elected a father provincial by secret ballot. I voted for Father Frémont because I think he is the one among us who best demonstrates the religious spirit.

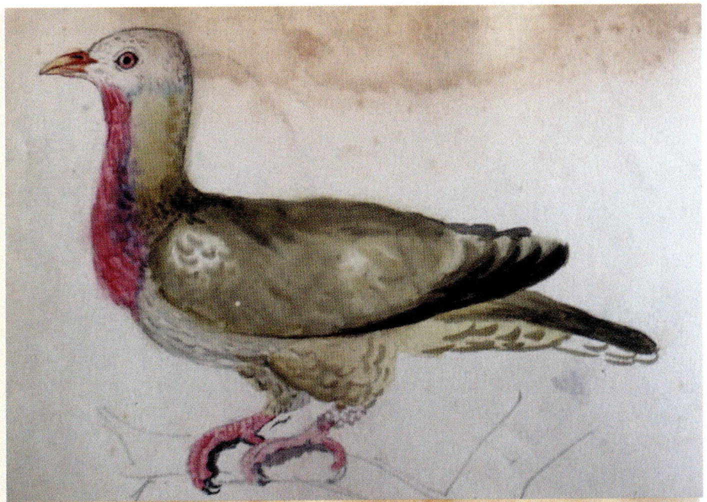

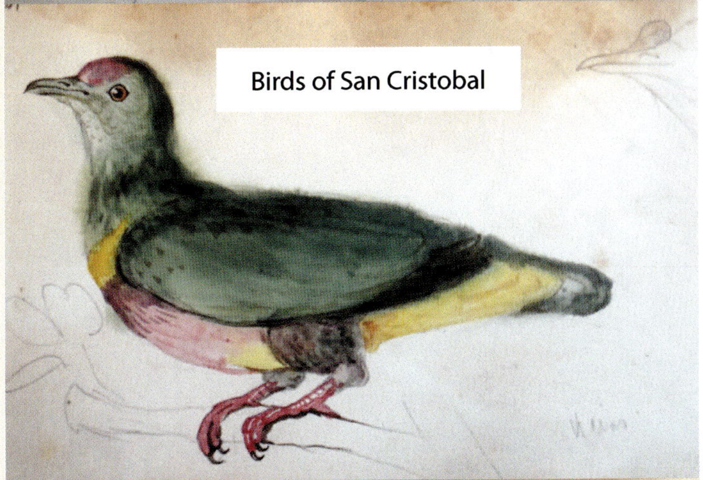

Birds of San Cristobal

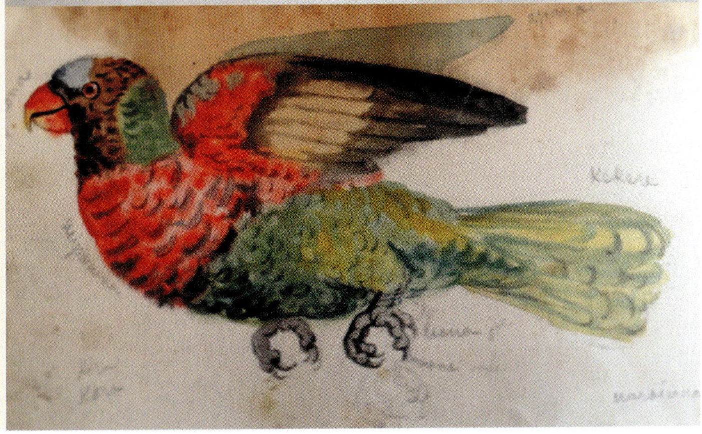

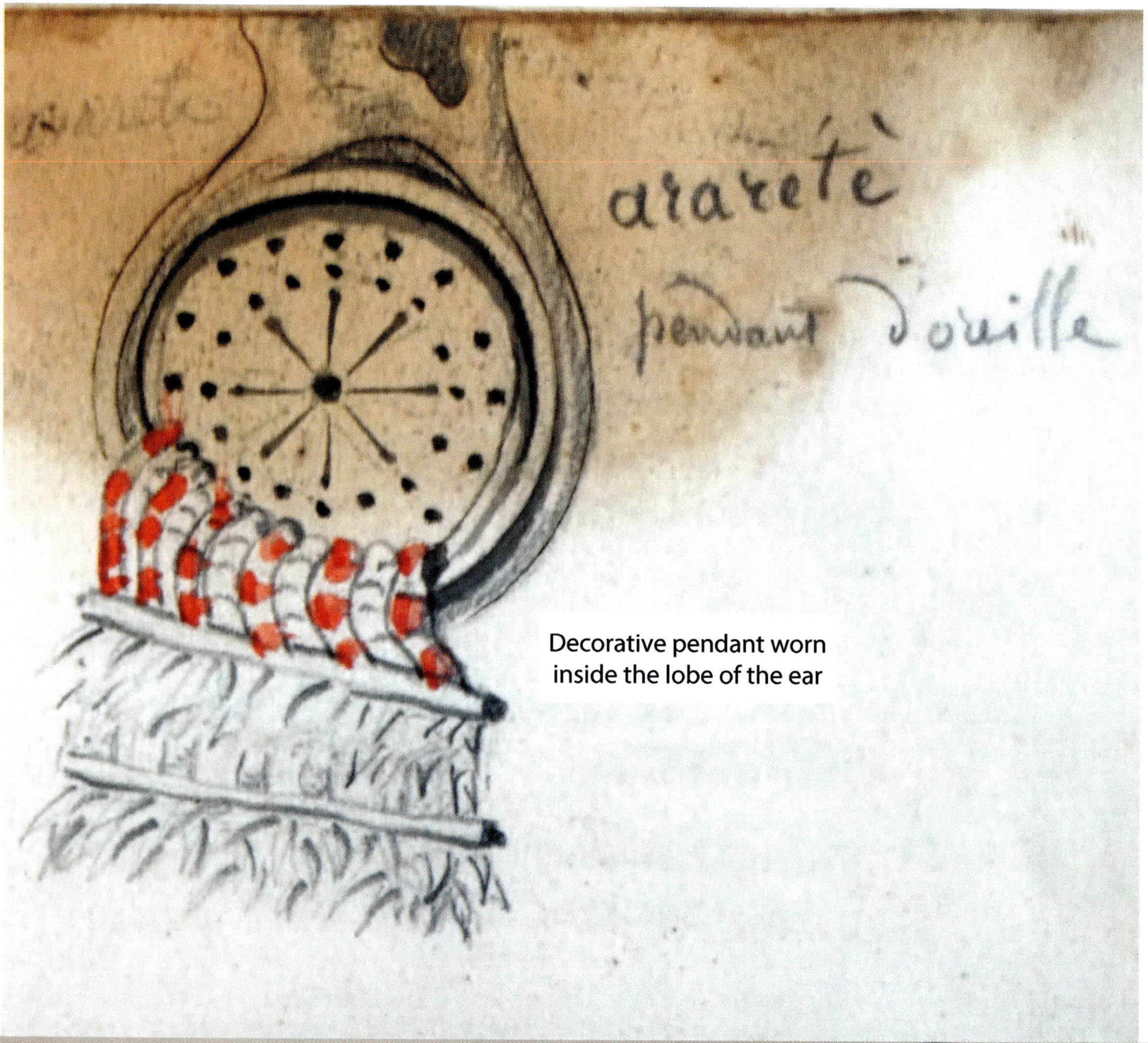

Decorative pendant worn inside the lobe of the ear

Orimanu
13 March 1847 - Fr Leopold Verguet to Fr Jean Claude Colin

...I am going to tell you a fact unimportant in itself but which is connected to another more interesting fact which occurred when we were starting to become established in this country. I want to speak to you about that native who injured Father Montrouzier. He is now one of our friends. Here is how God prepared the way for this reconciliation. I had the job of taking catechism to a tribe where he himself often went to visit his father-in-law. On the 28th of last October while on the way to take catechism to my parishioners, I saw on the sea shore four natives armed with spears. They were heading for the same tribe. I was in a canoe; I invited them to sit with me and help me paddle. Three accepted without difficulty; the fourth had me repeat the invitation several times before taking a seat. We soon crossed a little bay. There I asked my travelling companions their names. The one who had caused some trouble before getting into the canoe was Orimanu, the same person who had in the past wounded Father Montrouzier. I looked at him more closely; I found he had a gentle and pleasant countenance; he seemed to be about 25 to 30 years old. I invited him to come to see us at Makira; I promised him that not only would we not do him any harm but that I would even give him some iron and a red handkerchief. A refusal would have been dishonourable; to accept would cost him nothing. After washing in the fresh water and after gathering a good supply of amati (a very bitter leaf which is mixed with betel-nut), Orimanu and his companions escorted me as far as the summit of the mountain. There Ori-

> *"He was frightened of falling into a trap, so unaccustomed are they of forgiving one another*

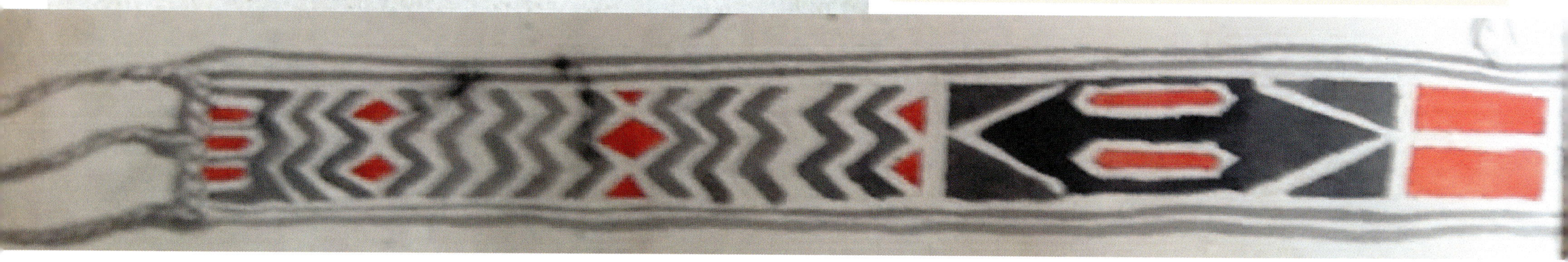

manu climbed a coconut palm belonging to his father-in-law and gave me sufficient to slack my thirst. After catechism he accompanied me out of the village and promised to come and see me in a few days. Since then I have met him several times in that tribe; he has always made the same promise but he has never kept his word. He was frightened of falling into a trap, so unaccustomed are they of forgiving one another their offences. On 19 September one of our neighbours, an old man of the Oné tribe passed away. He was the first Arossian who was baptized. After his death, according to the customs of his country, the natives put his body in the open air under 'vari' shells. They surrounded him with tree branches and coconut palms; they propped him up in a seating position using sticks from creepers and left him there for a fortnight so that his friends could pay their respects. Orimanu was among them. He came to visit him and eat coconuts in front of the cadaver. It was 20 September, and I was also in the tribe. I said to Orimanu that today he could not refuse coming to Makira. He said merely that he was frightened of being killed. I showed him how unfounded his fears were and asked him to tell me who was the man whom we had done the slightest harm to since the time that we were with them. He said that he did not know any. Ask those of the Oné tribe! They gave the same reply. Yet I pointed out to him that there were many of them who had stolen from us and that we would have been right to chastise them and that if we had not done so, it was to prove to them that we were good. That is true, said Orimanu, but instead of coming forward he stepped back. If you are still afraid, I said to him, take a lot of spears and bring along with you whom you like. I pointed out to him the son of one of the leaders of the area and by dint of pressing him, he got into a canoe and followed me to Makira. All our fathers and brothers were pleased to see him. How beautiful religion is, said a brother, there is a man who harmed us and we wish him well. Orimanu walked a little around the house and in the garden. He got a piece of iron and a handkerchief and retraced the route to Oné in peace. Having calmed Orimanu's feelings in that way, I no longer saw any difficulty myself in going into his tribe. On 23 or 25 October I made that journey with Father Thomassin. After walking for an hour and a half we arrived at the top of a high mountain quite crowned with coconut palms; the houses were built at the base of those palms. Orimanu's house was at the centre of the tribe. Orimanu's father-in-law acted as our guide. Orimanu and his men received us in a friendly fashion. They offered us coconuts. Orimanu lit a fire and let us lie down on his mats. Father Thomassin was struck with fever in that hut. We stayed about two hours at Orimanu's place; we gave him some presents; we were visited by the leaders of the area and we returned to Makira. Orimanu and four natives were keen to accompany us. They were a great help to us. Father Thomassin initially felt strong enough to make the trip but he was so indisposed that he was forced to lie down on a pile of wood in the middle of a field. Rain bucketed down. We were lucky to find a native who agreed to carry him on his back and take him as far as the sea shore. Orimanu and two natives climbed into the canoe and accompanied us to the mission station. The one who carried Father Thomassin was given a piece of iron, the other gave some yams in exchange for a large piece of beef (we had killed it two days previously because we did not have anything more to feed it). Orimanu got his share of it too. Since then he and those of his tribe come and see us without showing the slightest fear.

Léopold Verguet
Apostolic missionary
of the Society of Mary

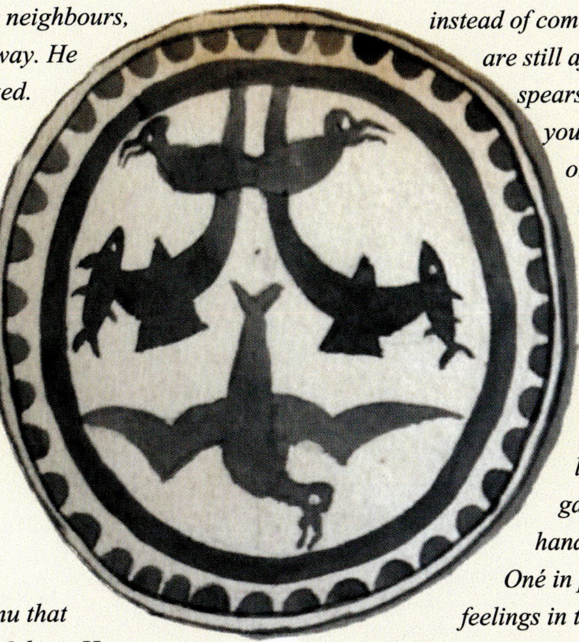

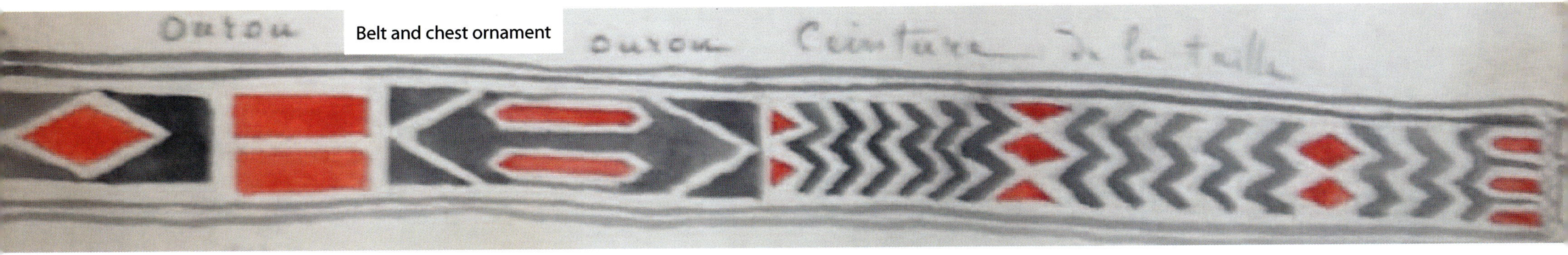

Belt and chest ornament

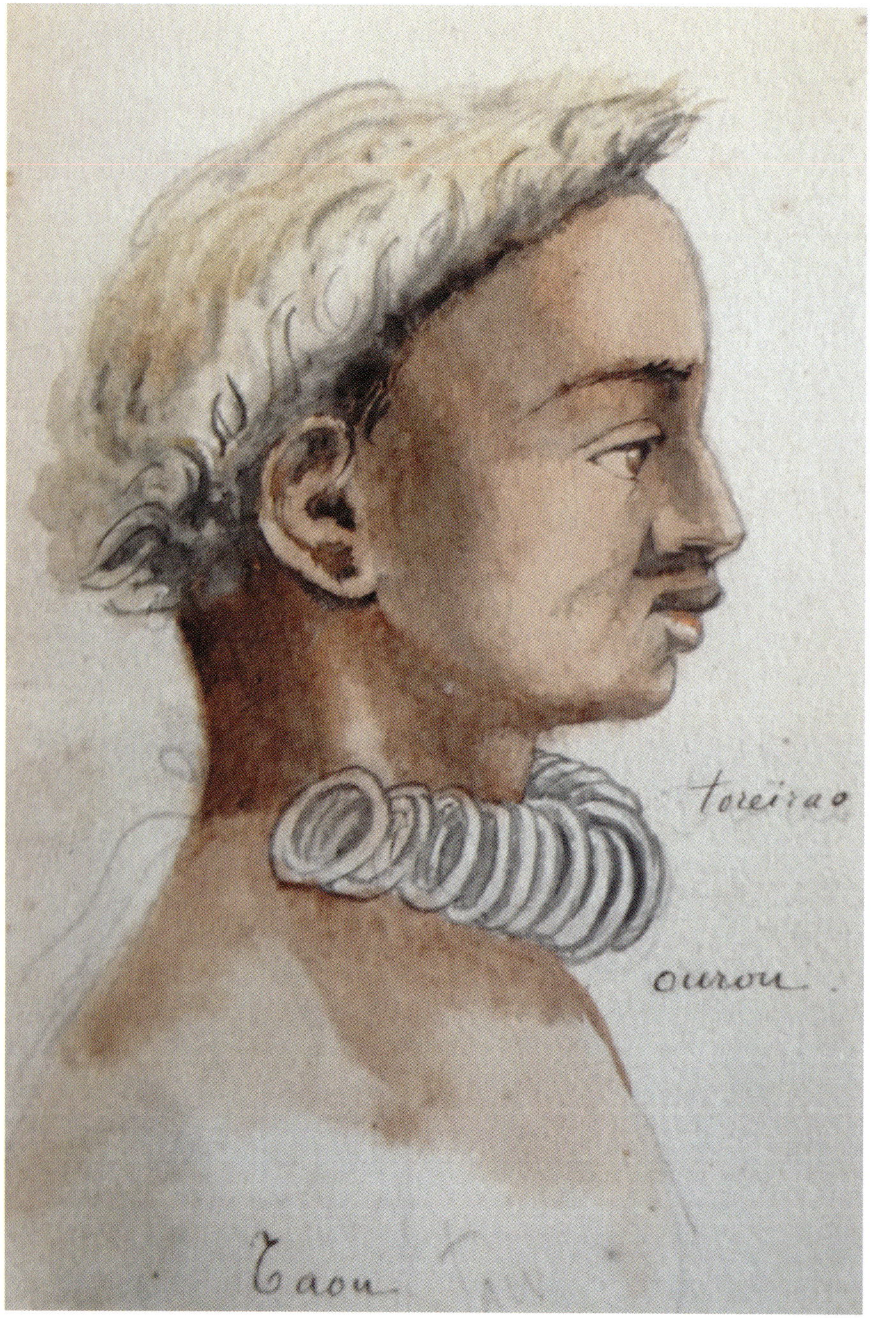

Taou of the Tribe of Lokou
on San Cristobal

The People of San Cristobal
24 June & 24 July 1846, Verguet to his father

Arosi, 24 June 1846

My dear father,

Today is your feast day. If I were with you, I would show you my affection by some proof inspired by my attachment to you. Although I am quite far from you, I have not forgotten you. Today I offered the holy sacrifice of the Mass for your happiness, and I am using the rest of the day to write to you with long details about the peoples among whom I am living. Your affection for me makes these things interesting.

It is impossible for me to speak of the idea which the inhabitants of San Cristobal have concerning the origin of their island. I do not know their language well enough. All that I have been able to obtain is the native name for this island which Mendaña, a Spanish captain, discovered in 1567 and to which he gave the name of San Cristobal, because he could not know of the name Arosi which the local people give it. The few bits of information which travellers have written about this island and which Mr. de Rienzi reports in the third volume of the work entitled The Universe, seem correct to me. It is regretful that they are so short. Mr. d'Uurville tells us that it is a big mountainous island, populated in this land which measures 72 miles (34 leagues) from the north-west to the south-east and 16 to 18 miles (4 or 6 leagues) wide. The east coast is not well known, from 10° 4' to 10° 53' latitude south and from 159° 2' to 163° longitude east. Port Saint Marie where the residence of the missionaries is located is situated at 10° 28' latitude south by 159° longitude.

> *"Generally there is nothing repulsive about their faces*

The Arosians are of medium build and have well-proportioned limbs. They differ from Europeans only by color, their skin is a very dark bronze, and by a few traits of their facial features; their forehead is slightly narrow and flat, the nose is open, not long, and contracted at the height of the eyes. While some of them have well developed jaws, most of them have a medium-sized jaw. Generally, there is nothing repulsive about their faces. Some of them inspire confidence at first sight and a fondness which cannot be explained. Their eyes are black and gentle. Their honey-tongued, often crafty speech causes the gentle name of friend to sound in your ear, or rather the name of good friend, malaou kou, of little brother torakou, words which fittingly find their way to the heart. There are some who speak like that only to deceive all the better, but others who speak sincerely and who prove their friendship when they bring yams, coconuts, bananas and other local fruit. The latter are quite sensitive to any show of friendship. If you refuse their present, such scorn can make them shed tears. If you offer them in exchange some cloth or a piece of iron, they want to accept it only as a brother or friend. ...

When they come with me on my errands, they are surprised to see me constantly looking for a place to put my foot. As far as they are concerned, they are never bothered; with lance in hand they are thinking rather of looking in the shrubs to see if some enemy is not setting a trap for them. Despite my precautions, it happens that I slip and fall; they laugh as they lend me a hand and tell me to take off my shoes because they are of no use for walking. "Let shoes be taboo for your feet and soon you will walk like us." When they see my bare feet on which the toes seem to be stuck to each other, they hold them up to ridicule, and they advance their own feet and spread out the toes, moving them in every direction, they dare me do so as much and are triumphant over my not being able to do so. Often, when I was in France, I used to make fun of the feet of the Chinese; it is quite just that the natives pay me back with the same thing, perhaps with no less reason.

You must not believe that the natives of these islands leave it up to nature to adorn their bodies. They really like to adorn themselves and show considerable good taste in the ornaments they choose. They cut their hair in different ways. The children have their heads shaved clean, except for a tuft of hair kept at the top of the head. The young people enlarge their foreheads by shaving a little of their hair; they let the rest grow and are careful to keep them combed up with a bamboo comb adorned with red feathers. Ordinarily they leave a space open in their hair so that the skull behind the head is visible. From a desire for cleanliness and also so that the sun should bother them less, they smear their hair with lime, which burns the hair and leaves a red colour at the edges. They seem to like this daubing very much. They use it especially when they go to visit some distant tribe. They want to appear in all their beauty and they would not forget either to powder their hair any more than a fashionable European would forget to arrange his beard and put perfume on his head in a similar situation. I have seen some who, in order not to disturb their hair, preferred to suffer the inconvenience of certain insects which are plentiful among them; they brought their hand to the lime in the hair and then withdrew it as if they had burned themselves. If the hurt were still felt, they would take a small rib of coconut leaves and would carefully stick it into their thick hair to harpoon the noxious guest. When they do not have their head beautified with lime, they go hunting and make a feast of all the game they can find. Some have a part in the hair so as to represent two crescents joined together on the inside by a straight line. Others let their hair grow naturally and highlight the blackness by the striking contrast with some pouri which they attach there. Pouri is their name for a shell about the size of an egg and white like porcelain.

The razor which they use to do their hair is a piece of fire-stone or a piece of glass. Almost all the Arosians have tattooed faces. Their tattoos differ from the tattoos of the New Zealanders in that they adopt the broken line instead of the curved line and thus they are all tattooed in the same way. They take as their model the coarse sculpted statues in the chief's house. This kind of tattoo is a series of zigzags, separated by straight lines which run parallel from the nose to the ears and which fill the whole face. On the middle of the forehead they trace a design which has some resemblance to the Malta cross. They tattoo only their faces. In rare cases some can be seen who are tattooed along the back spine; others have a fish drawn on their chest. I showed them a parrot which I had painted; one of them asked me to tattoo it on his shoulder. ...

The method used to make their pearls and their money is no less thorough. On a stone they wear down a seashell from which they get the pearls. They cut them up into small round disks, always by rubbing against the

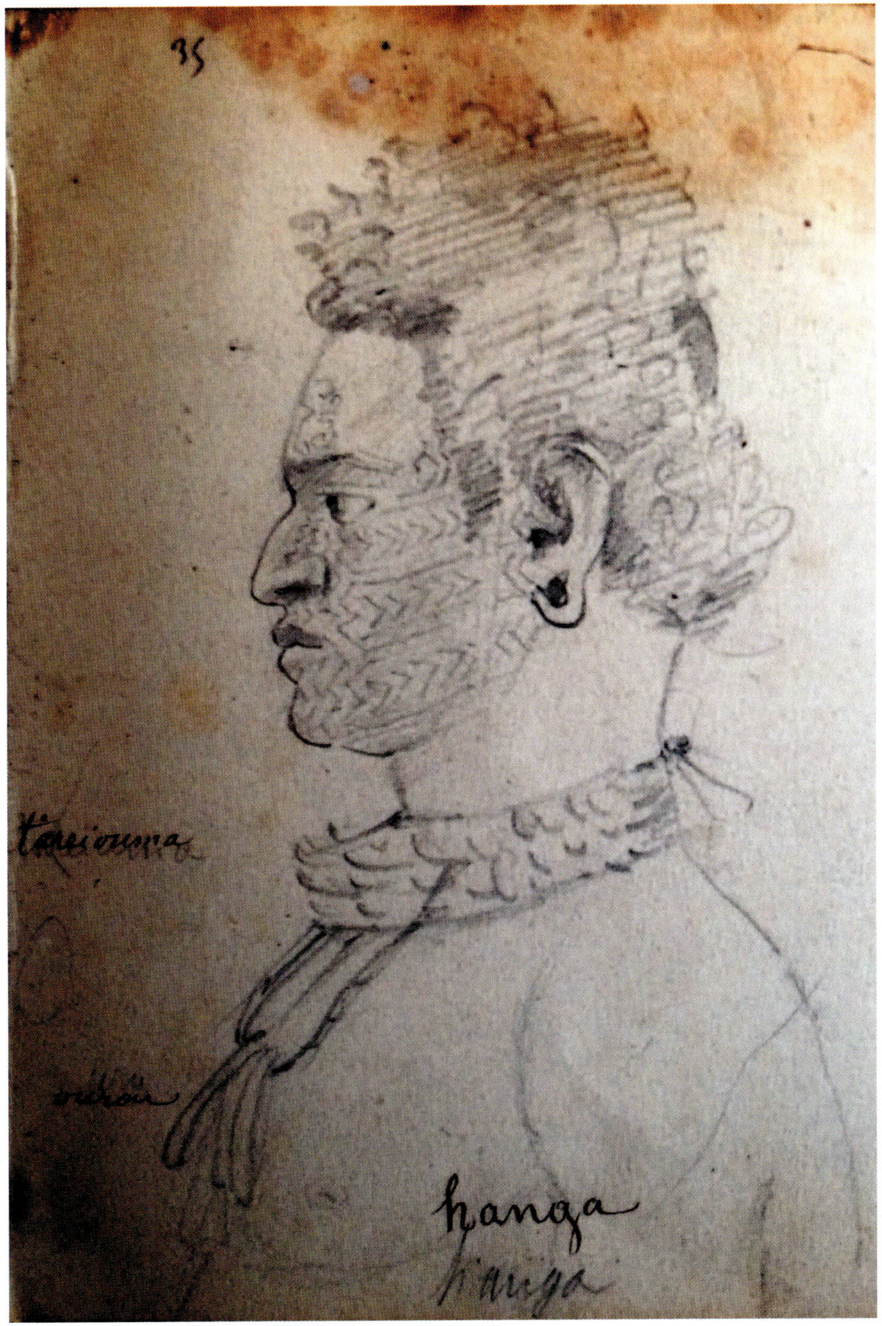

Hanga of the Tribe of Wasinpareo
at Port St Marie on San Cristobal

stone. They drive these disks into small holes made in a plank. Over the middle of the disk, they put a small rod with a very sharp piece of fire-stone at the end. They turn the rod very rapidly between their hands and end up piercing the seashell. The only thing left to do is to polish the pearl and put it on the thread. These pearls are the money current among them; they measure it on their arms. The lengths adopted in their exchanges are an elbow length, a half-arm's length and a full arm's length.

At the beginning, when we were bargaining with the natives to obtain from them permission to establish ourselves on their land, a native who speaks some English and whom we had taken as interpreter, said to us with assurance: "Although the proprietors of the land where you want to establish yourselves are not here, that does not prevent you from building a house even sooner. Go where you want; when the proprietors come, I am rich, I will take care of paying for you." We asked him what were his riches. He showed us an elbow length of rather coarse pearls. "How much is that worth?" we asked him laughingly. "It is worth a pound in Sydney" (that is, 25 francs), he told us with an imperturbable composure, and he added, without being disconcerted by our laughter: "I have a lot of them, and they are all at your service. ...

I have not said anything about the natives' clothing. That is because they do not have any, unless you want to consider as a garment that supple and narrow leaf with which the men hide a part of their nudity, and those small filaments of bark which the women hang from their lower belly and from behind below the belt. In New Caledonia I was revolted when I saw the women wearing so little. However, they are very modest in comparison with our Arosian women. I do not think that nudeness can be pushed any further than in these countries. The young girls go about completely nude. The married women wear the small transparent apron I spoke about. On Isabel Island, the women are covered with a blue cloth from the belt to the knees. The Arosian women have an adornment which distinguishes them from the men. It is a series of very white rings which covers their arm from the elbow to the shoulder. Aside from that, they cut their hair the same as the men. They pierce their ears and their nose at the end of which they sometimes place the feather of a pigeon or a parrot. Style is an unusual prejudice!

> *"I have not said anything about the natives' clothing. That is because they don't have any*

The houses of Arosi people are nothing but small cabins whose leaf-roofs are supported by a few stakes and whose sides are made of pegs close together or by superimposed palm branches. I will go into some detail. Before building his house, the Arosian begins by arranging the ground. He chooses four posts of the size he wants to give his cabin and puts then in a rectangle at the base. That is his first plan. He sticks a pike into the earth at each of the corners and rests on these pikes two other beams which support the roof. The ridge of the roof is formed by a long beam resting on two forked pikes fixed in the earth a little inside the house-plan. On this roof-ridge they attach small sticks with the bark removed. These sticks descend from the side beams to which they are securely tied. Once the framework of the roof has been set up, the only thing left is to cover it. They take palm leaves from which they have removed the leaf-vein. They fold these leaves around a reed to which they sew a rush, superposing them in such a way that each leaf covers half of the previous one. When they have a sufficient number of rushes thus prepared, they attach them across on the sticks of the roof framework going from bottom to top, putting them very close together. This covering is at once light, solid and waterproof. The roof of our house is made in the same way. At the roof ridge they place a large number of reeds so as to make a crest which gives the roof a certain elegance and much more solidity. The palm branches whose leaves have been used are not lost in the least. They use them to form the sides and the front of the house. Each house has two openings. Since the roof comes down almost to the ground, the windows are placed in the narrow sides of the house. These windows serve for both doors and chimney. In one of the corners of the house there is ordinarily a small opening next to the ground to let the dog go through. The interior of the cabin is as simple as its exterior. A few black stones mark the fireplace. Coconut-leaf mats stretched out on the ground serve as chairs and beds. On a small flooring, almost always covering only part of the

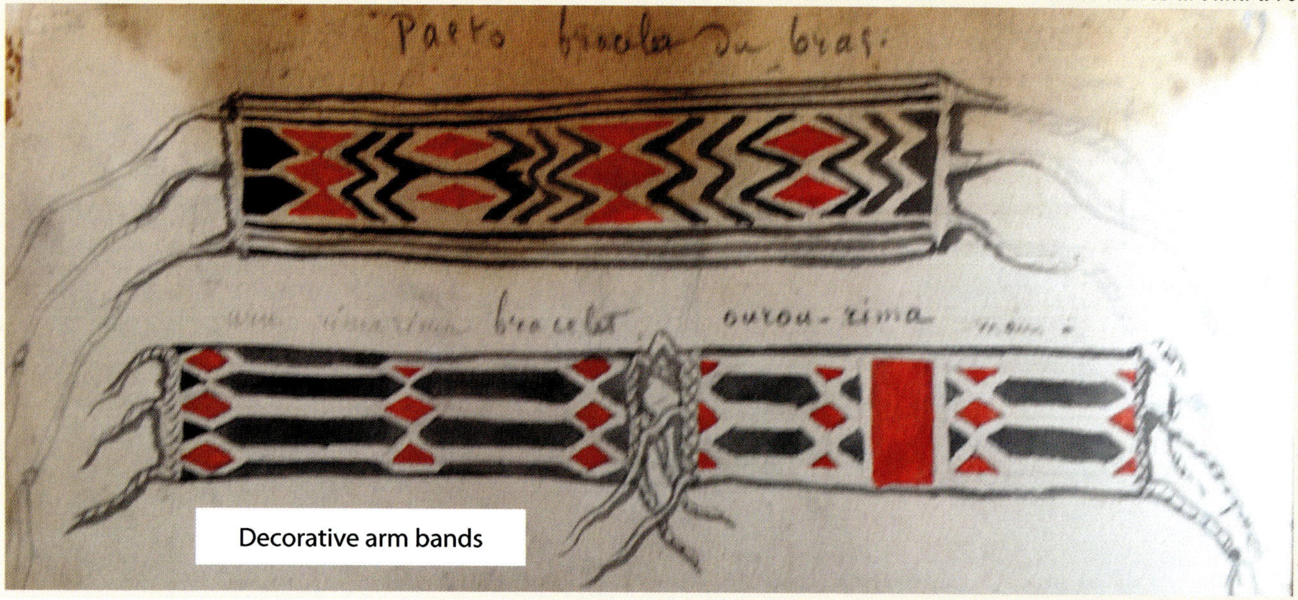

Decorative arm bands

ground, the food is placed. Weapons and tools decorate the walls.

All these treasures are sheltered from theft behind a simple mat which serves as the door. They bar it with a reed and go about their occupations, assured that no one would dare to break down this weak barrier. The master of the house has the right to kill anyone who comes into the house during his absence. One day, my ignorance of this custom made me expose the life of a native who was my guide. A certain Pahé had stolen a hoe from us. He was from the village of a young man named Toroa. I pretended to take a walk, but really I wanted to recover the hoe, so I invited Toroa to lead me to his village. I was with two of our Brothers. Toroa was leading me. I asked to see the house of Pahé, and he showed it to me. Pahé was absent. I entered unceremoniously and I looked everywhere for the stolen hoe. He had been careful to get rid of it. I did not find the hoe, but in Pahé's house I saw a small hatchet which had been taken from us without our knowing who the thief was. I left the hatchet and went back with the satisfaction of knowing about Pahé, in whom we had previously placed our confidence. The face of our guide became distorted when he saw me going into Pahé's house. One might have said that some sorcerer had changed him into a stone. "Get out," he said to me, "get out; Pahé will kill me. I got out, leaving the house open and Toroa led me back by another path. After walking for some time, we sat down in the shade near a waterfall. Toroa had not recovered from his fright. He was still saying: "Pahé will kill me..."

"No," a Brother said to him, "he won't kill us..."

"As far as you are concerned, that's true, he won't kill you, but as for me, he will kill me."

"So, this Pahé is quite terrible," I said to him. "Aren't you as strong as he; couldn't you defend yourself?"

"Yes, I am strong," he said, making a fist. "See, I'm a vigorous man," he continued as he flexed his arm to show us that he was hard muscled. "Let him come to get me, I will run him through with my lance. As he said this, his eye sparkled and he stiffened all the muscles of his body, as if he were getting ready to fight. He stayed with us all day long. In the evening, he went back to his village, and he promised me that he would come back the next day. I was very anxious to know how he had calmed his quarrel with Pahé. The next day, after our lunch, we saw Toroa coming. He told us that they had not gone to sleep at his own house but at Tiia's, our mutual friend. In the evening, during the darkest part of the night, he was seated before the door; his lances were in the house. All of a sudden, Pahé appeared and reproached him for his conduct. "You are the one who brought Perké [Verguet] into my house; now die from the blow of the lance." At the same time, without waiting for an answer, he threw the sagaye. Toroa, no less agile, avoided the blow by a quick movement. He threw himself into his house, seized the lances and ran in pursuit of Pahé. "He missed me," he said, "but if I had found him, I would have run him through."

"You are not courageous enough, you must have trembled like a leaf when Pahé approached.

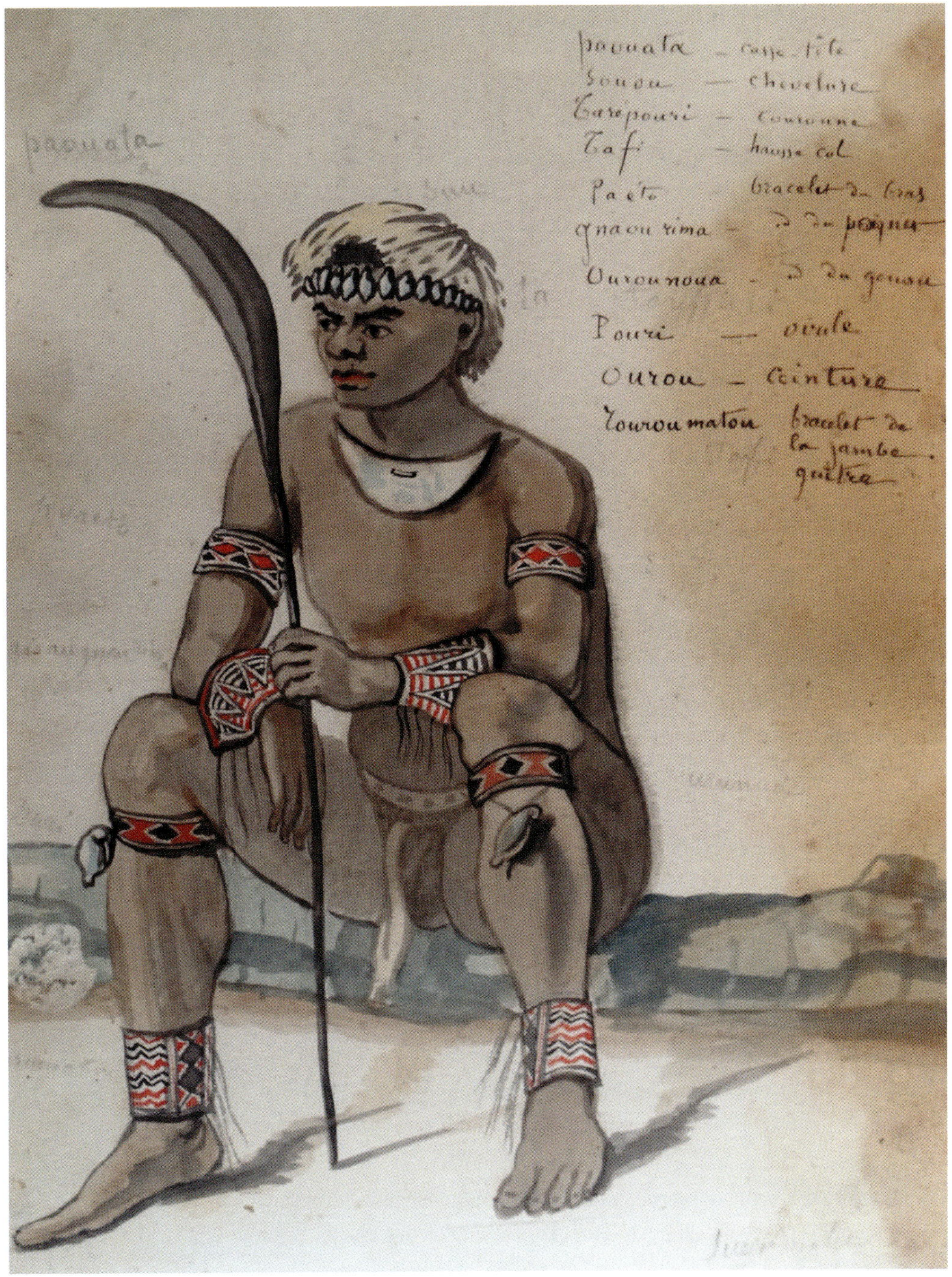

Portrait of Sourimahe

Your knees were knocking against each other, because you were so afraid."

"Should I tremble? Look at this arm, it's strong. If I had found Pahé, he would have felt it."

"Why did you not find him?"

"The night was too dark," he said, as he closed his eyes with great effort. "If there had been a bright moonlight, he would not have escaped from me." In talking about the moonlight, he opened his big eyes, he breathed heavily and spread his fingers as if rays were coming from his face.

"But you know well where Pahé's house is. Why didn't you go there?"

"Pahé is no longer at his house." Indeed, Pahé had gone away for three weeks. Then he came back and made peace with Toroa and with us. I have spoken too long about this thing of little importance, but it will help you to understand the customs of our neighbours." ...

The Arosi also have suspended houses in which they keep their provisions. These are store-houses for yams. These cabins seem very picturesque. They stand out elegantly in the middle of clumps of green, bamboos, coconut trees and sugar cane. And in each village you can see a large hangar endowed with everything that is most precious in the country and adorned with all that artists' imagination could invent, everything is most original. This is the palace of the main man and, so to speak, a royal palace. Only men are permitted to enter there. That is where strangers are received. It is a kind of forum where affairs of state are discussed. That is where prisoners of war are cut up and cooked. Their skulls and their bones, mixed with those of pigs and fish, adorn the ceiling of this palace! The palace of Mahémara, the chief of Oné, a village located at Port Saint Marie, is the most remarkable one that I have ever seen. It is about 24 metres long by 12 wide and 12 high. Each of the rafters is made entirely of a single piece of wood; the room is held up by 12 sculpted columns and placed in three rows. Each of the columns depicts coarse black statues embellished with all the ornaments known to the local people. They call these inoni -man. These "men" are all in about the same position. They are in a standing position, with both arms stretched out alongside the body. In the middle of the hangar, there is, I would say, something like a group sculpted from the same wooden post. This group portrays a man who has a fish on his head. This fish is devouring a child held crosswise in its long jaws. On the rafters upon which rests the middle of the roof, two images can be seen. One represents a victory over the mountain people and the other represents the capture of a large boat. This image had no depth: the men are all in the foreground, all the same size and pictured one after the other. The dead are depicted with the head below and the feet above. When the artist had difficulty fitting two fighters into the scene, he placed them above the others in the clouds. This tableau shows that drawing is not foreign to these island-people and that it is still in its early stages. They go into ecstasies when we show them engravings from our homelands. They express their admiration by jumping up and crying out. ...

Fishing is one of the main occupations of the local people. To catch fish, they have fishhooks, harpoons and nets. Their fishhooks are made of a single piece of mother of pearl. They use these to catch small fish. They can be seen in the morning nonchalantly seated in their outrigger pirogues, with the oar in one hand and the line in the other. They throw out the fishhook without bait; they make it run along the surface of the water. Its brilliancy attracts the small fish. As soon as these have bitten, the native pulls them out, deposits them in the pirogue when they fall off by themselves because the fishhooks do not have hooks at the end of the curve. The line is

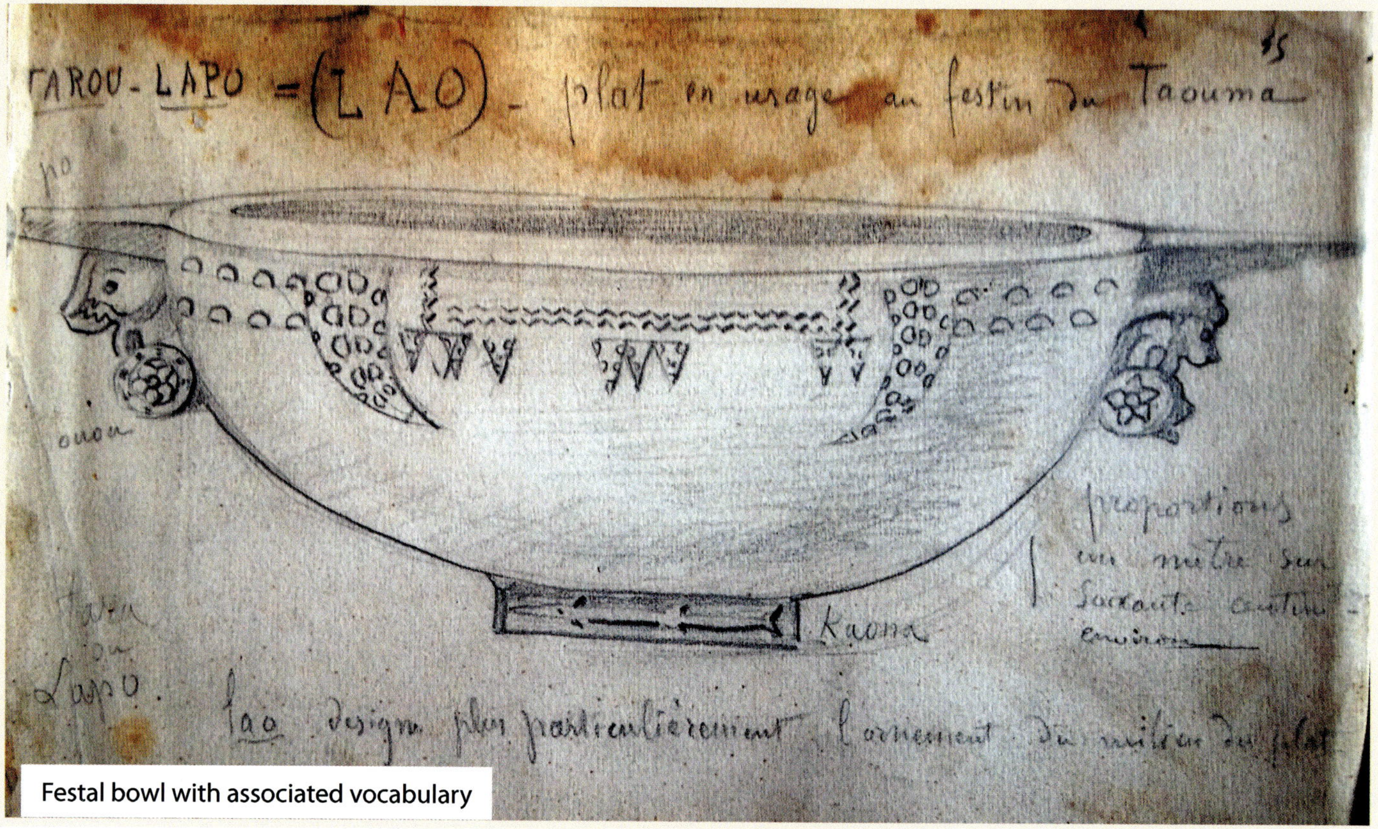

Festal bowl with associated vocabulary

immediately thrown back and in a few minutes they usually catch a dozen fish. The fishhooks used for fishing in the open sea are bigger and made from two pieces. One of these pieces is of tortoise shell and the other of mother of pearl. This kind of fishhook is curved and pointed. This kind pierces the jaw. With these fishhooks they catch fish weighing several pounds. They know the time when they should go fishing. ...

I have said only a little about the pirogues of the Arosians. They are so carefully and elegantly made that they deserve a separate treatment. They have three kinds which they call etea, ora, solima. The etea is a pirogue made with a single piece of wood. They make it by hollowing a tree whose wood lends itself to this kind of work; it is light, white, and resists cracking when exposed to the sun's rays. These pirogues measure around five metres long by thirty centimetres wide and forty or fifty centimetres deep. Across the middle of this pirogue there is a small seat for the rower. It would be impossible to keep this long and narrow boat stable if it were not fitted with an outrigger. The local people are very much attached to this kind of pirogue. From the seat and from the front of the pirogue are extended two parallel poles about a metre and a half long and which extend toward the left of the etea. At the extreme ends of these poles are fixed two half circles whose curvature is turned toward the sea. These half circles hold up a palm branch stripped of its leaves; it serves as the outrigger and counterweight for the pirogue. The front end of this palm branch extends beyond the front of the pirogue. It is lifted by a natural curve and is always out of the water. The etea is the kind of boat most used by the Arosians when they live on a quiet bay. They go to their farms in the etea by hugging the shore. They bring back the fruits, the wood and the herbs necessary for the household. They make use of the etea to go fishing along the coast. If, during the movements they are obliged to do, the etea happens to capsize, the Arosian is unperturbed as he returns to his pirogue by swimming, swings it above the water in order to begin to empty it. When the pirogue can float, he empties the water in it with a paddle which always goes with the pirogue. He swims to retrieve the oar, comes back to his pirogue, throws himself inside and continues fishing.

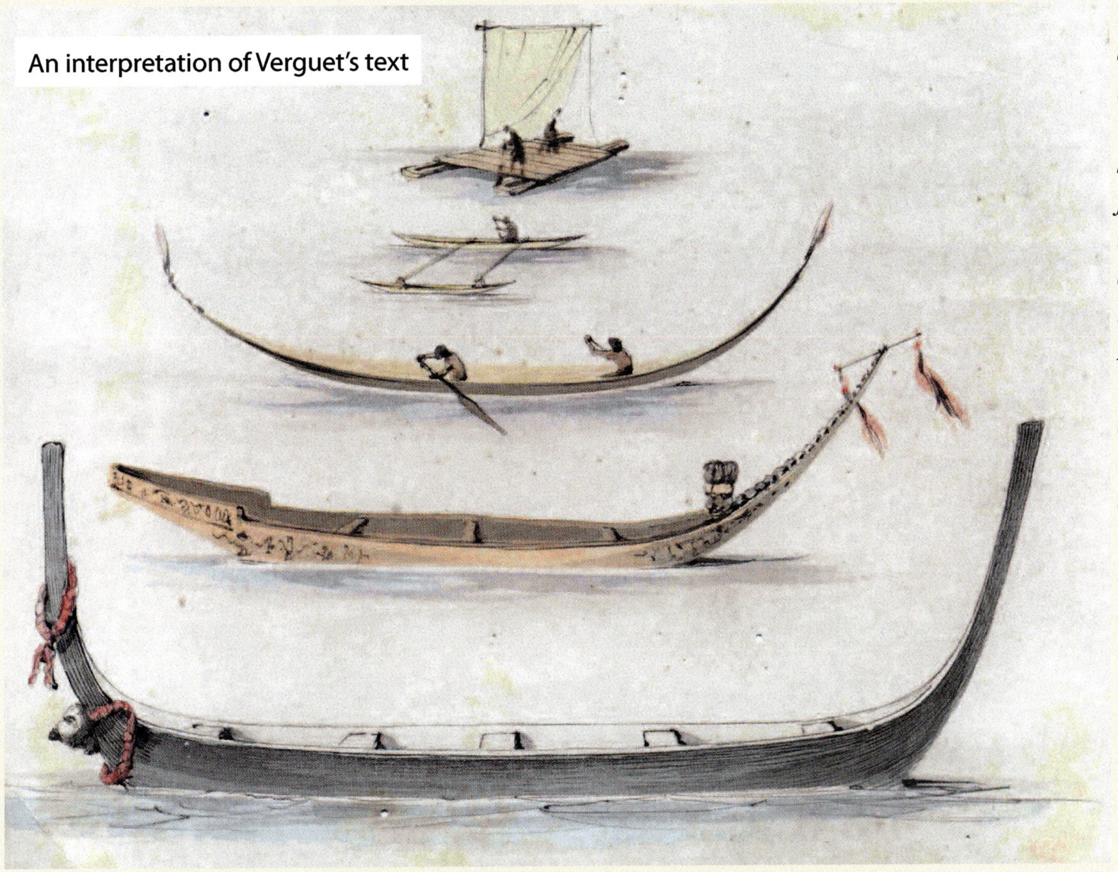

An interpretation of Verguet's text

The pirogue which they call ora is more elegant and seems to me to be more solid than the etea. The ora is made with long planks sewn together and tarred with the nut of a certain fruit, brown in colour, the size of a fist and shaped like an egg. They call this fruit puru. By rubbing it against a stone they obtain a paste which they place on the fault lines of their ora. Soon this paste hardens, turns black and looks like tar. The ora comes in different sizes. The average lengths are eight metres by seventy centimetres wide and about fifty deep. It is shaped like a crescent somewhat lengthened in the back. These canoes do not have a keel; they are extremely light. The least wave lifts them up; the smallest oar stroke makes them move a long distance. Three rowers in one of these boats would easily make several leagues per hour. The ora can hold up eight to ten rowers. You can imagine the rapidity of their course when they strike the water together and with all their strength. The seats in this pirogue are very low and rest on planks and are made of rounded pieces of wood carved from the interior of the boat. The point in front has two planks raised higher than the others so that large waves do not throw their foam into the pirogue. The ora is very graciously decorated. The point of the front crescent ends in a bird's head devouring a fish. From one end to the other it is embellished with festoons of pearls of different colours, with red plumes, and with mother of pearl shells. On the curve in the rear, there is the sculpture of a dog. The extreme end has small adornments of wood splashed with many colours. A succession of puru descend along the length

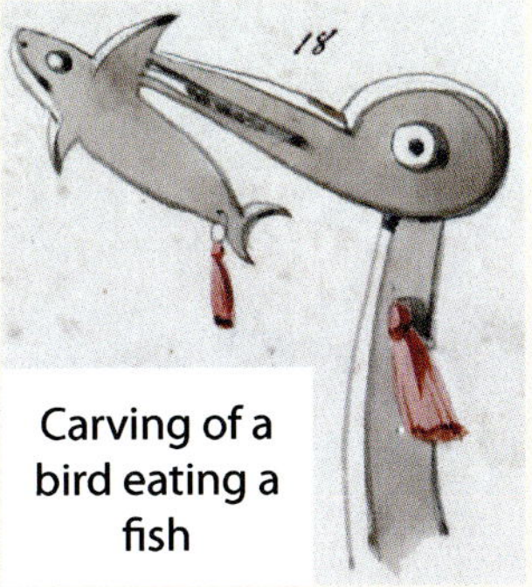

Carving of a bird eating a fish

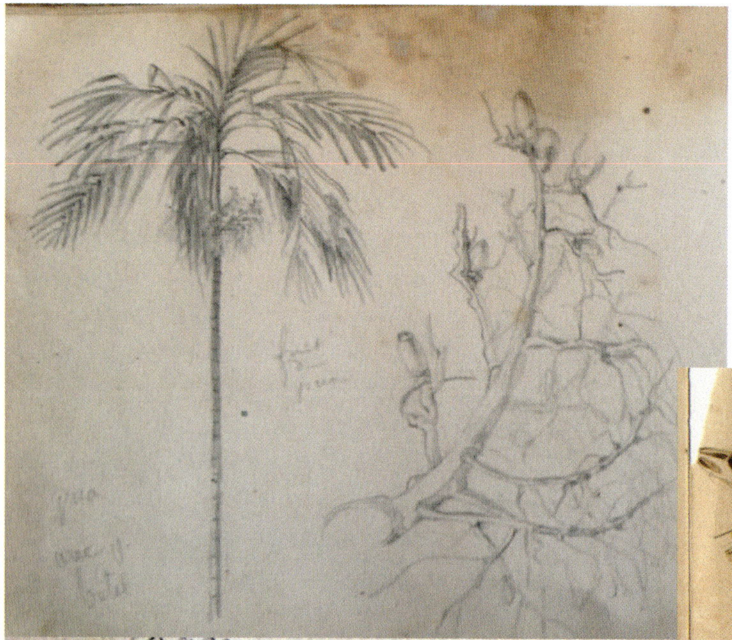

Betel nut
the palm
and the fruit

Carved dog

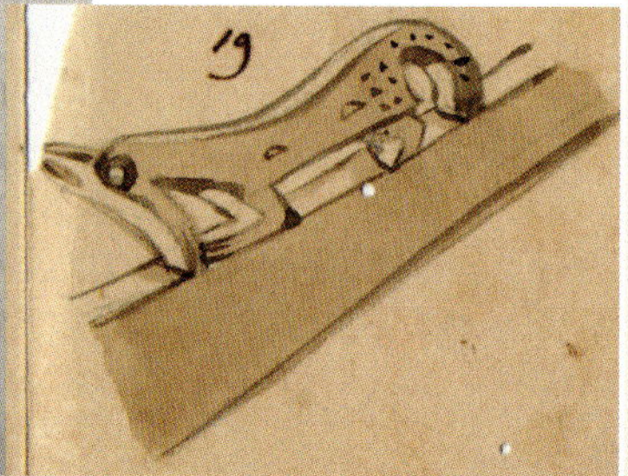

of the crescent. On the sides of the ora there are patterns of white shells stuck into the wood. These figures represent birds which spread out their wings and which seem to be shaking them on the surface of the water like swans or albatrosses. In these pirogues the local people venture far into the open sea to engage in commerce with ships. They also use them to go fishing for large fish.

The boat which they call solima differs from the ora only in size. It is a construction which is gigantic considering the fact that its builders have at hand only small blades of iron attached at the end of a curved piece of wood. The solima is about twenty metres long by a metre and a half wide. It has twelve or fourteen rowers' benches and can hold thirty to forty persons. Its ornamentation and shape are about the same as those of the ora. The Arosians ordinarily use these pirogues only for long voyages. They load them with arms and provisions and go to visit a friendly tribe about ten or fifteen leagues away. One fatiguing day is enough to make this long trip. They stay for several days with their friends, exchange their provisions, their arms, their tools and also the objects which they stole from us, and then return to spread before our eyes the gifts which they received. If sometimes we follow them to their friends', we find there a straw hat, a hatchet, a clerical frock-coat which we are obliged to respect because the present

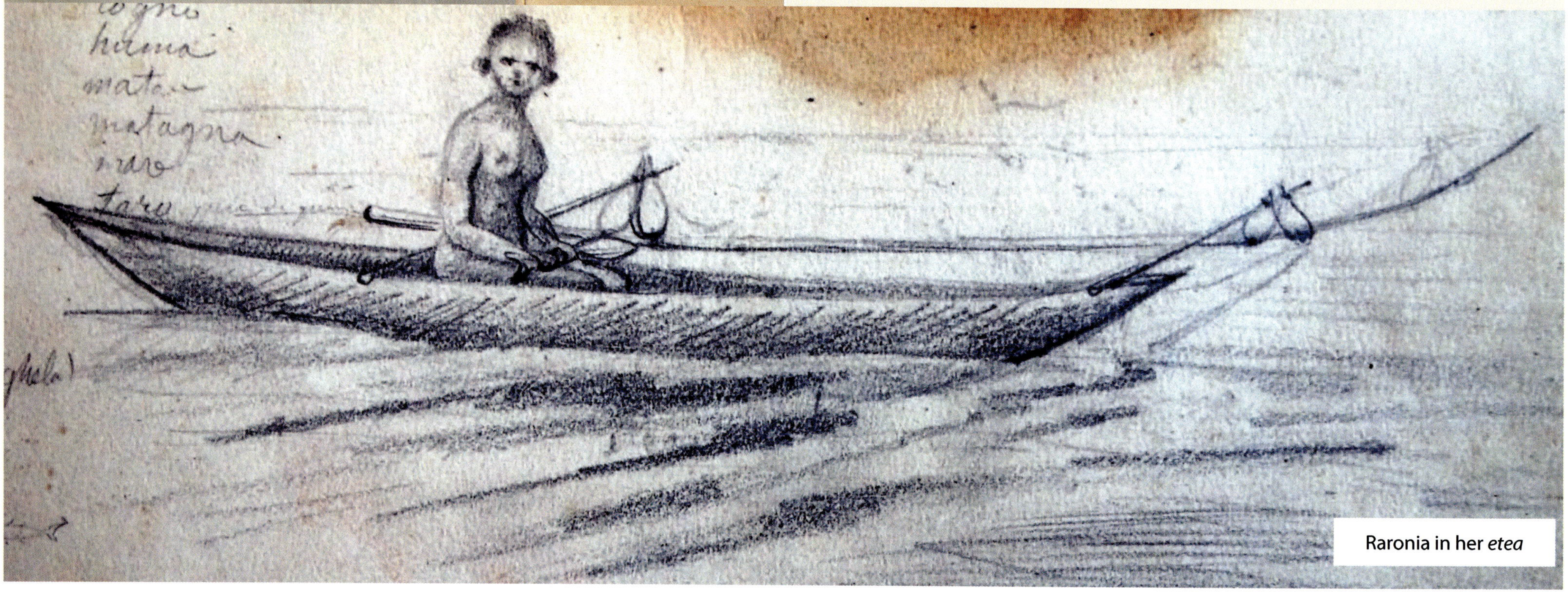

Raronia in her *etea*

owner has legitimately acquired these objects by paying for them with his money. ...

They take strength during the day by chewing betel; they make betel with bitter and aromatic leaves which they call auraté, with the fruit of the aru and other palms, and then, with the lime which they pulverize, they suck from the tip of a rod while they chew the auraté. That is the limit of what they need. The rest of the time is spent in visiting or dancing and very little in the cultivation of the land.

Their dancing is war-like; they always dance holding a small club. They arrange themselves in several ranks, jump forward and backward while always keeping the same distance from each other. They hum a melody full of violence and this helps them to dance in rhythm. They walk in rhythm with their club and with small globular bells of mother of pearl attached to their right hand. The whole of the movements creates all the beauty of this dance. After having jumped to one side, they suddenly turn around and jump to the opposite side. Their singing makes this dance rather distressing. Perspiration can be seen flowing down the length of their body, but they stop only when the singing and the manoeuvers have finished. This dance is forbidden to the women; they are satisfied with looking. ...

Such is the material life of the Arosians. But their spiritual life is deplorable. In this regard, they are worthy of pity! They barely recognize a superior being, about which they have but an obscure idea. It seemed to me that they call him Jona. He is a god who hears nothing, who sees nothing, but whom they address nevertheless when they plant their yams. They take the first yam, breathe on it, murmur a few words and put it into the earth. Until now, that is all that we have been able to notice about their belief and their worship. They are astonished upon learning that our God sees everything, that he hears everything, and that he penetrates even the most secret thoughts of our hearts, that after this life he will recompense us according to our merits or that he will punish us according to the gravity of our faults. This idea of a future life would bother them too much here below; they are anxious for us to finish speaking; they interrupt us or else they go away. They feel that our God is better than the one which they made for themselves, but in order to please him they would have to abandon cannibalism and polygamy, two great obstacles which we could not overcome except through a miracle of grace. I have enough confidence in the prayers of the associates of the Propagation of the Faith, in the merits of our Lord Jesus Christ, and in the mercy of God to believe that this time of grace is approaching and that the dawn of true happiness will rise upon these unfortunate islands.

I embrace you with all my heart, as well as my mother, my sister, my brother- in-law and my other relatives.

Your very affectionate son,

Léopold Verguet, apostolic missionary

Oneatare of Arossi

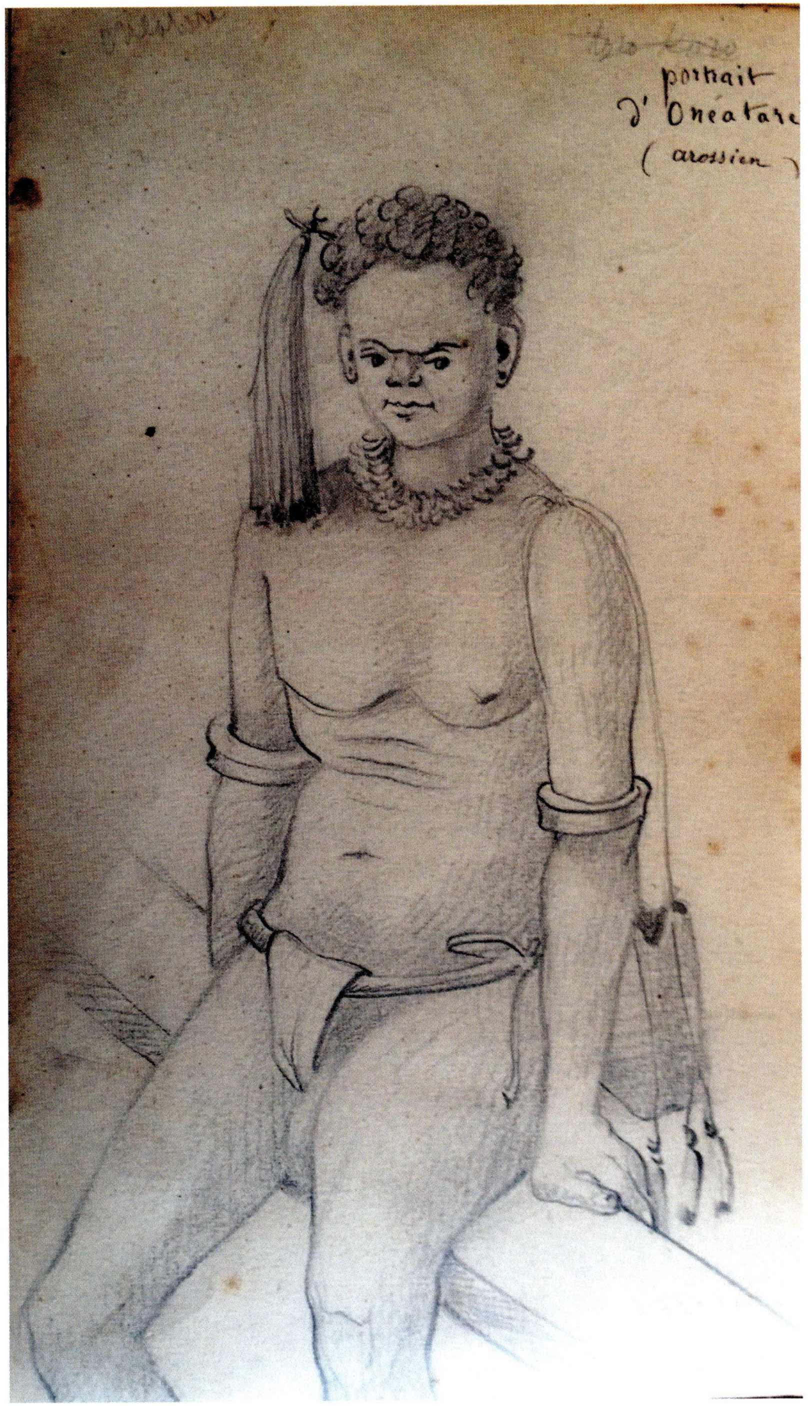

Verguet on his Art

In a letter to Colin, Verguet described artworks he sent back to France. Regretably, this collection did not survive as such. Through this letter Verguet allows us to visit him, as it were, in his atelier, his workshop, in the South Pacific.

5 January – 28 February 1846, Verguet, Port Sainte Marie, to Fr Colin:

My very reverend Father,

I take the liberty of sending you a little roll of drawings representing several aspects of our trip. My colleagues, in their letters, will doubtless speak to you at length about the subjects of these drawings. Here, I will only give you a short explanation, numbering them in sequence, sheet by sheet.

No. 1. View of the coast of New Caledonia. *I took it from Port Balade about a league from the house of Bishop Douarre. You can see that house on a slight elevation at the foot of high mountains. A little to the right you will notice on the shore between some coconut trees three native cabins. On the right of the picture there is a boat of that country. It is made of two pirogues held together by planks.*

No. 2. A close-up view of Bishop Douarre's house. *[See page 25] A: the missionaries' house; B: stables; C: site of the chapel; D: cabin sold to the bishop by the natives; that is where we slept during our stay in New Caledonia; E: garden; F-G: river and limit of the property. The house is surrounded by pastures. The river is navigable enough for a canoe to get up to the garden. There are great advantages to such a position.*

No. 3. Approximate map of Port Saint Jean-Baptiste and of Port Sainte Marie. *The former was named in memory of Bishop Epalle. The map is detailed enough to dispense me from further information. I put in a corner of the drawing a map of San Cristobal Island, called Arosi by the natives. At the north-west point of the island there are two bays (ab) (bc) which are interesting because of the good dispositions of the natives. The first (ab) has a ship anchorage which is not very good. The unloading of a ship is very difficult because of the way the raging sea breaks on the shore. Midway along the bay is the Marou tribe, next to whose village is a large river. Behind the village there is enough arable land for an establishment of the missionaries. The inhabitants all along the coast (a,b,c) until Port Saint Marie are friendly toward the Europeans and they speak the same language. At Port Saint Jean-Baptiste the language is different. The natives from the coast are at war with those from the interior. The coast (bc) is full of reefs and does not have any kind of port for ships.*

No. 4 *The bishop, after visiting Port Saint Jean-Baptiste, said he intended to send a map to Commander Duperrey. In order to make it easy for you to comply with the wishes of His Lordship I am including* ***another map*** *with the one I am sending you.*

No. 5 Portrait of Mahia, chief of the Marou tribe*, whom we have found to be well disposed toward us.*

No. 6 Young warrior from San Cristobal. *On his forehead he has a crown of seashells. His nose is pierced by a mother-of-pearl ring. The earrings and the necklace are made with dogs' teeth.*

Nos. 7 and 8 Heads of some inhabitants of Guadalcanal and Isabel. *The ends of their hair are whitened with lime-wash.*

The following drawings, very reverend Father, portray a very sorrowful subject, the death and burial of Bishop Epalle. I was afraid at first of grieving you by sending you these sketches, but I thought that you would overcome your sorrow so that you might know in detail all the circumstances of such an unexpected yet glorious death.

No. 9 The Bay of the Martyr, *which our captain [Captain Richards] calls the Bay of the Massacre, has a good port. I put a hatchet in the place where the bishop was struck down. In front of the Opi tribe, there is a bay where a ship can be anchored. The peak E serves as an alignment to locate the bishop's burial place. At the foot of this mountain there is a small bay where a boat can land without danger, an abundant stream, a good terrain, and a people who seemed to Father Paget and me to have peaceful dispositions. This is the Alitumbala tribe.*

No. 10 Scene of the fatal incident *of 16 December 1845 when bishop Epalle was killed. The picture is sufficiently self-explanatory. I should only point out that I should have put many more natives in the background of the picture. When the action began, there were about fifty natives; toward the end, the number had doubled; they kept coming out of the woods.*

No. 11 The wounds of bishop Epalle *and those who accompanied him. The two wounds (ab) (cd) should lean a little more toward the right, especially the wound (cd). This is what Doctor Guise observed. The doctor was born in the English colonies in India. His father was English and his mother Indian. In New Caledonia he asked to remain in the mission with us, but since the bishop's death he changed his mind. He is a Catholic.*

(No. 12) The night before the bishop's burial. *I was mistaken when I coloured the cassock violet. It should be black with red buttons. The shoes are black. His bishop's ring was forgotten.*

No. 13 The funeral convoy *is moving toward Astrolabe Harbour. The bier is in the second canoe; it is in red cedar wood; it was not covered with a shroud so as not to attract the atten-*

tion of the natives.

***No. 14** Drawings which may be used to find **the burial place** of bishop Epalle; they are well enough explained in the picture.*

*28 February 1846 — **No. 15 A few faces in colour of natives of New Caledonia and the Solomons**. In the background of the page I have drawn a few pirogues.*

No. 16. View of several houses of the Oné tribe.

*1. **Palace of the chief.** The roof is held up by 12 carved columns. They are statues embellished with all the natives' ornaments. On the back of the sheet I have drawn the head of one of these statues. There you can see quite well the kind of tattoo adopted by our natives.*

*2. **Small house held up on stakes.***

*3. **The most ordinary form of houses in the Oné style.***

***N. 17 One of the statues** of the palace of Mahemara with the names of the decorations with which it is adorned.*

***N. 18** Copy of a drawing which I found on a beam in the palace of the chief. This design, roughly executed, represents a **fight between those of the Oné tribe and the inhabitants of the mountains**; the latter are called Toro. They were conquered, and those of Oné perpetuated the memory of their victory by representing it in the ornamentation of the royal palace.*

***No. 19 View of the establishment of the missionaries** of the Society of Mary at Port Saint Marie on the island of San Cristobal (called Arosi by the natives).*

***No. 20. Portrait of the chief of the Oné tribe,** the one closest to the mission station. ...*

May I dare to ask you to assure our Fathers and our Brothers of my respect and my friendship. I commend myself to their prayers. I have the honour of being, very reverend Father, your very humble and very obedient servant,

Léopold Verguet
apostolic missionary

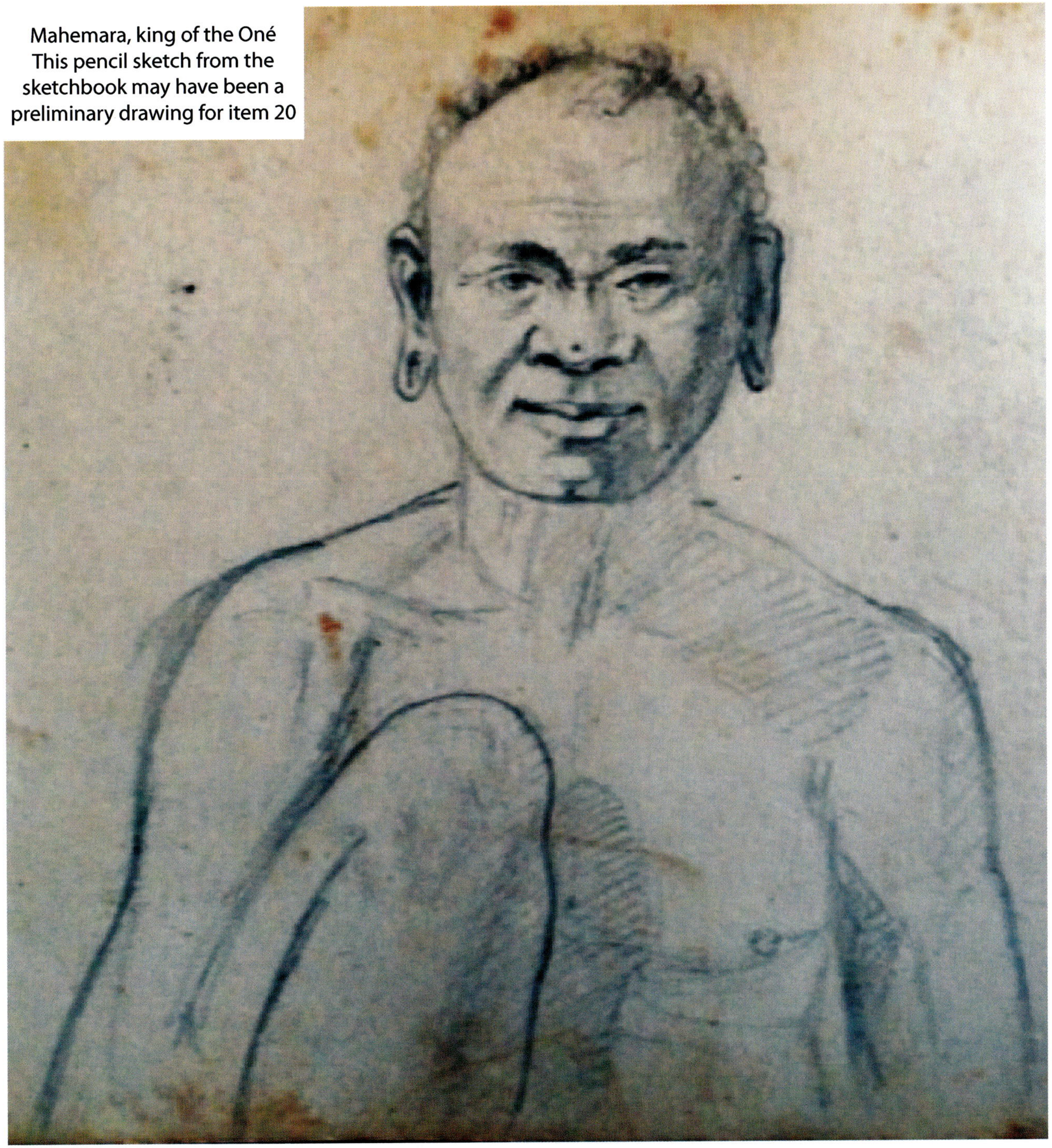

Mahemara, king of the Oné
This pencil sketch from the sketchbook may have been a preliminary drawing for item 20

Verguet on San Cristobal

Continuation of page 41

A month after the mission began Verguet, standing on the terrace in the evening, heard Montrouzier cry out – he had been speared. Apparently one of the sailors had "taken too much liberty" with the wife of a man called Orimanu. To avenge the affront, Orimanu had waited to ambush whoever came down to the stream.

Luckily Montrouzier was not badly injured but given the tropical climate the danger of infection was serious, so when the *Marian Watson* left in March for New Caledonia and Sydney it took Montrouzier, to give him a chance to recover. Fr Chaurain and Br Prosper also left at that time because they did not want to continue on San Cristobal.

Fr Pierre Rougeyron wrote from New Caledonia on 1 April that the ship of Epalle had returned to them, but when he asked if the Bishop were on board Montrouzier replied, 'He is in heaven.'

Verguet described at length in his letters the land, the people, their houses, canoes, tattoos and bracelets, can-

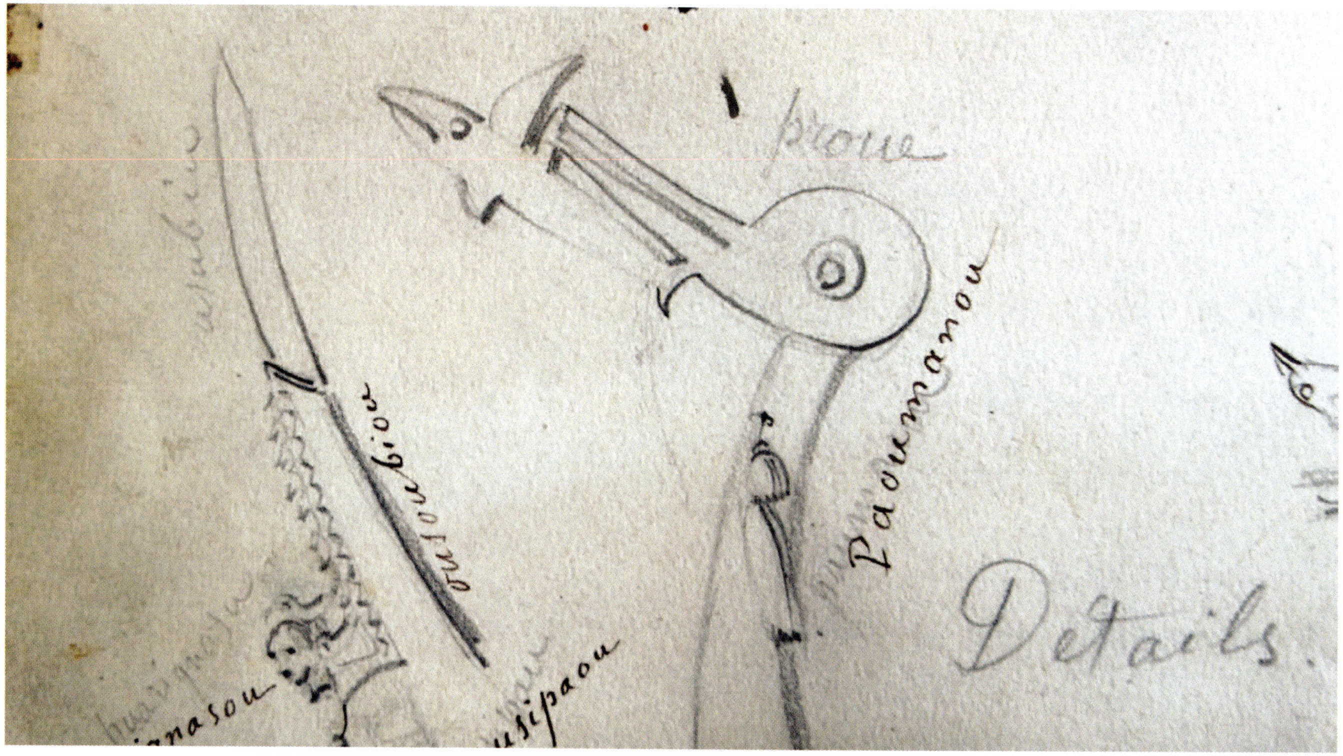

Above: Details of the canoe

Below: Ten-metre-long *ora* and the associated vocabulary

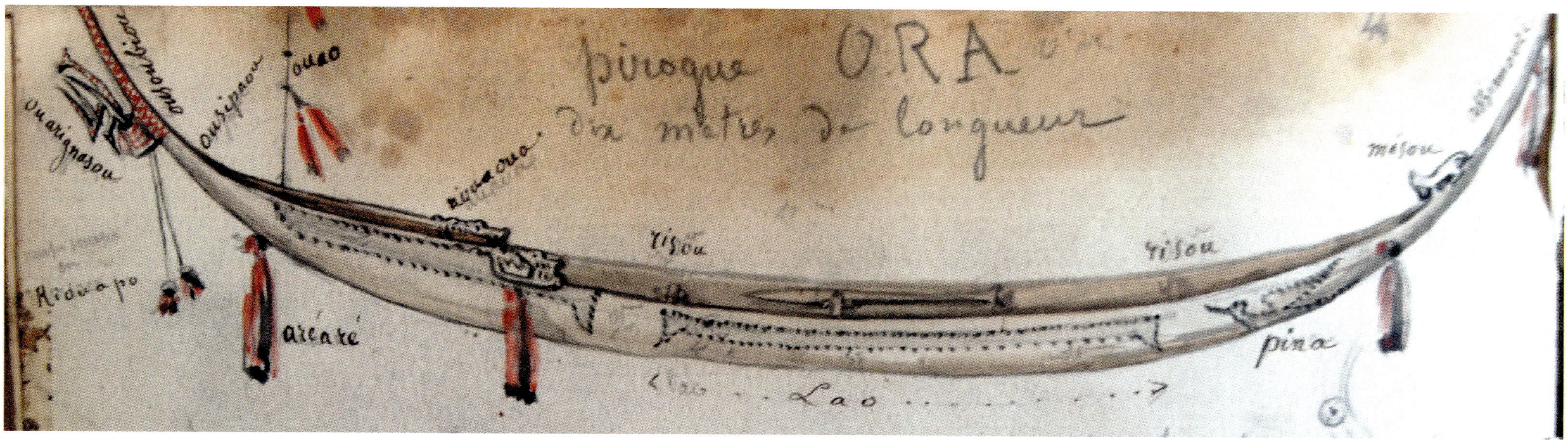

nibalism and funerals. His descriptions included little vocabulary lists. What Verguet called Arosi was the district in the north west of San Cristobal (Makira). In his book of 1854 he describes topography and plants and gives illustrations: trees, volcanoes, bananas, sugar cane, and coconut trees. He considers that the women were treated nearly as badly as in New Caledonia.

In the middle of 1846 they suffered badly from malaria. On 29 July, the *Clara*, a ship belonging to Bishop Bataillon from Wallis arrived with supplies to the delight of the men on San Cristobal. The next arrival was Bishop Douarre in August. Douarre wrote to Colin that he was happy to find the missionaries alive, but reported that 'eight of the nine are sick'. On 11 February 1847 the appointed successor of Epalle, Bishop-elect Jean Georges Collomb, arrived at San Cristobal. Verguet had been suffering for weeks from heavy malaria and asked Collomb if he could return to France. Br Charles made the same request. Collomb, who was now in charge, gave his consent so Verguet made a farewell visit to one of the villages and performed a baptism.

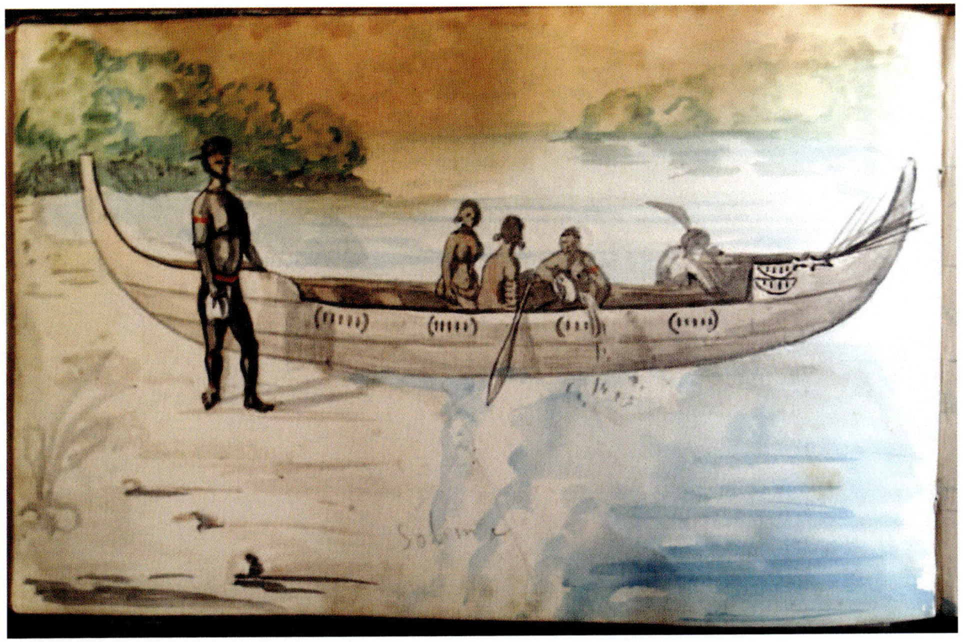

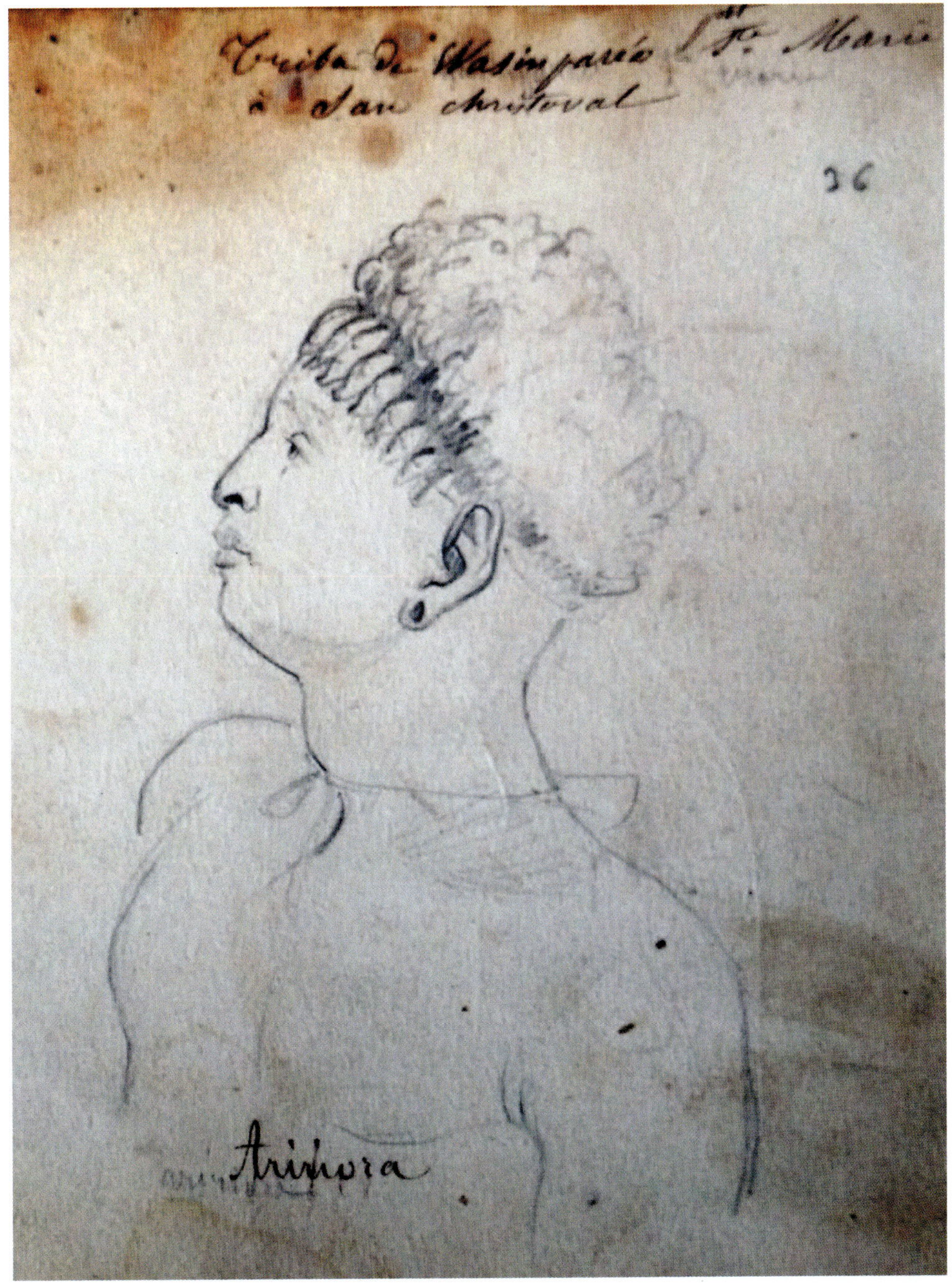

Aririora of the Tribe of Wasinpareo at Port St Marie on San Cristobal

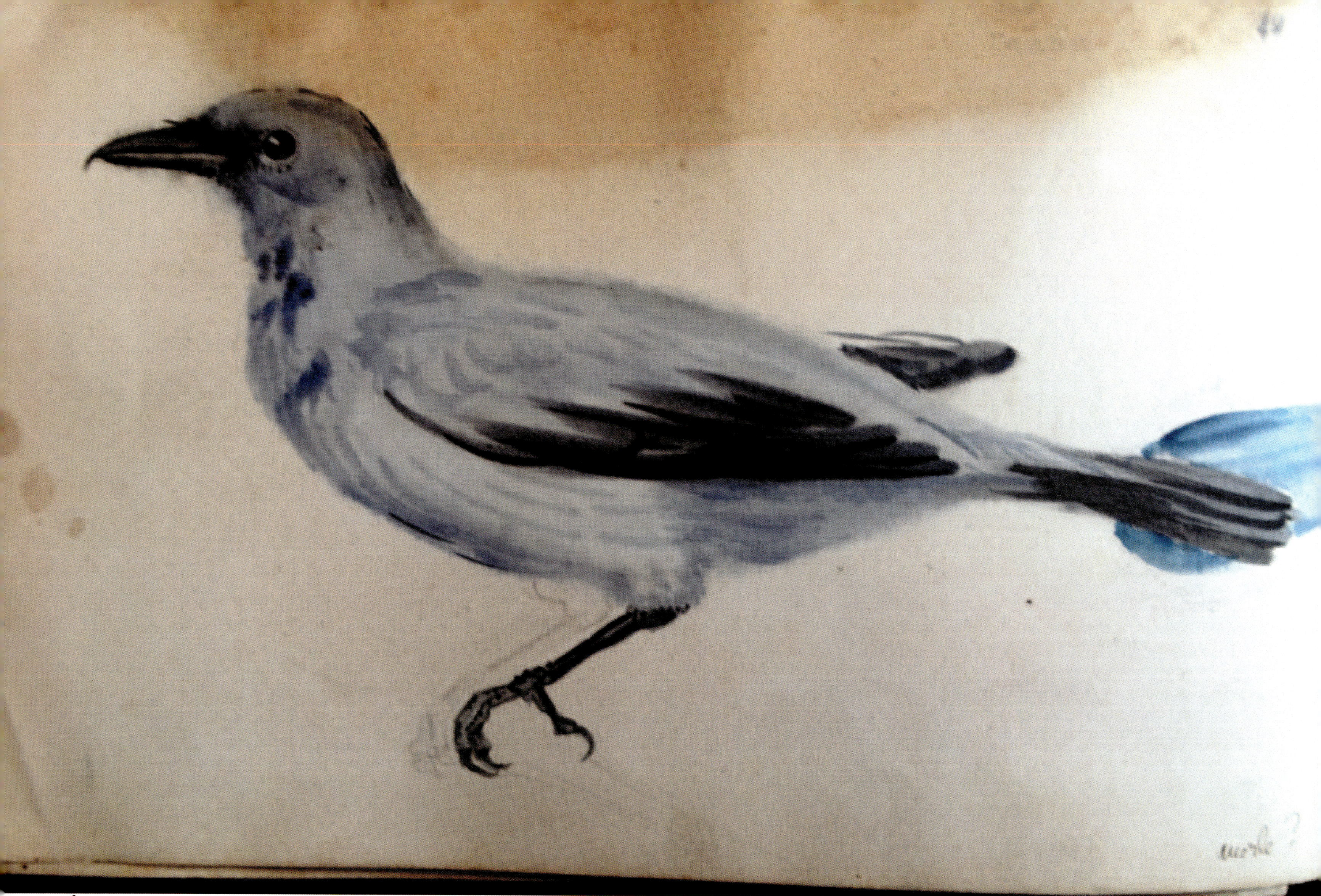
merle ?

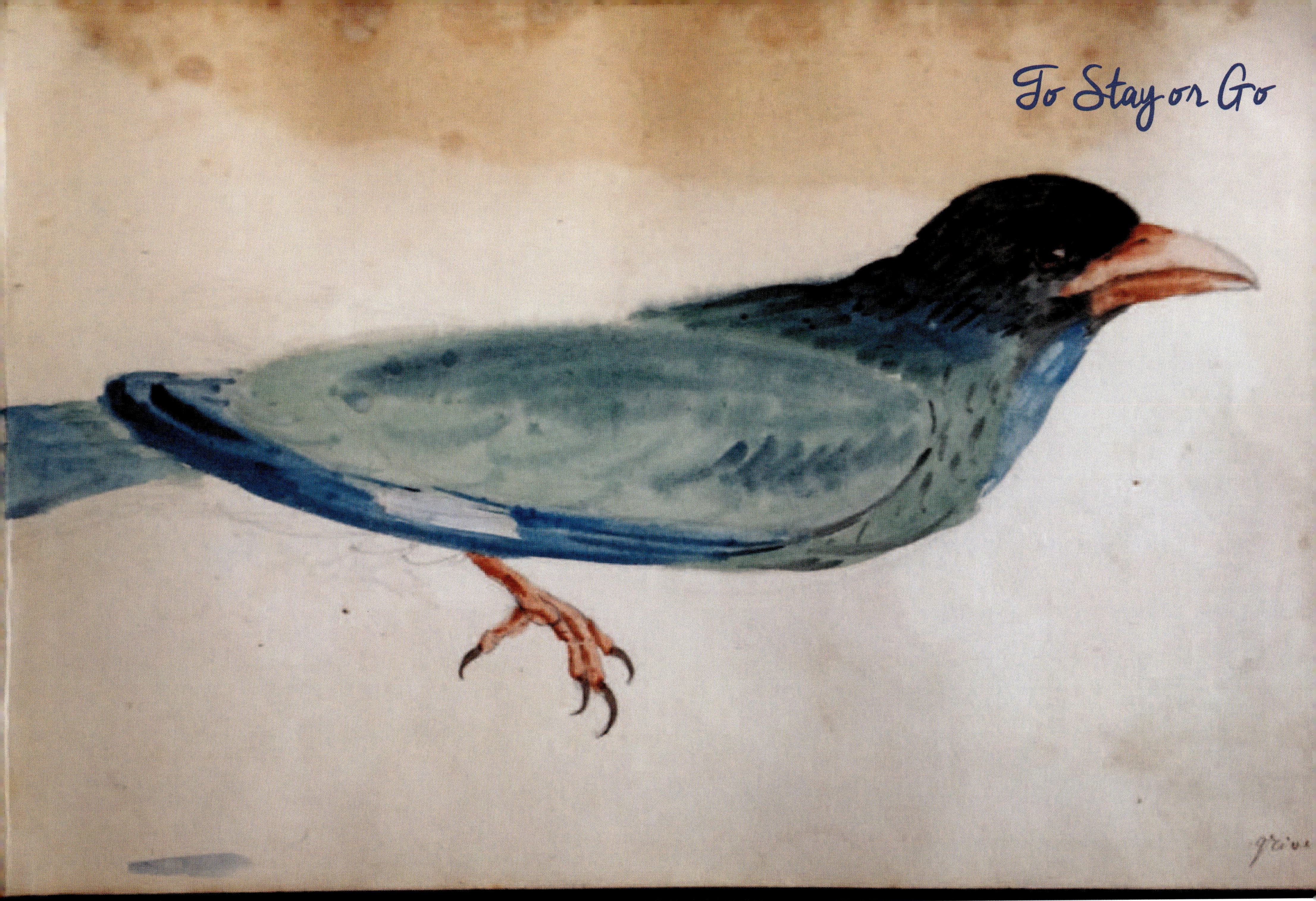

Burial Customs of the Solomons
Verguet to his parents, 4 June 1847, New Zealand

...In S. Cristobal the Arosi use another way of keeping the remains of the dead. They expose the corpse in the open air in the middle of the village on a pile of Nari (a sort of walnut) shells. They secure the body in an upright position by attaching it to two poles stuck in the ground. They surround it with a fairly plain palisade about six feet (two metres) high. When the process of decomposition has ended, they gather the remains and keep them in a tapu place. They like to attach to the rafters of their houses the skulls of the conquered enemies.

I have passed over too quickly the burial ceremonies of the Arosi. I should have told you that after the death of a man they cut down the coconut palms which belong to him, and that if this person is a chief, instead of leaving him to decompose in his upright position, they lay his body in a great flat-bottomed container with the wood decorated with festoons of mother-of-pearl [nacre] and big enough to hold him stretched out. The widow and her children observe mourning for two whole months. The woman, during this whole time, is obliged to wear a long white garment which comes down to her knees. The men must completely go without shaving and wear white necklaces and bracelets usually made from seeds called Job's tears.

SHIPPING INTELLIGENCE.

ARRIVED.

MARCH 6.—The French ship ARCHE D'ALLIANCE, 313 tons, Marceau, master, from Solomon's Islands the 19th February. Passengers, Rev. Monsieur Calon and Rev. Monsieur Verquet, Roman Catholic Clergymen.

The Australian (Sydney) 9 March 1847

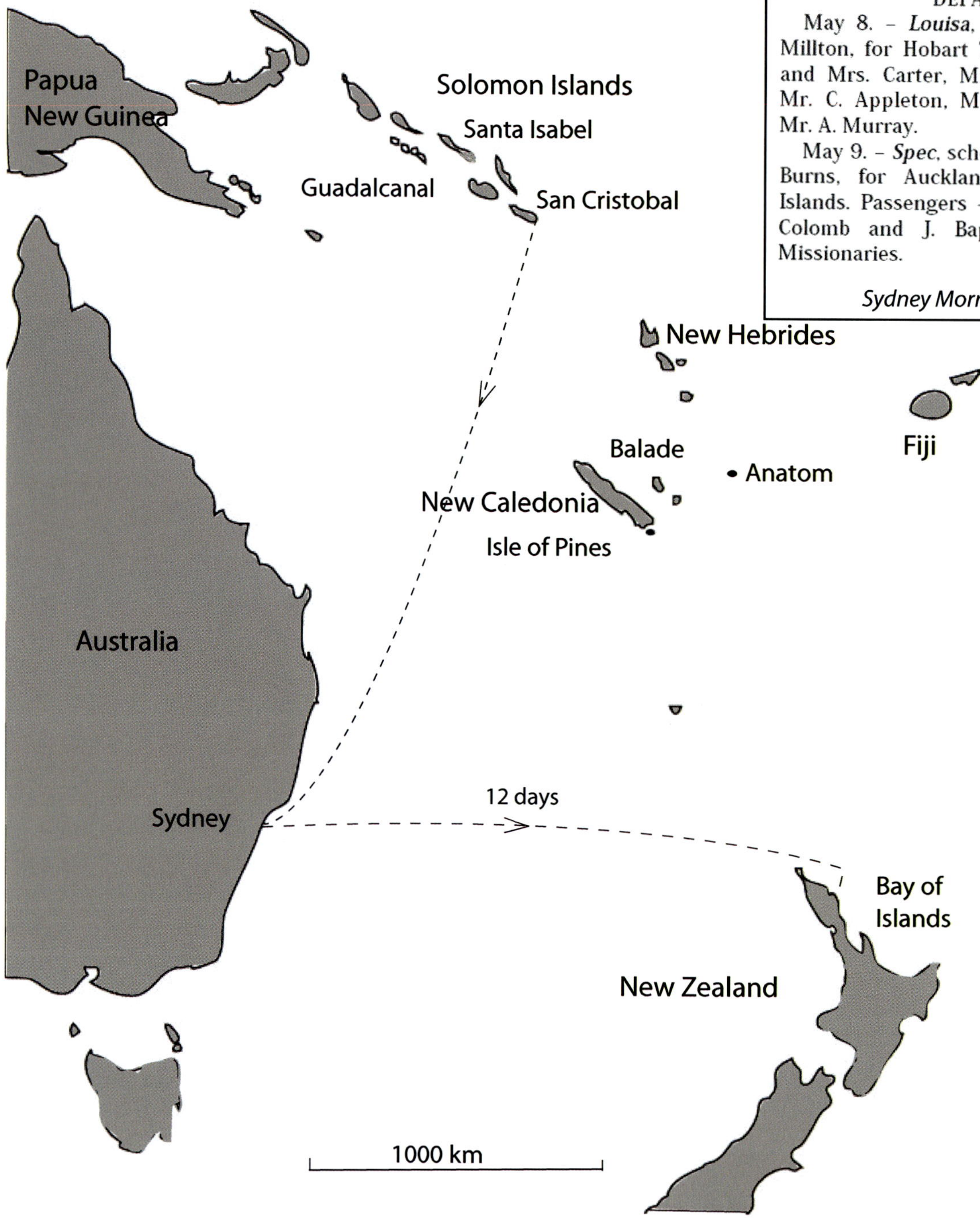

DEPARTURES.

May 8. – *Louisa*, brig, 182 tons, Captain Millton, for Hobart Town. Passengers – Mr. and Mrs. Carter, Mr. Leazley, Mr. Allwood, Mr. C. Appleton, Mr. J. Wigglesworth, and Mr. A. Murray.

May 9. – *Spec*, schooner, 169 tons, Captain Burns, for Auckland and the South Sea Islands. Passengers – Mrs. Burns, Revds. M. Colomb and J. Baptiste, Roman Catholic Missionaries.

Sydney Morning Herald 10 May 1847

Sydney and the Bay of Islands

February 1847

On 20 January 1847 another group of Marist missionaries had arrived in New Caledonia. They were Fr Jean Georges Collomb, Fr Cyprien Crey and Br Optat (Pierre Bergillon). A letter from Fr Colin informed Collomb that he was nominated coadjutor (assistant bishop) for Epalle – this decision had been taken before the death of Epalle was known. On 28 January he set off for San Cristobal accompanied by Crey and Montrouzier (who had been recuperating at Balade). One problem Collomb had was that he had been appointed as a bishop but not ordained as one, by church law he needed another bishop to consecrate him. He had hoped to meet up in New Caledonia with Bishop Pompallier of New Zealand who was on his way to Europe but they had missed each other.

They travelled on the *Arche d'Alliance* with Captain Marceau. This was a French vessel owned by a small company the *Société de l'Océanie* set up to support the Catholic missions. They found it a much more agreeable and prayerful means of transport than the commercial English vessels.

When they arrived at San Cristobal, after a slow trip on 12 February they found the mission in a fragile state. Collomb left Montrouzier there but took Verguet and Br Charles with him to Sydney. The group departed 19 February. Collomb was spending more time at sea than on land, but each day conferring with the missionaries meant holding up the ship and its crew, all of which cost money.

In the light of their sufferings from malaria the doctor on the *Arche d'Alliance* advised the Marists on San Cristobal to look for a healthier place than their initial site. As the role of the mosquito as a vector of the disease was not known, malaria, as the name suggests, was thought to be caused by 'bad air'. They moved to Pia, seven miles north of Makira Bay. The people of Pia were the enemies

Verguet to Colin, Sydney, 13 March 1847

Very reverend father,

I have just left the mission station of Saint Cristobal intending never to return there. All the time that I stayed there, I have not been able to bend to the rule of that mission station. The Father Provincial, seeing how little I was suitable to the religious life, suggested to me that either I changed my ways or I should leave. He spoke in that way in the first conversation which took place on Trinity Sunday, about three months after the departure of the ship Marian-Watson. He spoke generally but afterwards pointed out very clearly that not one of my colleagues was contemptuous of my attitude. About six months after that suggestion I still felt the same and moreover completely fed up with the mission station, I made him aware that I wanted to leave the Society and return to Europe. Father Frémont told me that he did not have the authority to release me from my vows but he would allow me on the first opportunity to leave for Sydney and that from there I could return to Europe and obtain a dispensation from my vows.

I used the passage of Mister Marceau to come to Sydney. Weak health brought on by some bouts of fever which reoccur from time to time and which have been going on for about eight months was the excuse for my departure. I am supposed to have come to Sydney to recuperate there. Some days after my arrival at the supply base, I informed Bishop Collomb and Father Rocher of how I felt, as far as the missions and the Marist Order were concerned. Bishop Collomb would like me to leave with him, something I can't decide on; Father Rocher also gives me the same advice, but he adds that if I don't want to return to the mission field, I can stay at the supply base and that I should not confuse my distaste for the mission field with a distaste for the Marist Order. He said, "The first should not entail the second; they are two very distinct matters. If you don't return to the mission station, you will stay at the supply base; we will find you a job waiting for your health to be restored. From here you will be able to write to the Father Superior; he will always find some job to keep you happy be it here or be it in Europe; above all, I beg you, don't think about leaving the Marist Society." In fact since then I am trying not to think any more about it and that is all I am capable of doing, for I find it impossible to make any decision; the only thing is that I am determined not to return to Saint Cristobal. While waiting for your reply, I shall stay at the supply base. I will learn by your letter whether I have to return to the mission field and to which one because the climate of the tropics is hardly compatible with my health; or if I have to stay at the supply base, I will soon know enough English not to be useless there; or if I have to return to Europe to take up some work for the Marist Society; or if I would not do better to leave the religious vocation for which it has been recognized that I have not the aptitude. I suggest writing to you from time to time to inform you of my feelings and to allow you to judge my case better. At the moment my preference would be to choose: firstly to be released from my vows and to return to the ordinary ministry; secondly to return to Europe to take up some job in the Marist Society; thirdly to stay at the supply base in Sydney; fourthly to return to the mission field but somewhere else than in the tropics; and finally and only as a fifth choice to return to the mission station at Saint Cristobal.

Reverend Father, excuse the liberty I take in writing to you. I would think my letter perfectly useless if I did not open my heart to you, however weak it is.

I have the honour, revered Father, of being your very humble and very obedient servant,

Léopold Verguet, Missionary of the Society of Mary

of the Oné who were very unhappy with the missionaries moving out from among them.

On board the ship travelling to Sydney, Verguet showed his drawings to some of the crewmembers. They showed him sketches of theirs and he copied pictures of people from the Magellan Strait and the Marquesas. Also in the sketchbook and dating from this period are three rough sketches of coats of arms. They have been identified as the arms of Epalle and Collomb and possibly Viard, but the identifications are all wrong. It is more likely that Verguet drafted up some ideas for Collomb as to what he could choose for his episcopal coat of arms. A dove (visual pun for Collomb) above the intertwined MA symbol for the Virgin Mary, or the Immaculate Conception and the Immaculate Heart with a palm tree. What subsequently eventuated was that Collomb's arms were the first depicted, wrongly identified in the sketchbook as those of Epalle: a gold radiant star in a field of blue above two crossed laurel branches with the motto '*Clamamus exules*' meaning 'We refugees cry out'. The phrase is from the famous *Salve Regina* hymn, where in full it is '*ad te clamamus exsules filii Hevæ*'. The translation in the *Hail Holy Queen* renders that line as 'To thee do we cry, poor banished children of Eve.' The device is therefore intended to represent the Virgin Mary under the familiar title of 'Star of the Sea'. In the midst of the Pacific, a long way from their homeland, Verguet and Collomb are pondering what the emblem of Collomb's episcopacy should be. As exiles they call on Mary, the Star of the Sea, to guide them.

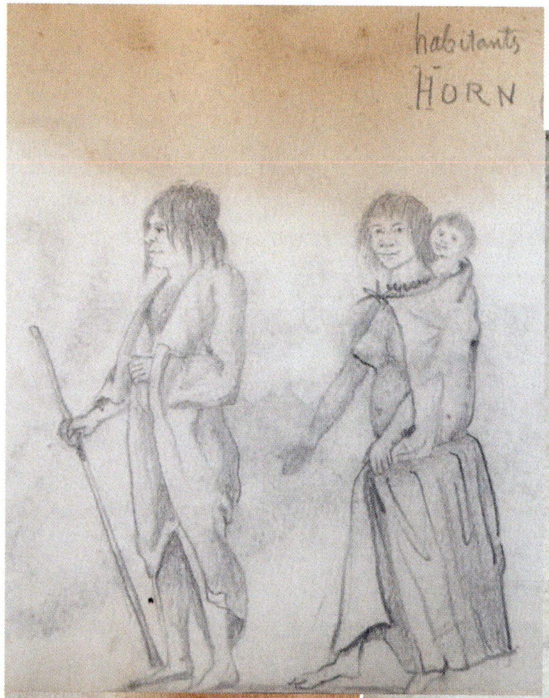

Unlike most of the material in the sketchbook these are not drawn from life

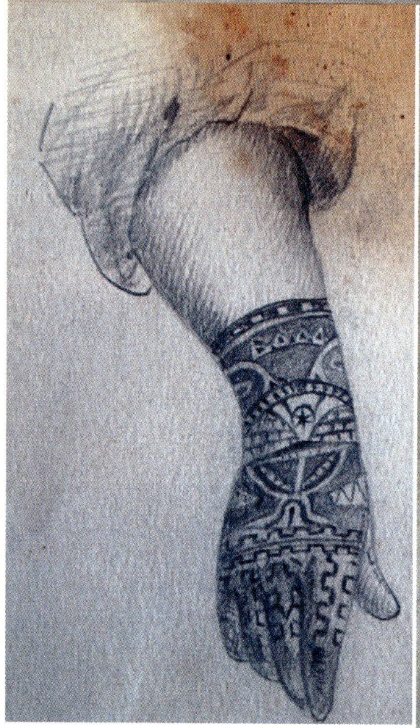

A hand tatooed in the style of the Marquesas

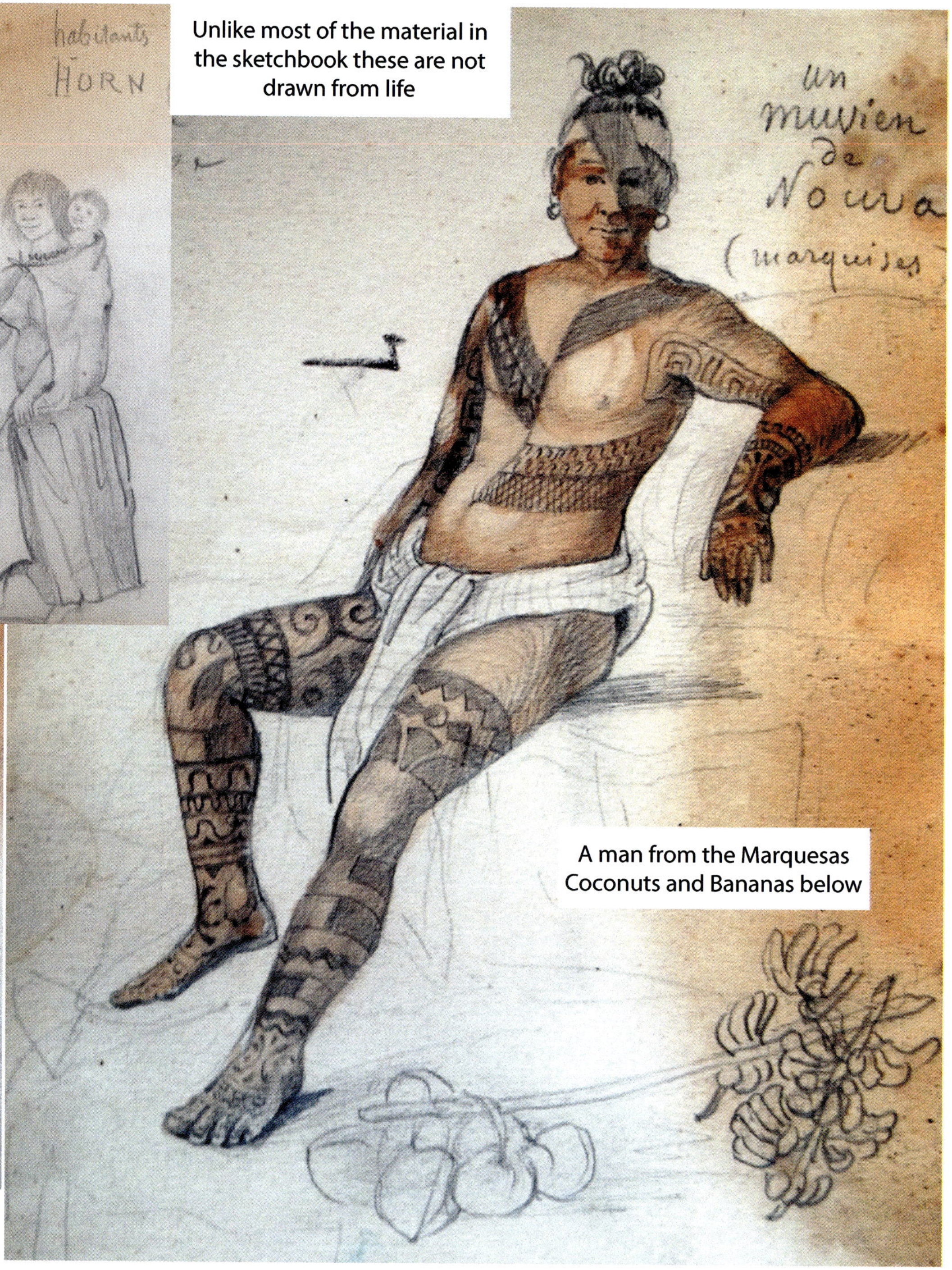

A man from the Marquesas
Coconuts and Bananas below

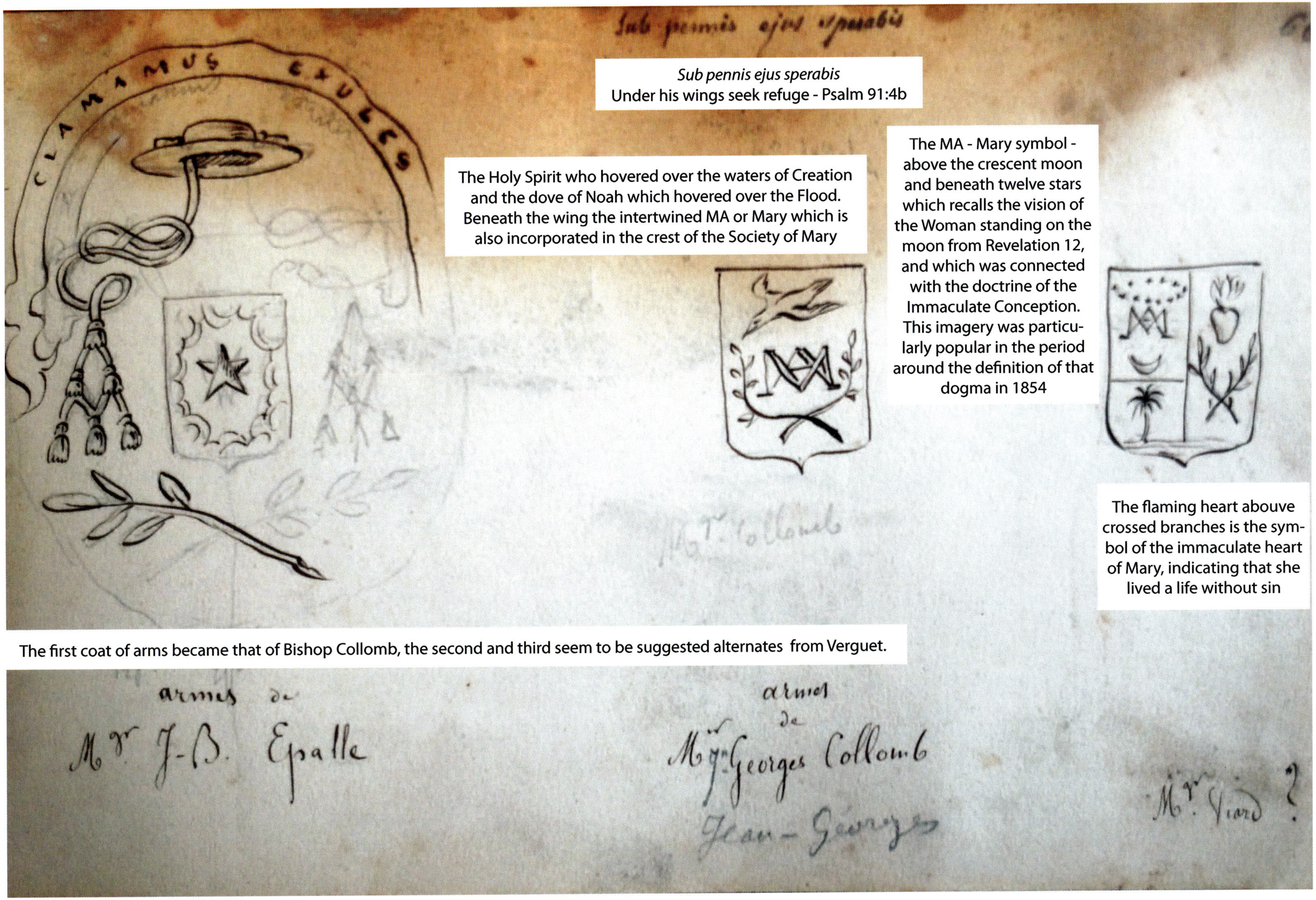

Sub pennis ejus sperabis
Under his wings seek refuge - Psalm 91:4b

The Holy Spirit who hovered over the waters of Creation and the dove of Noah which hovered over the Flood. Beneath the wing the intertwined MA or Mary which is also incorporated in the crest of the Society of Mary

The MA - Mary symbol - above the crescent moon and beneath twelve stars which recalls the vision of the Woman standing on the moon from Revelation 12, and which was connected with the doctrine of the Immaculate Conception. This imagery was particularly popular in the period around the definition of that dogma in 1854

The flaming heart abouve crossed branches is the symbol of the immaculate heart of Mary, indicating that she lived a life without sin

The first coat of arms became that of Bishop Collomb, the second and third seem to be suggested alternates from Verguet.

March to May 1847: Sydney

On 6 March they arrived in Sydney. Collomb found the official letters about his episcopal appointment were waiting for him, but Bishop Polding was absent. He still needed to find a bishop to consecrate him. They were accommodated at the Marist Procure. Verguet was so unwell that he spent the next two months in bed. On 23 March, Collomb wrote to Father Colin mentioning that Verguet wished to return to France or even leave the Society of Mary. His main problem is religious life, in particular the vow of obedience. This may have to do with his provincial, Father Frémont, a rather strict man. The fever had left Verguet but he was still weak.

By then, on San Cristobal, his replacement Fr Crey was already dead. He had contracted a fever and died after a short illness on 15 March. The Marists on San Cristobal decided to try for a still healthier location and opened a house on Wango a mountain on the north coast of Makira Bay. Fathers Jacquet and Paget and Brother Hyacinth went there on the 20 April. On the way they were killed by the Toro and eaten. Verguet later said: "Father Paget had incomparable zeal but, like Bishop Epalle, he did not see the thousandth part of danger." From June 1847 on the Marists were practically under siege on San Cristobal.

In Sydney, on 28 April, Collomb visited both the French consul and the Vicar General of the Diocese to inform them that he was to be the successor to Bishop Epalle. He had arranged by mail with Bishop Viard, the coadjutor to Bishop Pompallier for his episcopal ordination to be done in New Zealand. He bought provisions for the New Zealand Marists and sailed on board the *Spec* on 9 May. To the surprise of Father Rocher, according to his letter to Colin, Verguet went with him. With the recovery of his health had come a new desire to continue as a missionary, as long as he could avoid malarial zones.

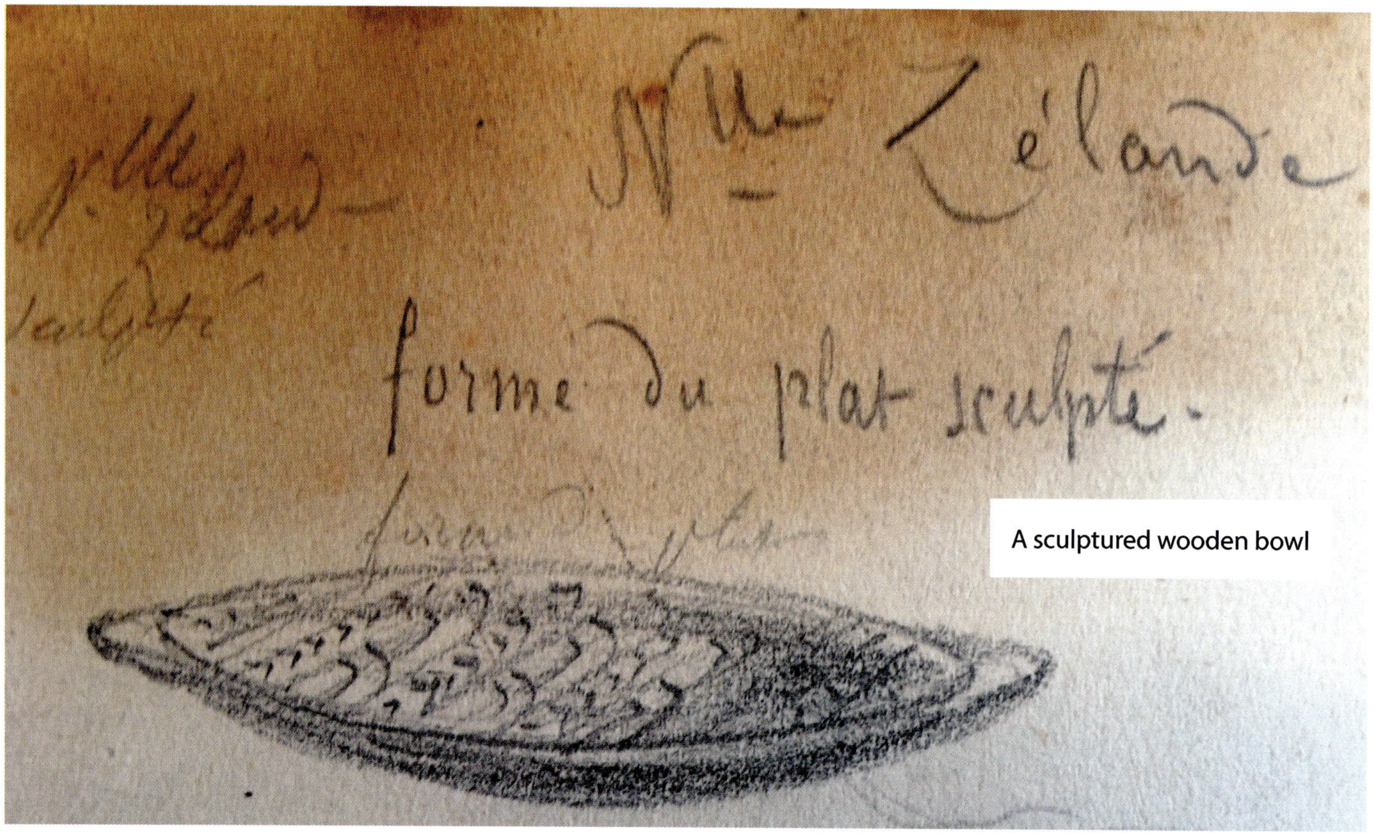

A sculptured wooden bowl

May and June 1847: New Zealand

On Pentecost Sunday, 23 May 1847, the first catholic episcopal ordination to take place in New Zealand was celebrated in the little wooden chapel of Saints Peter and Paul at Kororāreka (now Russell) in the Bay of Islands. The township was still recovering from the destruction caused by Hone Heke having sacked it two years before in the "Flagstaff War". Verguet, who had been present at Epalle's consecration in Rome, attended the consecration of Collomb, his successor, in Russell. As Viard preached on the 'unity, perpetuity and Apostolical character of the Episcopal office' Verguet must have reflected on how dangerous it was to be appointed Vicar Apostolic of Melanesia and Micronesia.

Verguet wrote to his parents about New Zealand, the tattoos, the people, their canoes, the township, its troubled history and how Pompallier had tried to mediate between the Maori war party and the British. He gave an account of the 11 March 1845 attack on Kororāreka. He reflected on the chances for Christianity and civilization in New Zealand. He mentioned having joined an expedition 'to the interior' on which he had seen villages and tombs. Verguet sent portraits to France: for Colin a man with a pipe and with a New Zealand mantle, and of a woman and a small child; a copy of the same for the *Société Orientale*, Paris; and finally a bigger portrait of a 'sauvage', for his brother at Carcassonne.

With Collomb he spent a fortnight in New Zealand. The *Spec* had gone down to Auckland to deliver a cargo of stone. After its return they left the Bay of Islands on 2 June 1847, their next destination was New Caledonia.

NEW ZEALAND:—The Right Rev. Dr. Collomb, who had recently spent a few weeks in Sydney, and who had been appointed by the Holy See to succeed the venerated Bishop Epalle, was consecrated in the neat wooden Church of SS. Peter and Paul, at Kororarika, Bay of Islands, on Pentecost Sunday. The Bishop elect went into retreat on the feast of the Ascension, and spent the succeeding days in spiritual exercises, preparing like the Apostles, for the coming of the Holy Ghost whom he was to receive by the imposition of hands at his Episcopal Consecration. The Right Rev. Dr. Viard, Coadjutor Bishop, of New Zealand, assisted by the Very Rev. Pere Baty, Vicar-General, and the Rev. Pere Rozat, performed the solmen rite of consecration, the Apostolic Bull having first been read by the Secretary, the Very Rev. Petit Jean. The Consecrator then delivered an instructive sermon to a large congregation, consisting both of Protestants and catholics, upon the unity, perpetuity, and Apostolical character of the Episcopal office. The ceremony commenced at ten, a.m., and was not concluded until one.

The new Bishop, after his consecration, baptised three children, born of English parents, and administered the sacrament of confirmation to three adult New Zealanders who had become converts to the Catholic faith. His Lordship seems to have entered with the spirit of the Apostles upon his arduous duties, and to have determined upon offering himself as a holocaust to promote the glory of God and the salvation of his fellow-men, among the benighted heathens of the South Sea Islands. On the 15th June he sailed for New Caledonia, where he will tarry for a few weeks, and he will then depart for the Islands of San Christoval, which, with the neighbouring islands, is to be the sphere of his future labours.—Correspondent Sydney Chronicle.

Wellington Independent 29 September 1847

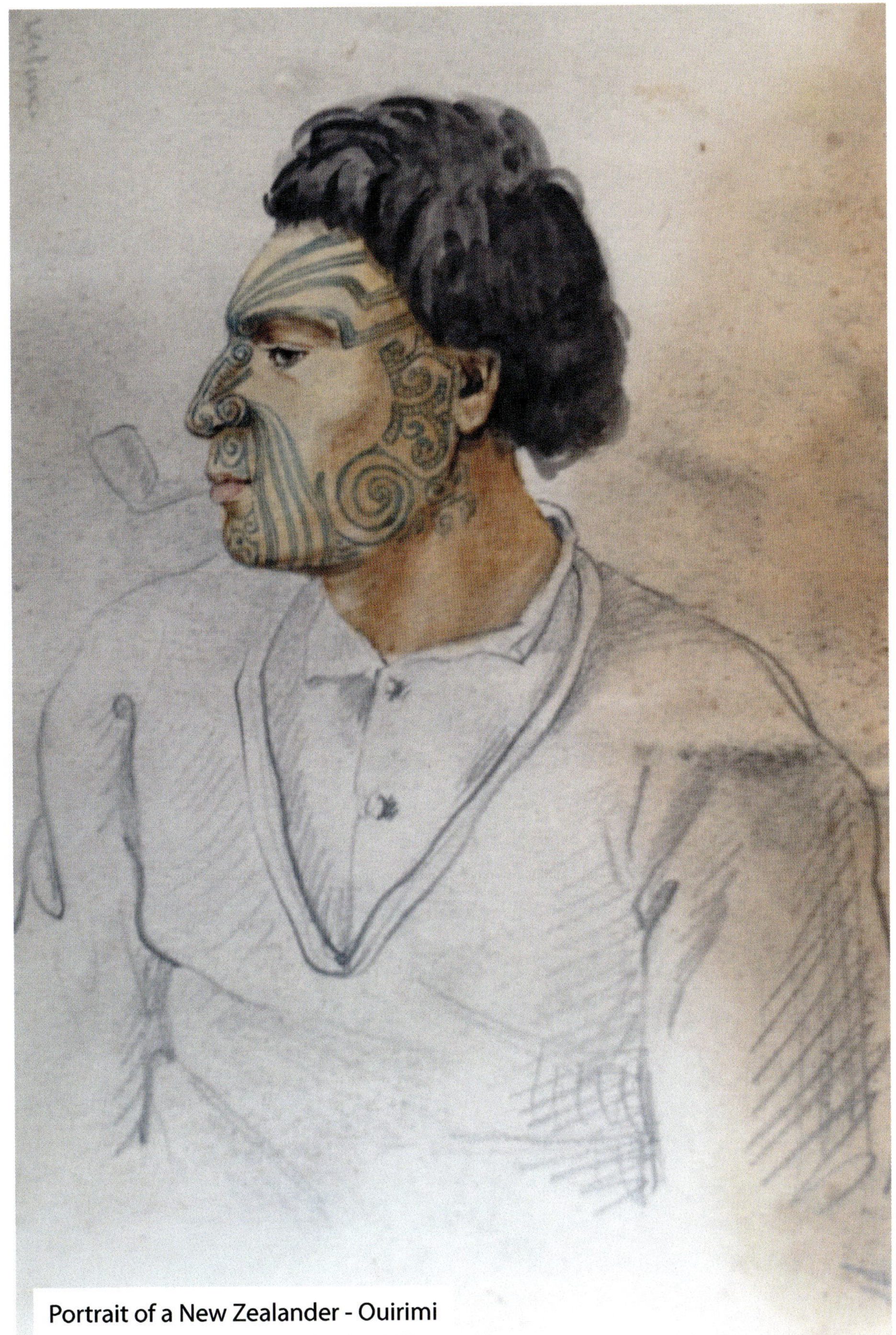

Portrait of a New Zealander - Ouirimi

Crossing the Tasman
4 June 1847, Verguet to his parents, from Kororareka

My dear parents,

I arrived in New Zealand on the 20th of last month after a good 12-day voyage. The wind was favourable, and we had no bad weather. The seasickness I experienced this time with more severity than ever, no doubt because of my weakness, has been an excellent remedy for me. Since our arrival my health has so improved that I am, today, pretty much as well as at the time of my departure from France. Bishop Collomb also enjoys good health. He was consecrated as a Bishop last Sunday, the 23rd May, Pentecost Sunday. Now we are waiting for our ship which has gone to Auckland – a town about 40 leagues from Kororareka – and which, when it returns, will pick us up to take us to New Caledonia. There, there will be another ship for the Bishop's use.

New Zealanders and their Tattoos

Verguet to his parents, 4 June 1847, New Zealand

"...Since my arrival in New Zealand, I have been busy sketching the curiosities of the country, I draw the natives' faces with their tattooing, the canoes, the houses, the graves etc.

The tattooing gives the faces of the New Zealanders a ferocious look. It consists of tracing on their skin, which is usually brown and tending to be sallow, blue indelible lines following directions dictated by custom. They are almost the same on all the faces. You always notice four wide blue lines which rise like great wrinkles [rides] above the eyebrows; others equally wide leave the nostrils and come down onto the chin. The rest of the face is more or less covered with circular festoons according to the patience of each individual and the desire he has to get pleasure out of being noticed. To prevent the beard from hiding their facial good looks, they are careful to pluck the hairs from it as they grow.

Tattooing is very painful. For this process the New Zealanders use a piece of sharpened iron which they strike with a little wooden hammer to dig it into the skin. In this way they stipple the line that they want to mark, being careful from time to time, to dip the point of the iron into the sap of a tree which has the property of colouring in blue. They draw on the face without marking beforehand, and nevertheless achieve a perfect symmetry. During the operation the blood flows abundantly, and the man being tattooed makes not the least movement. The next day and the following days, the wounds he has received become inflamed, and the skin which has endured the tattooing swells considerably. I have seen a lip which had just been tattooed: it was monstrous. To better endure these pains, the New Zealanders have their tattooing done on different occasions. The mature men are distinguished by the extent of their tattooing. The young people have barely a few lines in the middle of the lip.

Tattooing here is very different from what it is in the Solomon Islands. There they tear the skin with a piece of bamboo, and add nothing to colour it, so this tattooing is hardly visible. It leaves a slightly reddish mark on the black skin of the Melanesians. The people of Cristobal, for example, use a broken line. Their tattooing is only a series of zigzags which at intervals go from the nose to the ear. They are separated by straight lines and cover the whole face. On the nostrils

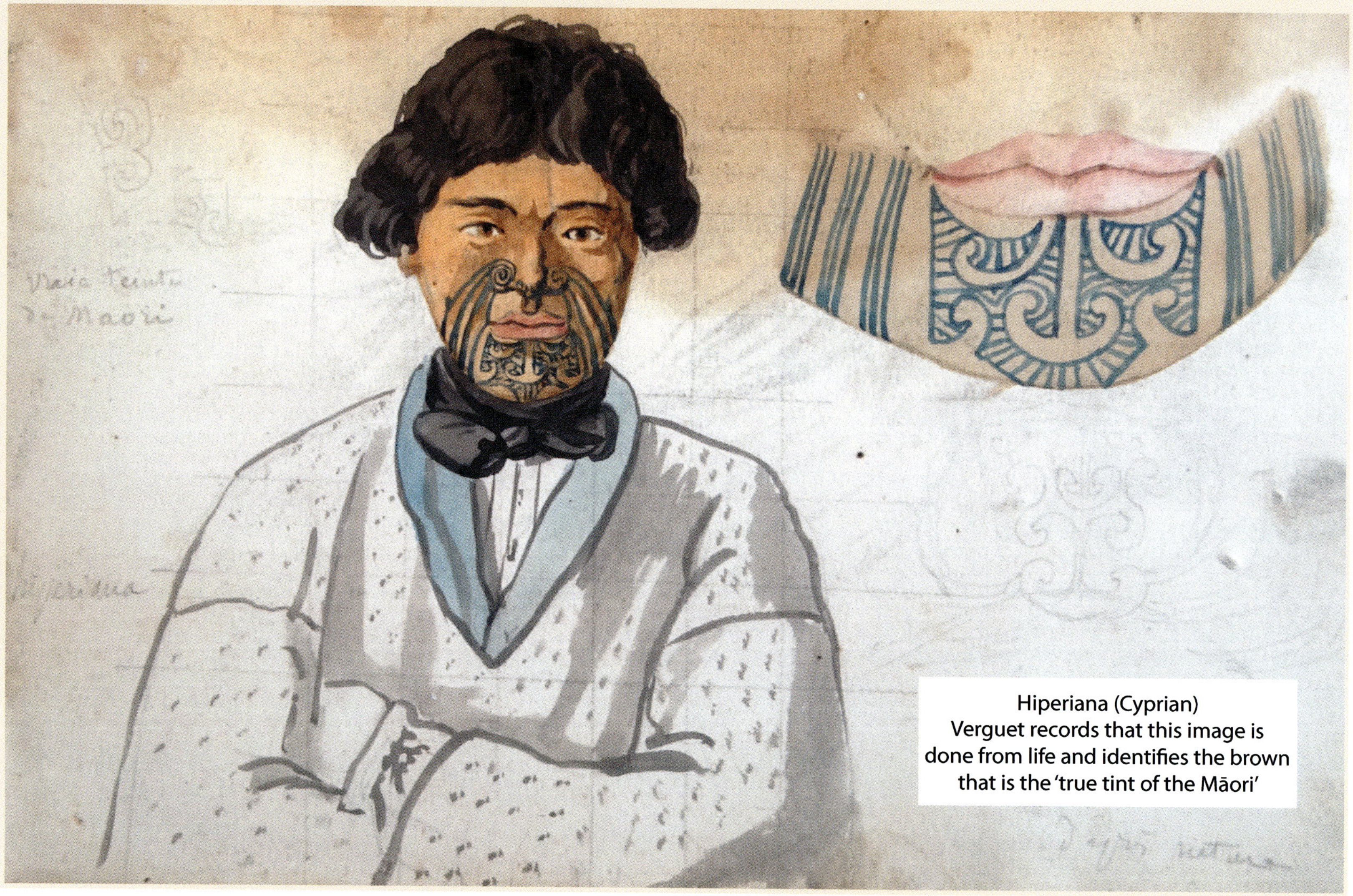

Hiperiana (Cyprian)
Verguet records that this image is done from life and identifies the brown that is the 'true tint of the Māori'

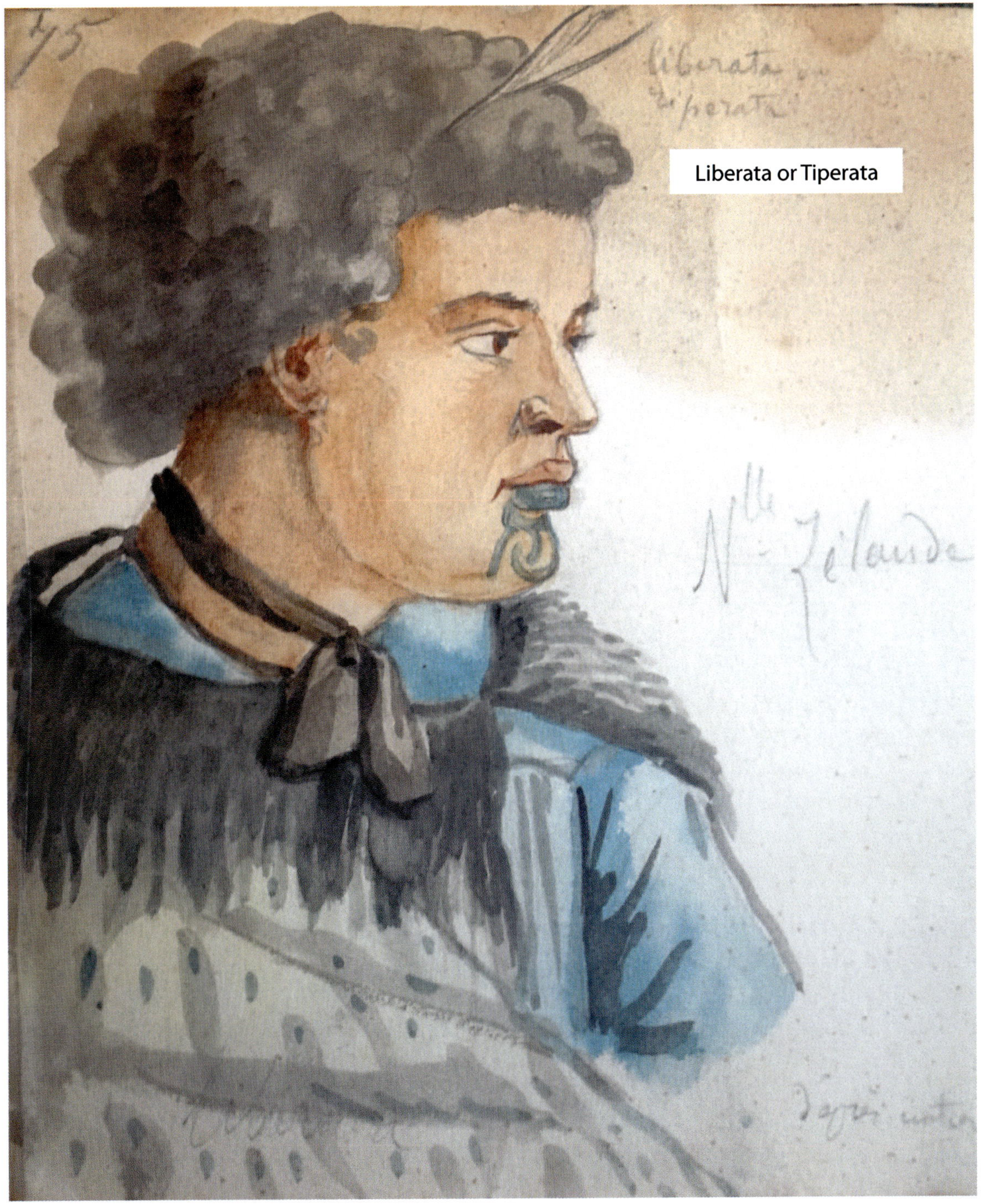

Liberata or Tiperata

of the nose the broken lines go down in the same way to the lips and the chin. On the middle of the forehead they draw a figure which bears some resemblance to a cross. This broken line which you can see on their carvings, their houses, their canoes and which covers their faces – what does it mean to the Cristovalians? I think that they make these designs to imitate the sinuosity of the snake, and that it is in its honour that they tattoo themselves in this way. I have noticed that in several tribes the snake is for them a divinity.

It is not only on the face that the Maoris are tattooed. They are tattooed as well on the thighs and on the legs. To see these tattoos you have only to look at their idols. The buttocks are covered with great blue lines in the form of circles, on the backbone a distinctive tattooing is drawn. I think it is a repetition of the tattoo which is found on the middle of the forehead. This tattoo is, as it were, the name and the title of the person bearing it. When a New Zealander wants to show his nobility, he uncovers himself and shows this tattooing.

Maungaroa, the son of a Protestant minister, got himself tattooed on his buttocks and he also uncovers himself to show off his particulars. The tattooing on the thighs is parallel to their length. It consists of long straight lines which end by curving towards the middle of the thigh in another hook shape by the latter. It is followed by a straight line which goes down to the knees. The space between these two lines is filled with blue tattooing. The legs bear the same tattooing as the thighs. The great chiefs alone have the privilege of having it.

In the southern part of the island, I am told, they tattoo figures of lizards on their legs; on the idols, tattoos on the arms and on the bodies, and the same as that on the thighs; only on the body it takes a different direction – it is transverse.

If the New Zealanders wanted to complete their tattooing, they would not have a single part of the skin free of colour. They ought to tattoo their tongues since those of their idols are tattooed. The women have only the two lips and the chin tattooed. The bluish colour of the mouth, a result of tattooing, pleases the New Zealanders; in Europe it would arouse disgust.

The New Zealanders, on becoming Christians, are ceasing to get themselves tattooed. Those who before baptism underwent this operation retain its indelible marks, but they have only that of a savage. They are good, happy and have a childlike simplicity. There is a Christian woman who takes delight in adoration in front of the Blessed Sacrament. Often she weeps when she is at the foot of the altar. If she is asked what is the cause of her tears, she naively replies that it is the love of God.

Religion, Baptism & Penguins
Verguet to his parents, 4 June 1847, New Zealand

...Going one day to catechise a village in my district I told them to adore Jehovah (that is how we name God) and to pray to him. I made them get down on their knees, and they repeated after me this act of charity: "Jehovah, I love you." One of them, who was not pleased with this prayer, said that Jehovah was for us, and not for them; that their prayers consisted of doing what I was going to see. At the same time he took a wooden dish in which there was some coconut milk then taking from the fireplace one of the stones used for heating food, he plunged it into the liquid with bamboo tongs. It boiled immediately, and the white vapour which was given off rose up in front of a very crude statue. "Are you without any understanding?" I said to him, "to offer your prayers like this to a piece of wood? What can this wood, which has no life, do for you?" "This wood has no life, it is true," he replied, "but come and see another which does have life." He pointed out a plank carved in a broken line ending in a triangle. I did not realise that with this crude design someone had wanted to represent a snake, whose head was formed by the triangle. "I see only wood," I told him again, "and this one is no more alive than the other." "Yes, that one is not alive, but the snakes that slide along the ground, aren't they alive?" So it is in honour of the snake that they made this carving, and it is to it that they offer their prayers. In another tribe I noticed that they offered fat to dogs. What unfortunate people! They adore the devil under the form he chose to seduce our first parents: they have his image everywhere, even on their faces.

I have told you nothing about the little children. I saw several of them while on a walk. They are all very fat. They have noses so flattened that, if seen from side on, they can hardly be seen. They are concealed by the cheeks and by the lips. With children the lower part of the face is the most developed. While travelling, the women carry the little children on their backs – these put their arms around the necks of their mothers, who hold them by wrapping them around the lower back with woollen blankets which they use as cloaks.

We had the happiness, before returning home, of baptising a child. The ceremony took place in a very poor but clean hut which serves as a chapel in the village where we were. There were only a godfather and two other people there. I answered the missionary when he spoke in Latin, the Maoris answered when he spoke to them in their language. A woman was carrying the child in her arms. She was squatting down near the priest. The godfather was sitting on the ground against the wall. The priest was obliged to bend down to do the anointings and to pour water on the child's head. Never did the sacred ministry seem to me so beautiful. I believe I saw in the person of the priest Our Lord Jesus Christ making himself small to save others. There was, outwardly, nothing impressive in that chapel. Great simplicity was its entire decoration, but how consoling it was to think that I was present at the rebirth of a soul. In circumstances like these, the missionary is well recompensed for his efforts. How then would he regret his exile when he thinks that without him, the souls whom he baptises would have been forever deprived of the sight of God. Since the Catholic missionaries have been in New Zealand they have baptised about 8,000 Christians.

After the baptism of this child we embarked on the journey back to the house. The sea was calm. I saw above the water the neck and head of a bird, the rest of whose body was hidden. I expressed my surprise to the missionary, who told me it was a koru – a penguin and was good to eat – reka [sweet] – hence the name Kororareka given to the British settlement in the harbour of the Bay of Islands, where these birds are very numerous. I recall having seen penguins at the Cape of Good Hope; it is an aquatic bird whose wings have no feathers and resemble flippers. When it is on land it uses them to strike at harmful creatures or to defend itself from those who would want to take hold of it. The Maoris hunt them. They wait for them at night when they go to find shelter in holes in the rocks on the edge of the sea, and stun them with blows from sticks.

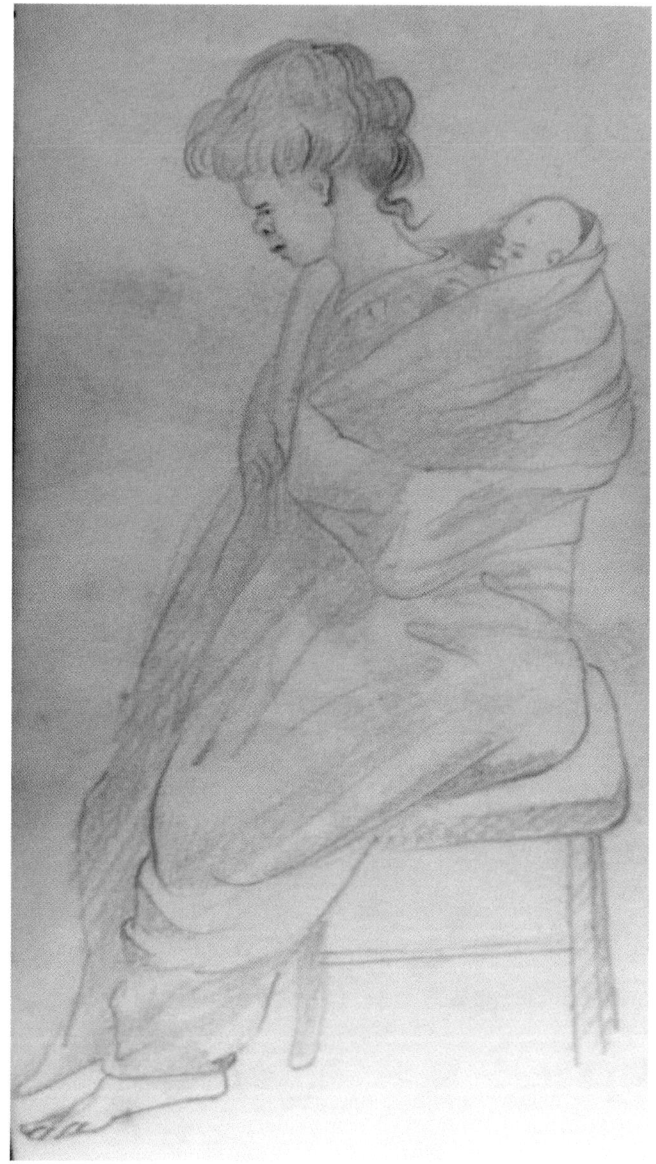

Māori mother and child

The Māori Greeting

Verguet to his parents, 4 June 1847, New Zealand

...Embracing, here, involves pressing nose against nose. When it is done only in passing by, it is soon done. You press noses, holding your breath, and when you are almost out of breath, you go to embrace another person. When people have not seen each other for a long time, the embraces go on and on. To do that, the natives crouch down on their legs, and press nose against nose, and remain so long in this position that one day, being a witness of this sign of friendship that two young people were giving each other, I did not have the patience to wait until they had finished.

When they question me, if there is no interpreter, I cannot answer them. My silence greatly amazes them. "How can you not understand the New Zealand language?" they say. "This language is so easy!" When they tell a funny story and I maintain a serious look, they clearly realise that I do not understand, they say, otherwise I would laugh.

Flax and Whares

Verguet to his parents, 4 June 1847, New Zealand

... We do not have many natives at Kororareka. Since the war they have gone away a bit, and those who remain near the settlement are very much affected by European influence. They wear clothing that is half European and half Maori. Their houses are built half and half in each style.

A little further into the interior, you do not come across this strange situation – there you find Maoris in their natural state. Their houses are all made of wood, roofed with phormium tenax. [flax] They are low, and have two openings – a door and a window (Catholic chapels in the interior are hardly more sumptuous).

Phormium tenax is a swamp plant which has very long flat leaves, like a spear with two cutting edges. The lobes of these leaves are very tough while still being very pliable. The natives use them for making elegant cloaks. They are white in colour. They are made more colourful by little black threads, fixed at intervals into the fabric. The circumference of the cloak is edged with black fringes. Phormium is also used by them to make mats and ropes. The New Zealanders highly esteem the uses this plant offers them. After having listed them, they say to the foreigners listening to them, "There is nothing like it in your country".

The British wanted to try to make fabrics out of phormium but the attempt failed – this plant is too tough. It also has the disadvantage of being damaged by rain.

To cover their houses the natives use phormium leaves which they attach to the framework. They make this layer about half a foot [about 15cm] thick. Above that they lace a lay of reeds thick enough to prevent the rain from penetrating through to the phormium. The sides of the house are also stopped up with phormium.

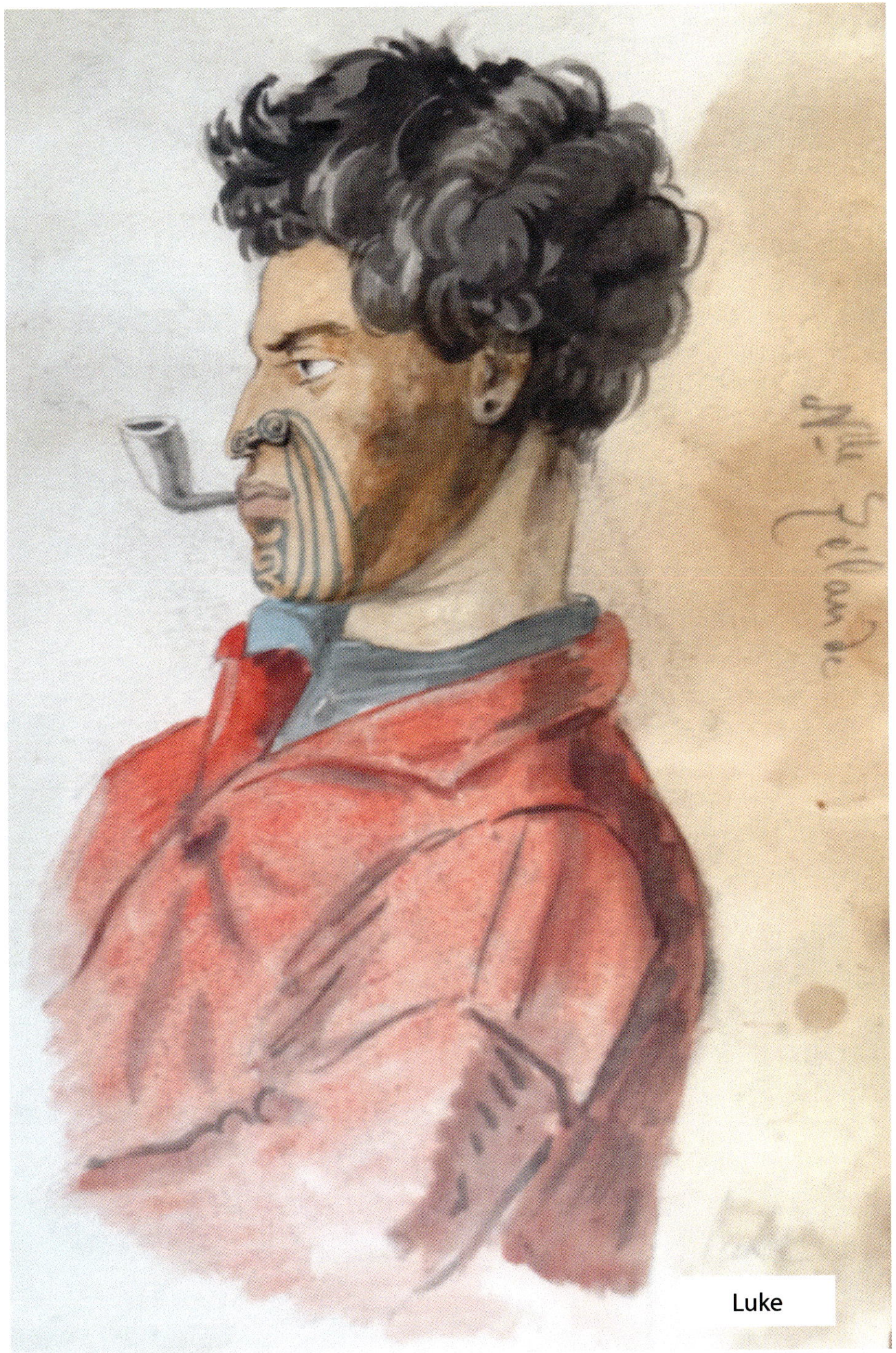

Luke

A Māori Pa
Verguet to his parents, 4 June 1847, New Zealand

...During a journey I made in the company of a missionary in the district surrounding Kororareka, I was able to see the sites that the Maoris give their villages. They place them indifferently by the seashore, or on the top of a hill. In every case they surround them with high and strong palisades, which give them protection against a sudden attack. Each village resembles a small fortress. Apart from the general palisade there are other smaller ones which separate the (individual) properties and isolate each house. You go between these rows of pickets as between two walls close to each other. The entry gate in this surrounding wall is raised above the ground and is rather like a window.

In one of these villages I saw the tomb of a chief's daughter: her remains were resting in a red box, carved in the style of the country. It was four metres up on a platform made of planks nailed together. The whole thing was decorated with pigeon feathers and sheltered by a roof lined underneath with mats of different colours. This tomb was surrounded by a double palisade. It is forbidden to go through this wall. When they have lost one of their relatives whose remains they want to keep, the Maoris enclose the body in a box, and carry it away to an open air site where there is always someone to watch over the box. If some of the remains fall from it, the person watching over the box notices it and has them burnt, and preserves the ashes which later on he will put in the tomb with the dried out remains.

Shrunken Heads
Verguet to his parents, 4 June 1847, New Zealand

...The New Zealanders preserve not only the skulls but the whole heads of their enemies, along with the flesh and the hair which they preserve from corruption by a process they know. Since the arrival of the Europeans in New Zealand this custom has, little by little, disappeared along with cannibalism, traces of which remain in the northern areas. To call them cannibals is to insult them. When a Christian New Zealander comes to die, his relatives let him be buried in the Catholic cemetery. It sometimes happens that they come back to ask for the body. They go and disinter it and take its remains away to throw them off a great inaccessible cliff where the remains of their ancestors already lie.

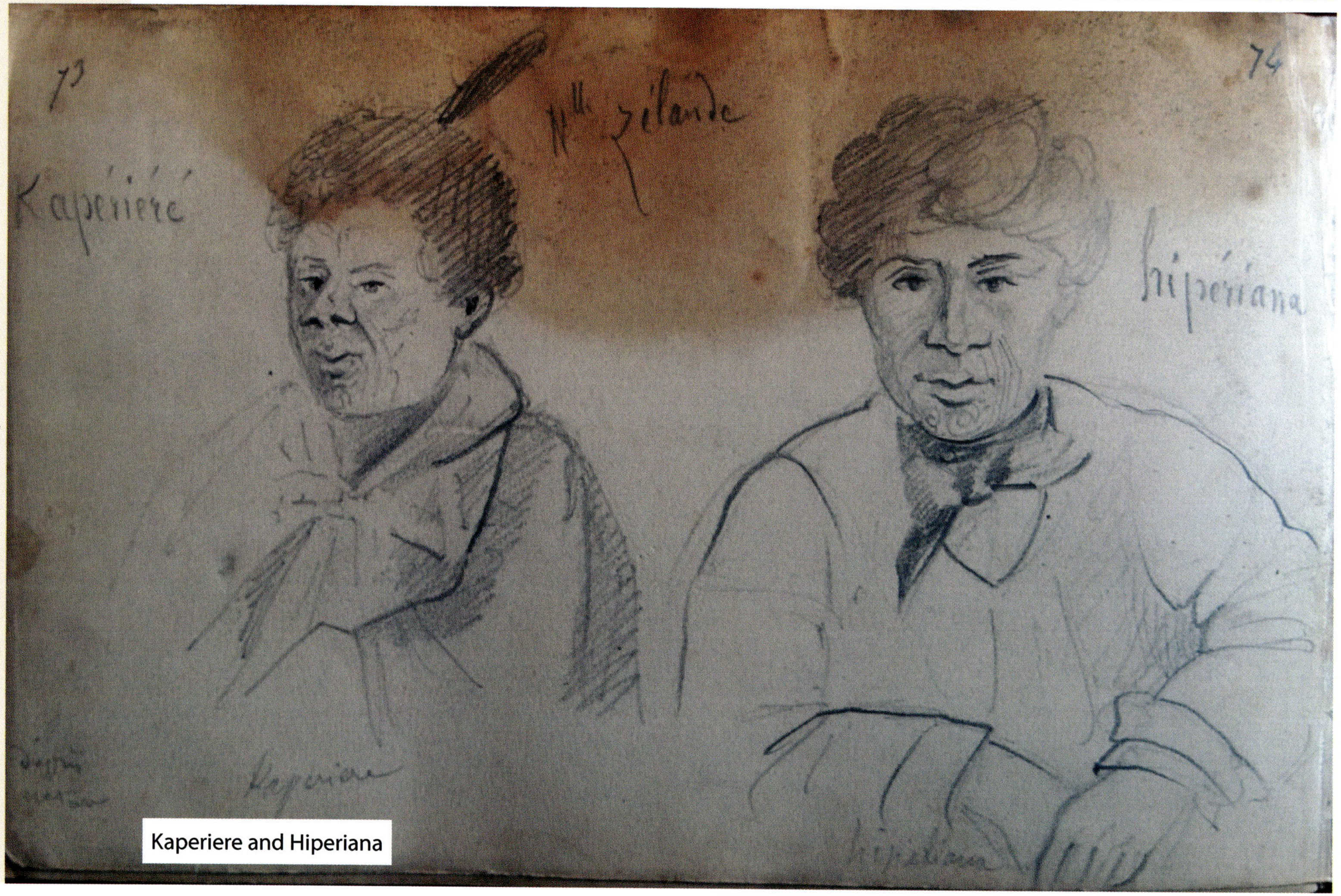

Kaperiere and Hiperiana

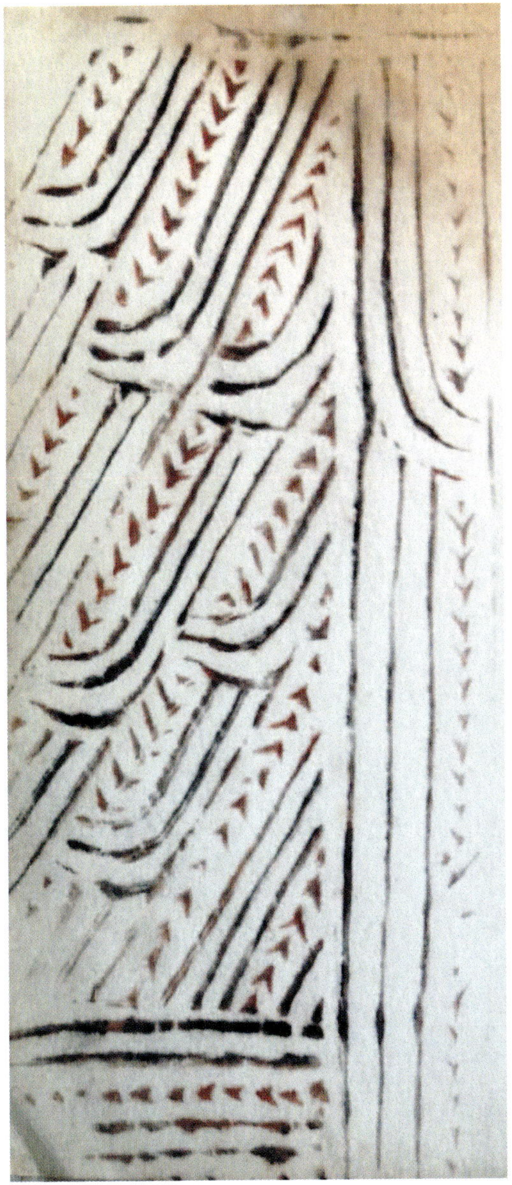

Verguet's copy of the carving design on a Māori bowl

Maori Carving
Verguet to his parents, 4 June 1847, New Zealand

The New Zealanders have the reputation of being skilful in working in wood. You would not say that if you saw their carving in the northern part of the island. There is nothing really extraordinary. Their statues are even more poorly done than the one I saw on San Cristobal. The heads of their statues equal a good third of the body, and the rest is also so lacking in proportion that sometimes you have to spend a long time looking to guess at the different parts. Although they seem to be unaware of the laws of proportion and perspective, there is so much

> *"Their statues are even more poorly done than the one I saw on San Cristobal*

symmetry in this apparent disorder that the eye finds it pleasant to study their work. I particularly like the two carvings which they place at the prow and stern of their canoes. On the prow they put the head of a man or of a devil remarkable for its disproportionately lengthened tongue, for its big eyes made of mother-of-pearl, and for its hair made of pigeon feathers. The stern post of the canoe rises sharply at a right angle. It is a board about two inches thick, a foot and a half wide, and about a metre high and carved in an open work style. The human figure, grotesquely disfigured, is always the subject of the carving. The whole canoe is 15 to 20 metres in length, two metres wide and one metre high. It can carry 80 to 100 people. It has one or two sails made of reeds which fold like fans. These canoes are made of two great pieces of wood lashed together with phormium tenax and tied to a strong plank. The oars are small and resemble a rhombus shape at the end of a handle.

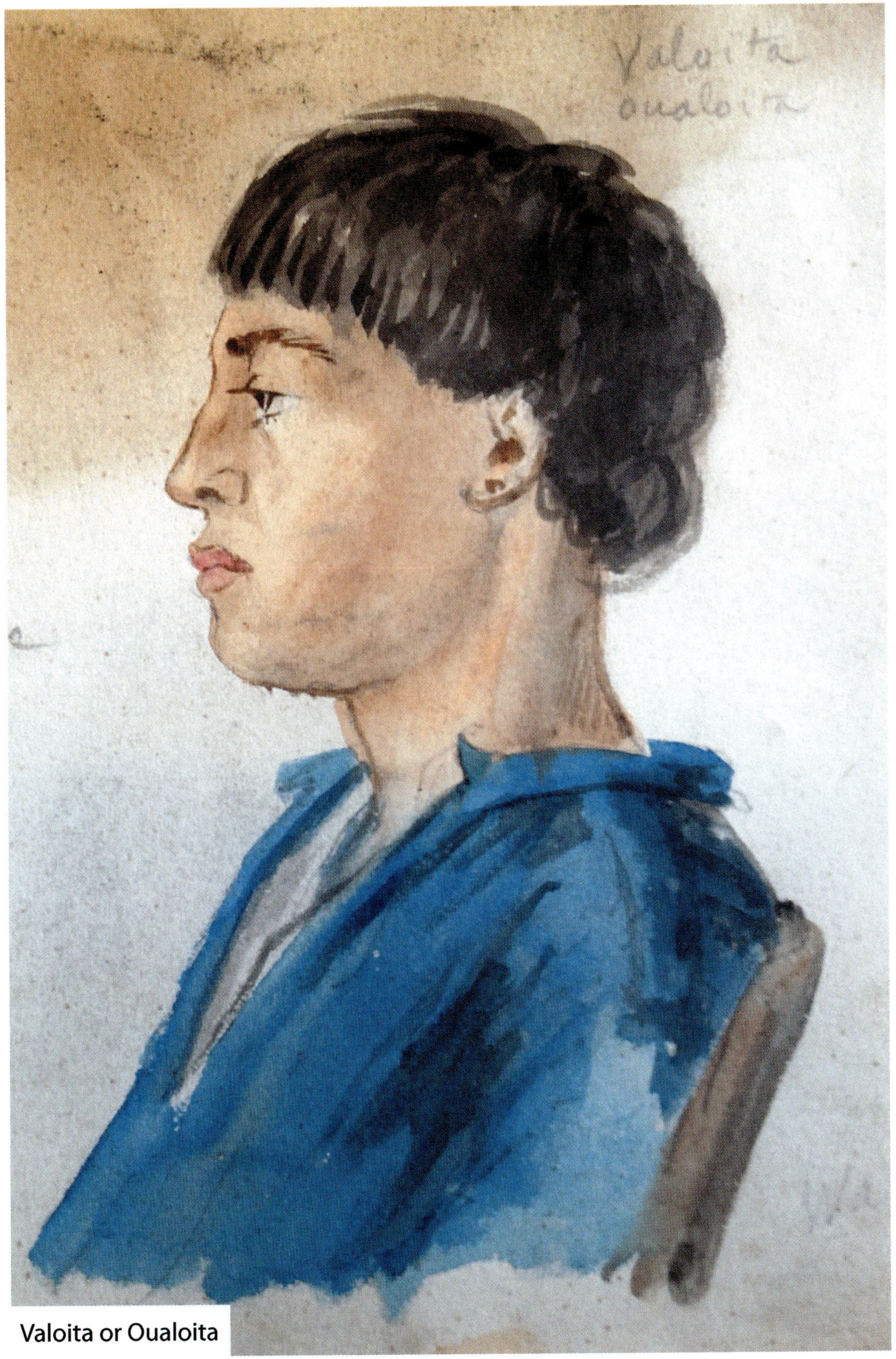

Valoita or Oualoita

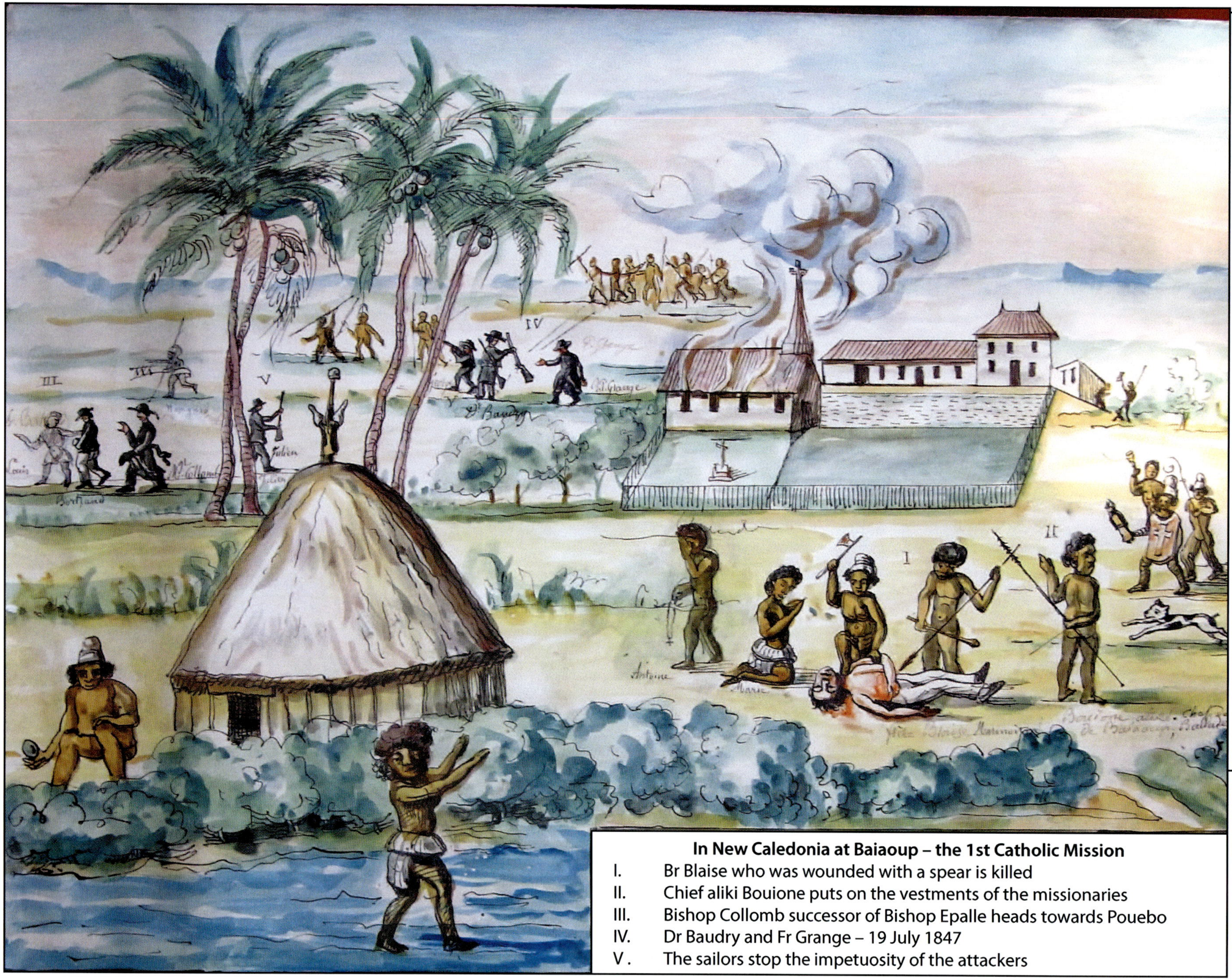

In New Caledonia at Baiaoup – the 1st Catholic Mission

I. Br Blaise who was wounded with a spear is killed
II. Chief aliki Bouione puts on the vestments of the missionaries
III. Bishop Collomb successor of Bishop Epalle heads towards Pouebo
IV. Dr Baudry and Fr Grange – 19 July 1847
V. The sailors stop the impetuosity of the attackers

Facing Page

In New Caledonia the crew of *La Brillante*, commanded by Du Bouzet, rescue the besieged missionaries at Pouebo.

I. *La Brillante* – 24 guns
II. Frs Rougeyron and Verguet
III. Captain De Trogof
IV. A savage killed
V. Sailors versus savages
VI. The ambush
VII. Canoe

Note. Bishop Collomb left New Caledonia for San Cristobal aboard the *Anonyme*, Captain Rabaland, 21 August 1847.

Sketch done at Carcassonne 30 May 1906 by L Verguet, canon.

These watercolours were done by Verguet when he was 89

Under Attack

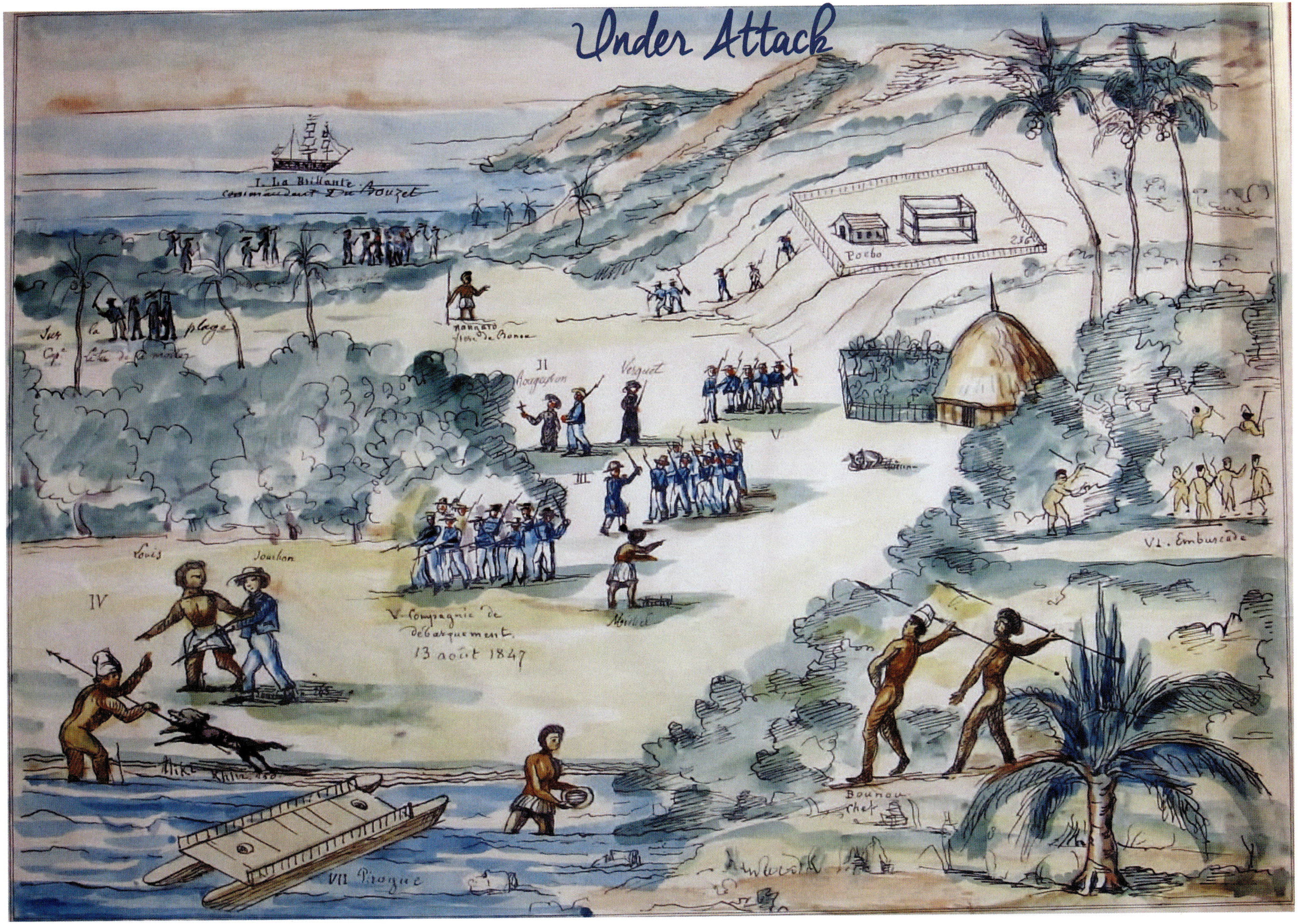

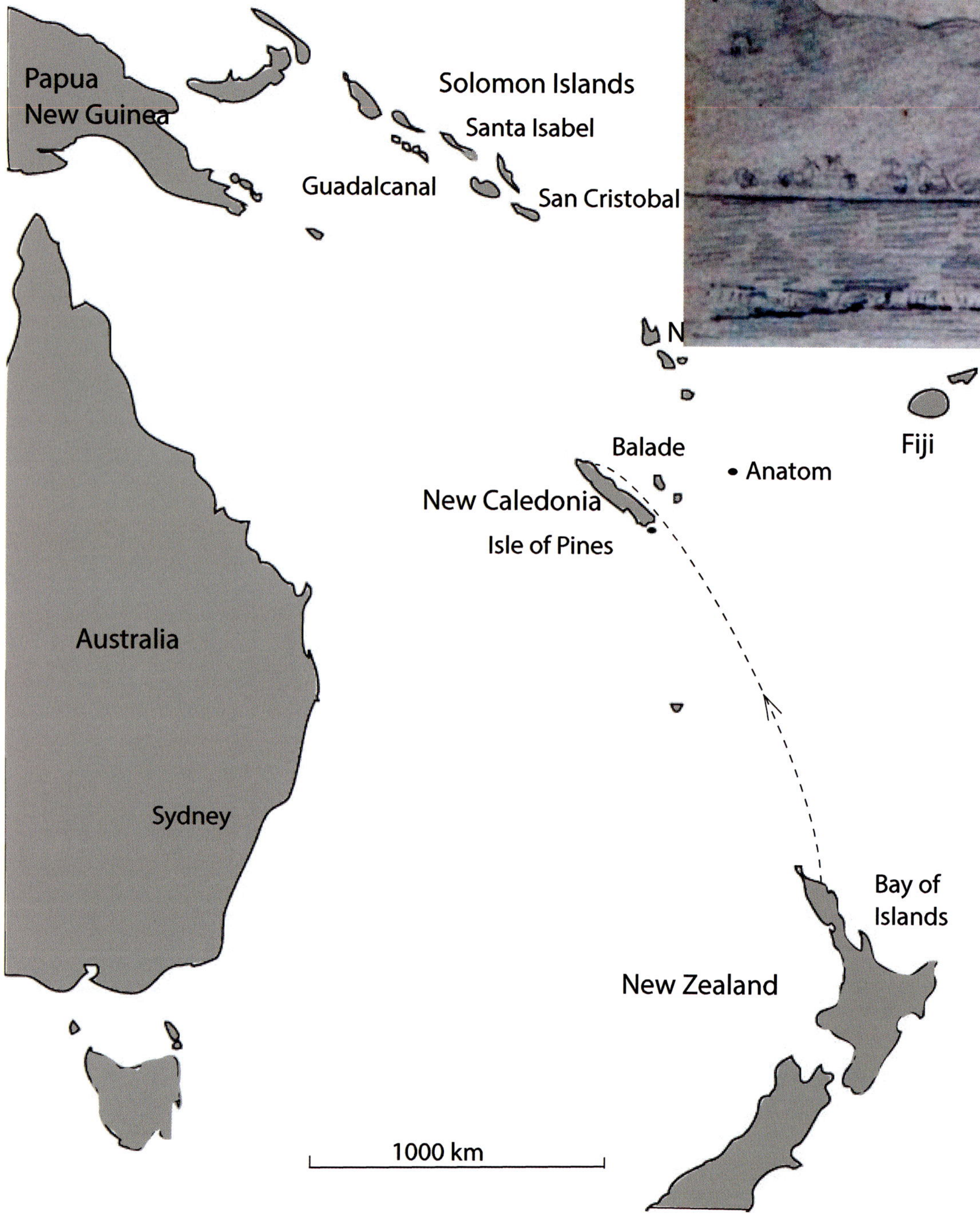

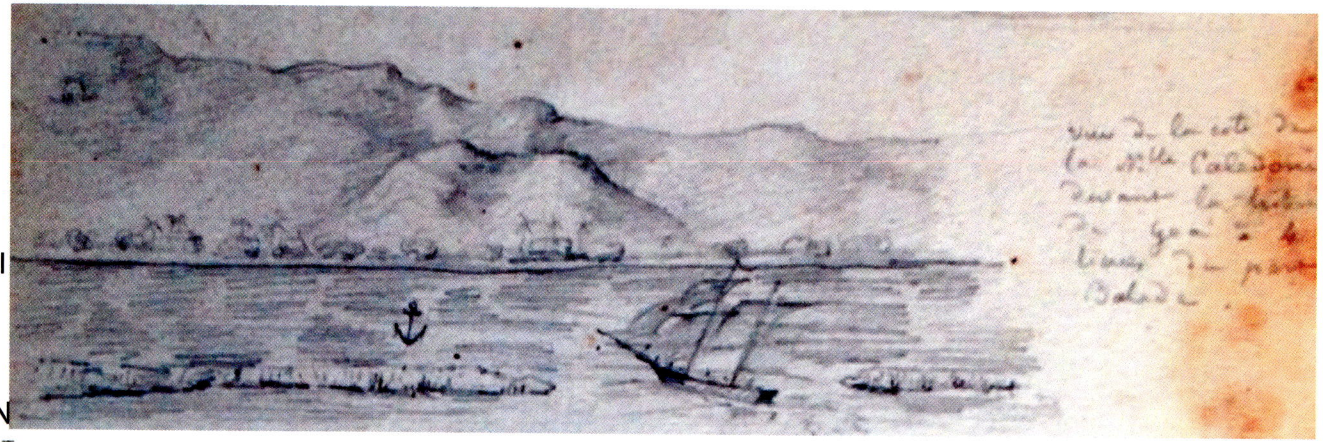

View of the coast of
New Caledonia
opposite the tribe
of the Goa at 4 leagues
from Port Balade

New Caledonia

June 1847

Douarre, the Bishop of New Caledonia, was in Europe seeking manpower and funds for his mission. There had been a famine, particularly affecting the Balade region. The flourishing mission plantation had been repeatedly raided by locals, the previously good relationship between the missionaries and the people they were working with had deteriorated.

The main mission station at Baïao had just been resupplied by the *Anonyme* not long before Bishop Collomb and the *Spec* arrived on 29 June. They had intended to connect with the *Anonyme*, and were carrying goods for the Solomon Islands mission, supplies for the New Caledonia mission station, and various items for transhipment on the *Anonyme*. These were off-loaded by the *Spec* over the next fortnight and carried by locals into the Balade chapel to await the return of the *Anonyme*. The locals considered this to be very valuable cargo and wanted a share. The more important goods were transferred into the mission storehouse. On 10 July, in the evening, the chapel was robbed of fabric and trade goods, about 300 francs worth. Given that theft and the garden raids, it was thought that their animals might be safer at Pouebo than Baïao, the Balade base, so on 15 July, Verguet, guided by a young convert helped drive some of the livestock to the other station. Verguet intended to spend some days with Rougeyron, the superior of the mission in the absence of Bishop Douarre, and to discuss the prospects of his joining the New Caledonia mission. There he heard rumours that the tribes intended an attack on the Balade mission, Baïao, once the *Spec* had departed. He wrote a note to Collomb at Balade relaying this disturbing news, but such rumours had been in circulation for months. On 17 July, the *Spec* left for Batavia (Indonesia). The same day, two children, Antoine and Marie, friendly with the missionaries, gave them another warning about an imminent attack; they too were not taken seriously.

July to August 1847

The day after the departure of the *Spec*, Sunday 18 July, a large group of locals, under the pretence of returning stolen property, attacked the mission station of Balade. Present there were: Bishop Collomb, Fr Jérôme Grange, Br Blaise Marmoiton, Br Bertrand Besselles, Marie Julien a carpenter, George Taylor a Scotsman who was converting to Catholicism, and Doctor Baudry who had been left by the *Arche d'Alliance* to do some scientific exploration, plus some sailors who had survived the shipwreck of the *Seine*. The attack was driven off by Br Bertrand firing a random shot but not before Br Blaise received a chest wound from a spear and Father Grange took a less serious injury. The chapel was set alight and burnt to the ground.

Meanwhile, not very far away at Pouebo, Rougeyron and Verguet were out walking. The local people seemed peaceful and welcoming but a young catechumen, informed them that the topic of discussion was whether or not it would be a good idea to kill them then and there, so they headed as quickly and discretely as they could back to the mission house. Once there they received news about the first attack on the base at Balade.

The attack that had been rebuffed on the Sunday was renewed on the Monday. Large numbers of the Pouma tribe gathered outside, while the missionaries within made their confessions and conditionally baptised George Taylor. When it seemed that the house was going to be stormed, they distracted their attackers by throwing to them the keys of the storehouse. As the attackers were looting the storehouse the group at the Mission fled out the back. In the confusion Br Blaise could not keep up and he was killed, the others made it safely to the Pouebo house where they were welcomed by Rougeyron and Verguet. There they stayed daily expecting attack. There were some confrontations which they drove off with the threat of firearms. They were in constant fear of attack in the Pouebo station and being worried that the people of Balade would ambush the crew of the next ship to arrive the

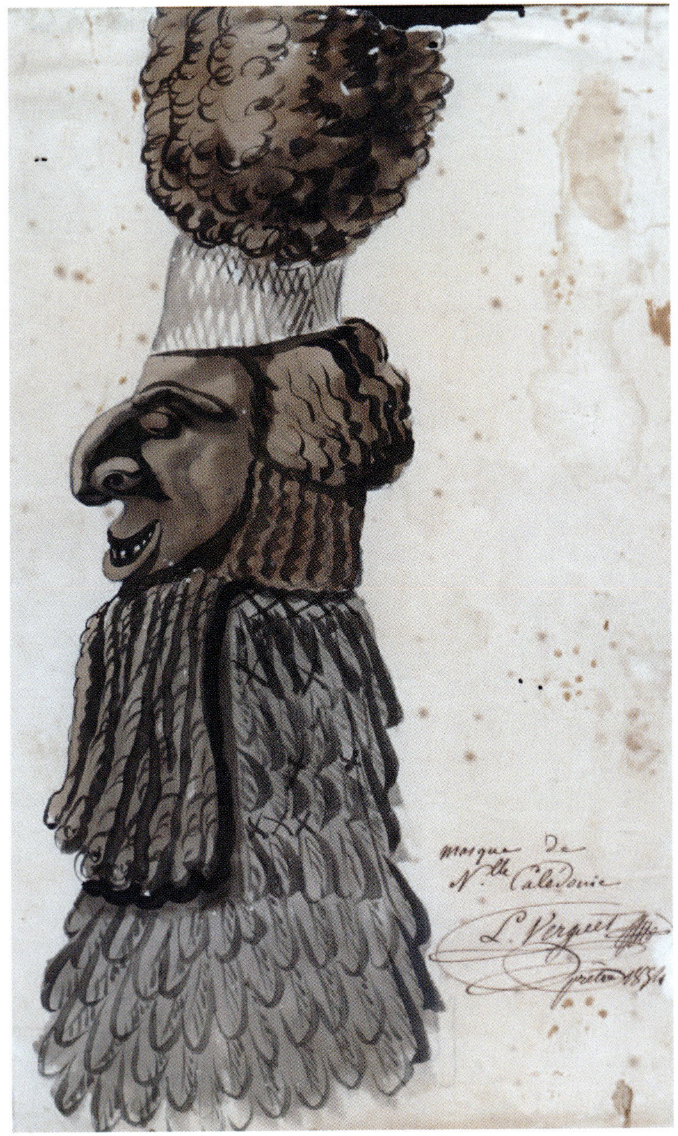

Mask of New Caledonia
a watercolour done by Verguet in 1854
on the basis of a sketch in the sketchbook

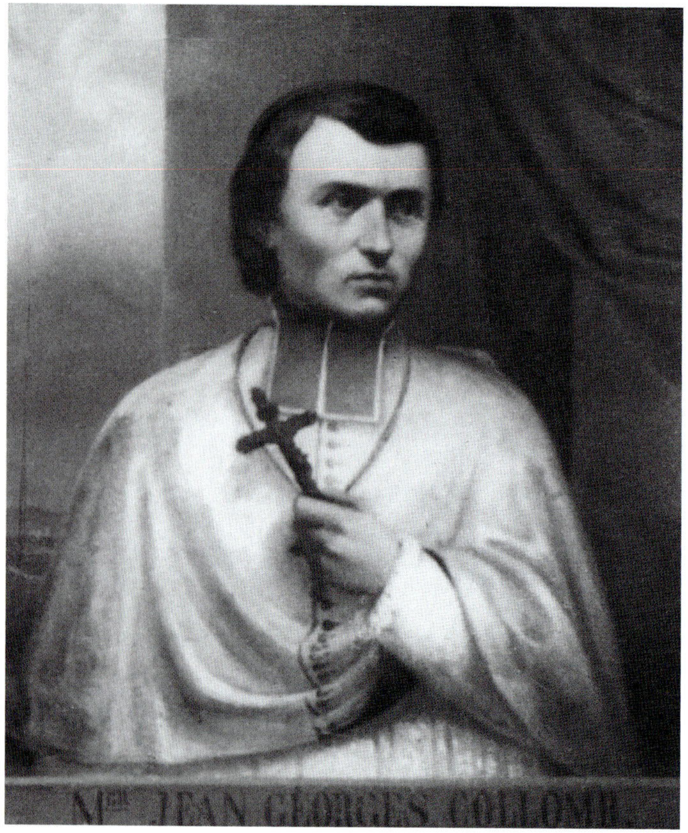

Bishop Jean Georges Collomb SM
1816 - 1848

missionaries sneaked back and set fire to the ransacked mission house at Balade on 5 August, so that anyone arriving would be warned.

On 9 Auguste they saw the *Brillante* approaching. Some, including Collomb and Grange, went to Balade to warn them of the situation and were taken on board when the ship anchored in the bay the next day. It was a French naval vessel under Commodore Eugène Du Bouzet with orders to take Bishop Collomb to the Solomons. This was the second time that Du Bouzet had arrived just after the death of a Marist missionary; in 1841 he had taken Bishop Pompallier to Futuna to collect the remains of Pierre Chanel. Pompallier had dissuaded him from taking punitive action then, this time he was resolved that the honour of the French nation and the safety of her citizens required it.

On 12 August, the *Brillante* reached Pouebo. Collomb, Grange and 30 soldiers went on land to gather the men and their material. They were attacked and locals as well as soldiers were wounded. The next day, the soldiers took the missionaries and local Christians of Balade on board. Years later Verguet did a watercolour of the turmoil. On 15 August, the *Anonyme* arrived at Pouebo with Father Roudaire. Three days later, both ships sailed to Balade. Du Bouzet enacted punitive measures on both places: the soldiers burned trees and plantations. The Marists protested in vain.

Finally, all left. The *Brillante* left New Caledonia and took most missionaries among them Verguet to Anatom (Vanuatu) and then Sydney. Collomb left on the *Anonyme* for the Solomons. Collomb wrote to France: The attacks of 18 and 19 July cost us 20,000 francs – but I would say much more. They had lost Br Blaise, and the work of years. The New Caledonia Catholic mission was temporarily abandoned. Their catechists and Christians helped them during the siege, warned them of attacks, and tried to protect them in the face of their own people. Louis, Augustin, Raphaël, Nangara, Koïne went with Rougeyron to Sydney. Michel, Grégoire, Antoine, Victor, Raphaëel and Magdeleine stayed in New Caledonia. There were about six hundred persons who knew the prayers but who were not ready for baptism.

In the midst of all this was Verguet; after the traumas of the Solomon Islands he had thought to continue as a missionary in New Caledonia and seemed to have stepped from the frying pan into the fire. There is an inscription on the back cover of Verguet's sketchbook, it reads: 'This sketchbook is battered by use and thereby its value increased. It spent a month in the hands of the savages of New Caledonia in July 1847 after the looting of the Baïao house. - L. Verguet 1881' The wonder is that it was returned to him before their departure. One of those 'savages' must have appreciated how important the sketchbook was to Verguet.

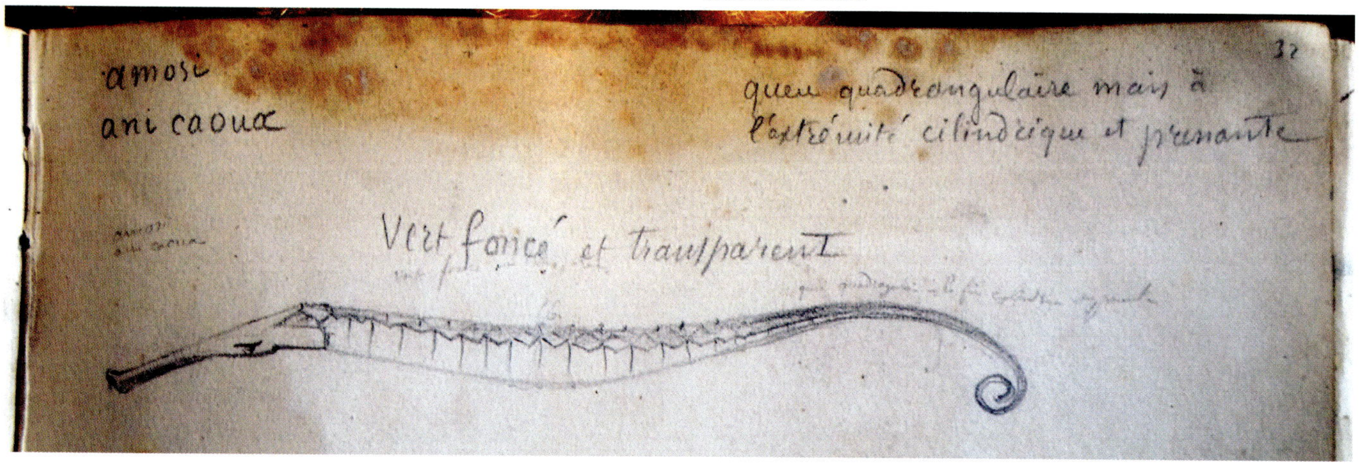

"amosi
ani caoua"'

Tail quadrangular but, at
the extremities, cylindrical and flattened

Dark green and transparent

Going

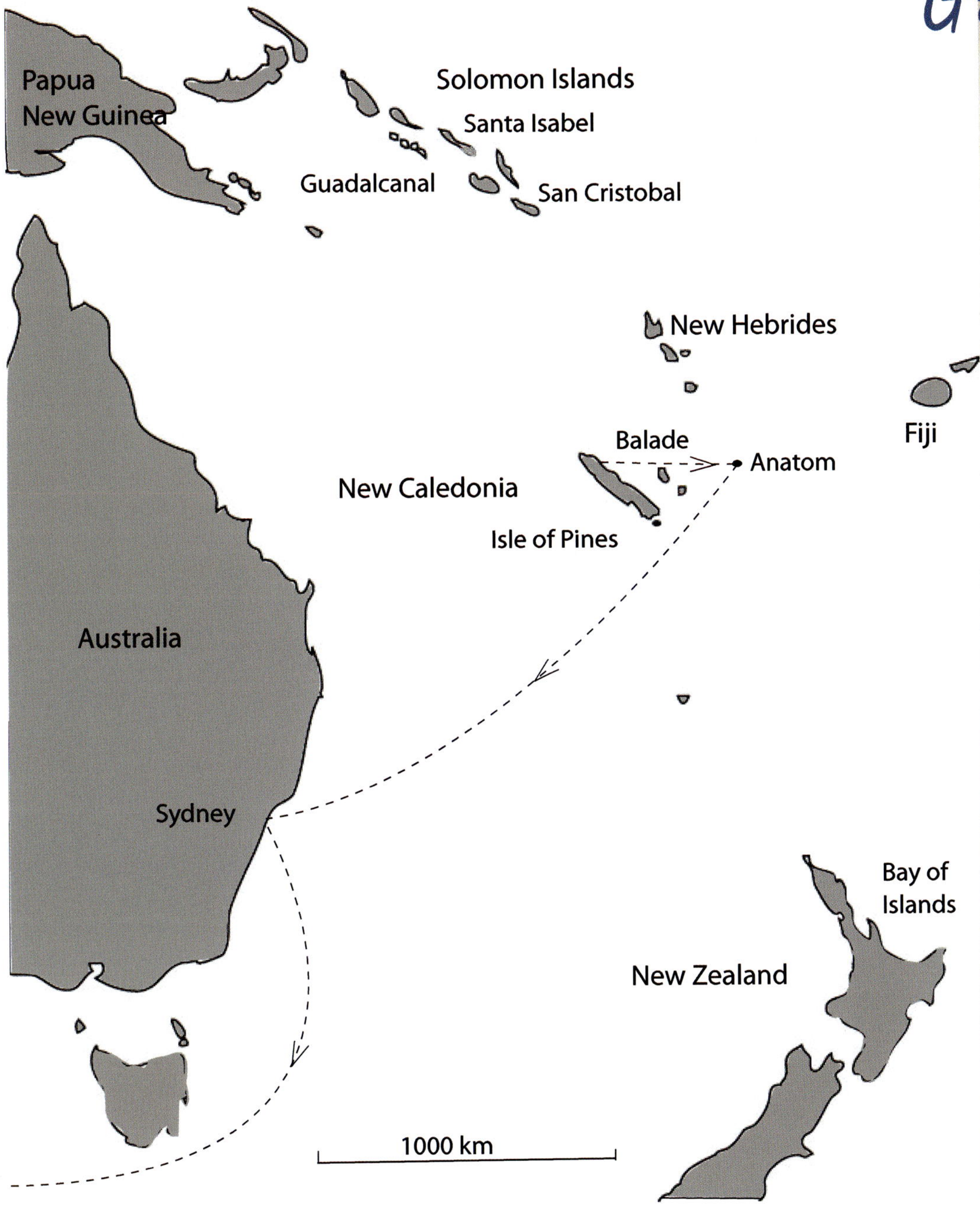

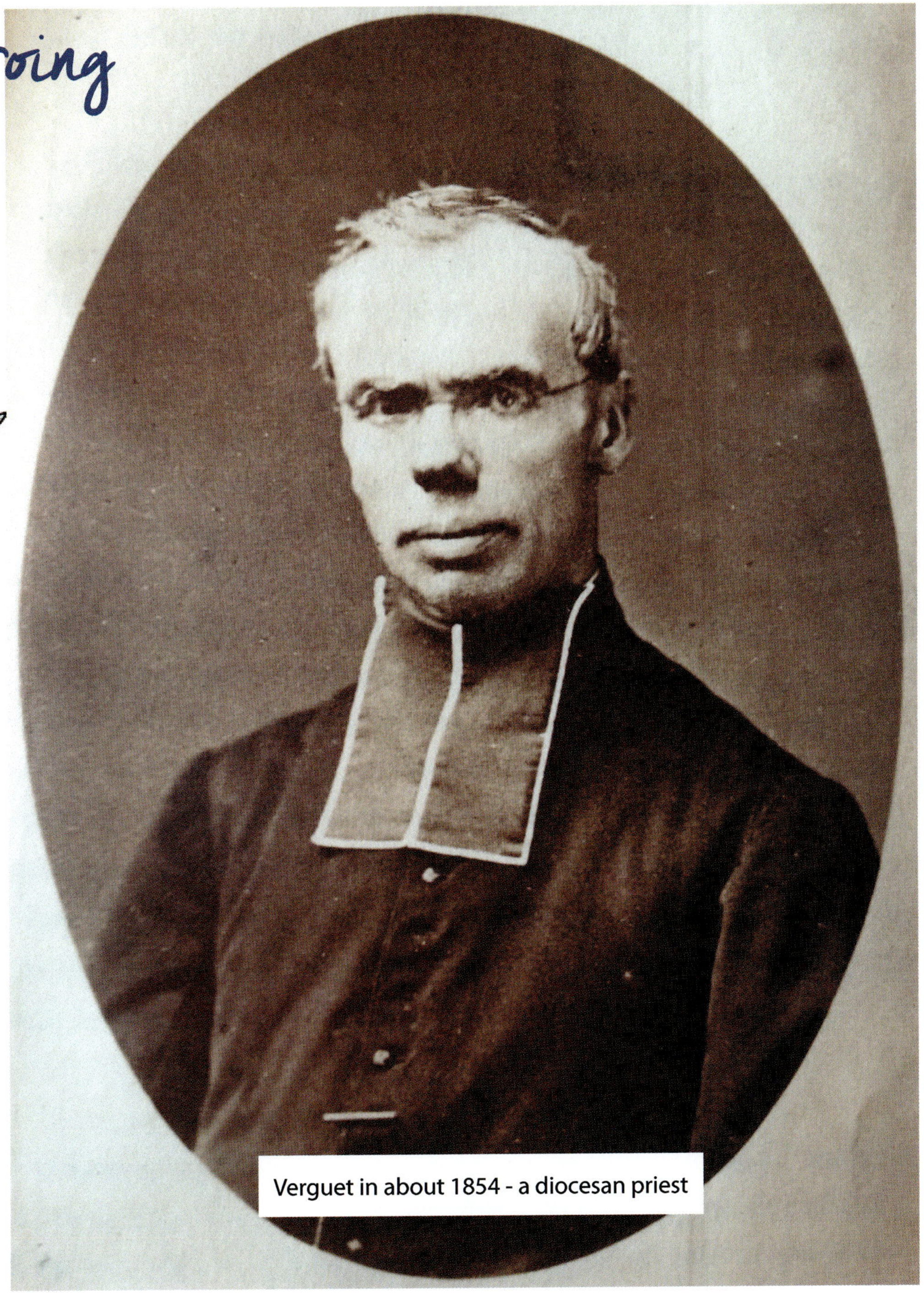

Verguet in about 1854 - a diocesan priest

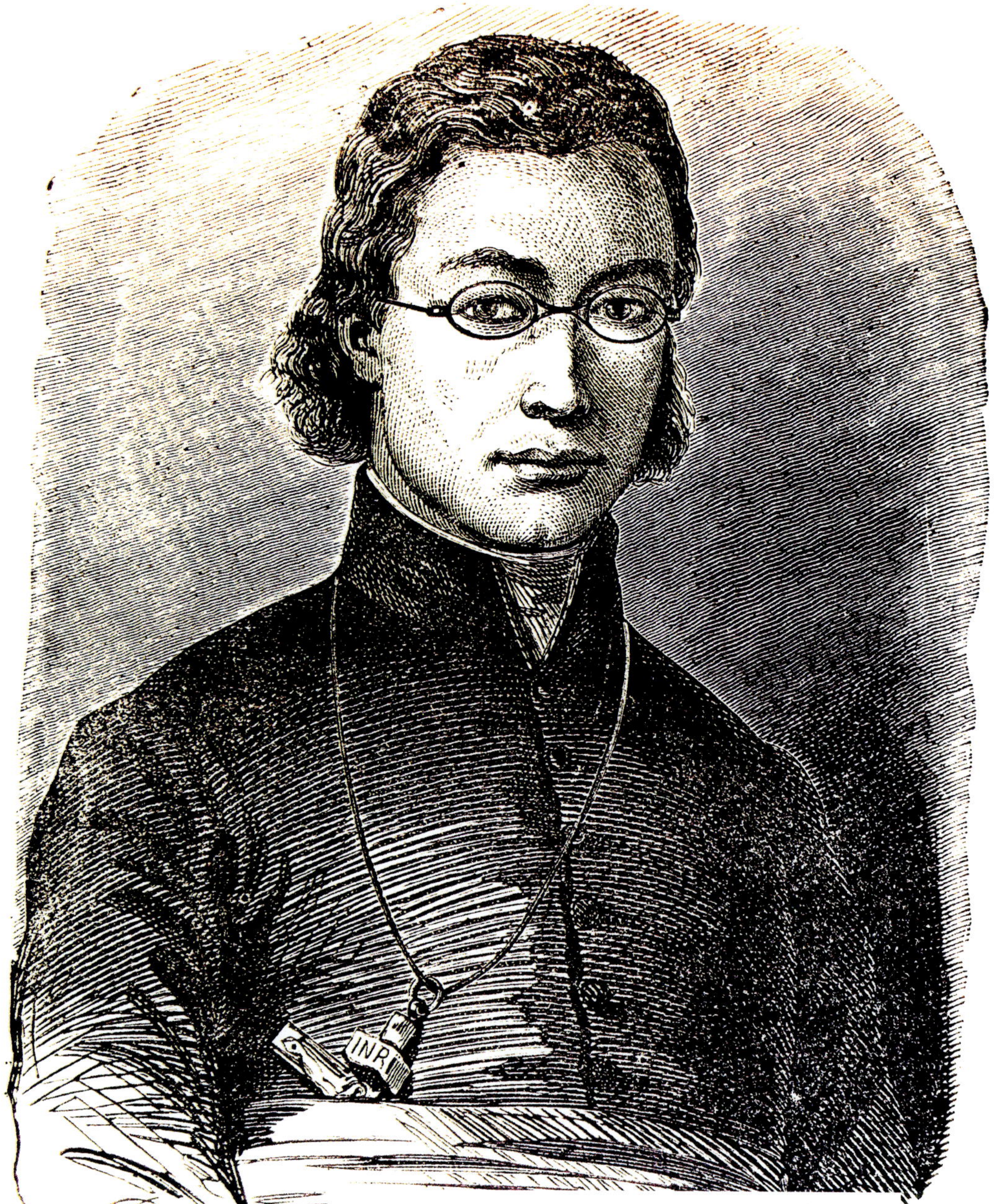

Verguet's author portrait for *L'Histoire*
Verguet, Apostolic Missionary of the Society of Mary
1844-48

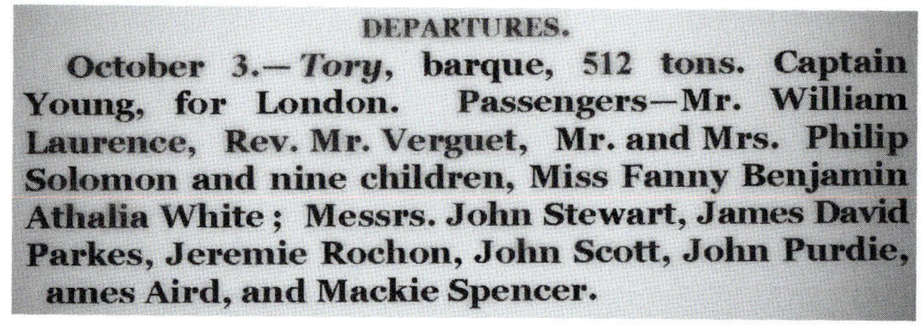

DEPARTURES.

October 3.—*Tory*, barque, 512 tons. Captain Young, for London. Passengers—Mr. William Laurence, Rev. Mr. Verguet, Mr. and Mrs. Philip Solomon and nine children, Miss Fanny Benjamin Athalia White; Messrs. John Stewart, James David Parkes, Jeremie Rochon, John Scott, John Purdie, ames Aird, and Mackie Spencer.

Sydney Chronicle, 5 October 1847

Return to France

August 1847: Sydney

When Collomb wrote a report to Fr Colin on 21 August from aboard the *Brillante* off the coast of Balade he mentions that Verguet is not going to go with him back to San Cristobal but will stay with the other priests. They will try to start a mission on Anatom (Vanuatu) and Verguet hopes to stay there five years, but if that does not work out he will return to Europe and leave the Marists. Collomb thought this latter course likely as Verguet has acquired a dislike for the foreign missions and for religious life, which he joined only in order to go to the missions. This annoyed Collomb because he had been under the impression that Verguet would go back with him to the Solomons. He also felt that Verguet should have consulted him, his bishop, on these decisions. The relationship between Verguet and the others was good and remained so.

On 15 August the group with Verguet landed on Anatom but did not stay. They continued to Sydney arriving there on 27 August. They were divided about what the next step should be. Fr Grange wrote to Fr Colin: 'The two Fathers [Rougeyron and Roudaire] wish to return to New Caledonia with just three people, taking with them a house made of iron, some canons and some rifles so as to be able to defend themselves if needs be. But I am morally certain that we will be obliged to make use of these arms or else be massacred ourselves.' He went on to ask

Frustrations in the Solomons

19th July 1847 - Father Xavier Montrouzier to his brother, Henri Montrouzier, SJ

You cannot imagine how difficult it is to extract words from the savages once one has used up those that apply to material objects. So although we have been here nearly two years, we have not yet been able to learn the word for "love".

"although we have been here nearly two years, we have not yet been able to learn the word for "love"

[...] A month after having installed themselves with the Pia, Father Crey succumbed to an illness of which he died within a few days. On Thursday Father Jacquet and I had gone to the new establishment to take a few vegetables from our garden; he seemed tired but we did not think there was any hint of danger. He expressed the wish to return to Makira. So as not to tire him we tried to return by sea, but quarter of an hour out from shore, we were caught in a storm that obliged us to turn back and soaked us to the skin. This left him more unwell. On Monday, Father Frémont wrote to us asking us to go and administer the last rights to our dear colleague. We hurriedly set out, overwhelmed by this blow that we certainly had not anticipated. The Pia did not want to allow Father Crey to be buried in their village; the reason they gave was that his "ataro", (spirit) having never killed anyone during his life, would inevitably kill many people after his death. So we carried the body to Makira and in the evening we conducted the funeral with church prayers. Several days later we placed a cross and some flowers on his grave, which we protected with a little fence. Father Crey had not had more than one month at the mission. He was still very young and had looked forward to a long career. God had required of him only some of his aspirations. He did not wish him to help us bear the burden of evangelism. May His goodness be forever blessed. But I must say it is a very harsh blow to a missionary when he sees one on his colleagues, who are already too few, carried off so rapidly and he feels himself surrounded by so much need spread amongst so many islands that, for lack of disciples, languish in faithlessness and savagery.

permission to return to France once the *Arche d'Alliance* comes back in five months. With their Bishop still in Europe the little group decide to await the decisions of higher authorities. In fact, Grange returned to France in 1848 and continued to work there as a Marist.

On 3 October 1847 Verguet left Sydney on the barque *Tory* destined for London. He had to borrow money to pay his fare. The Captain was a friendly Scotsman by the name of John Young. Verguet found the journey monotonous. He enjoyed the stop over at Saint Helena on 6 January, where he visited the house and tomb of Napoleon. He arrived back in London on 6 March. In March of 1848 Verguet was back in Lyon, staying initially with the Marists. He left the Society of Mary and re-joined the diocese of Carcassonne.

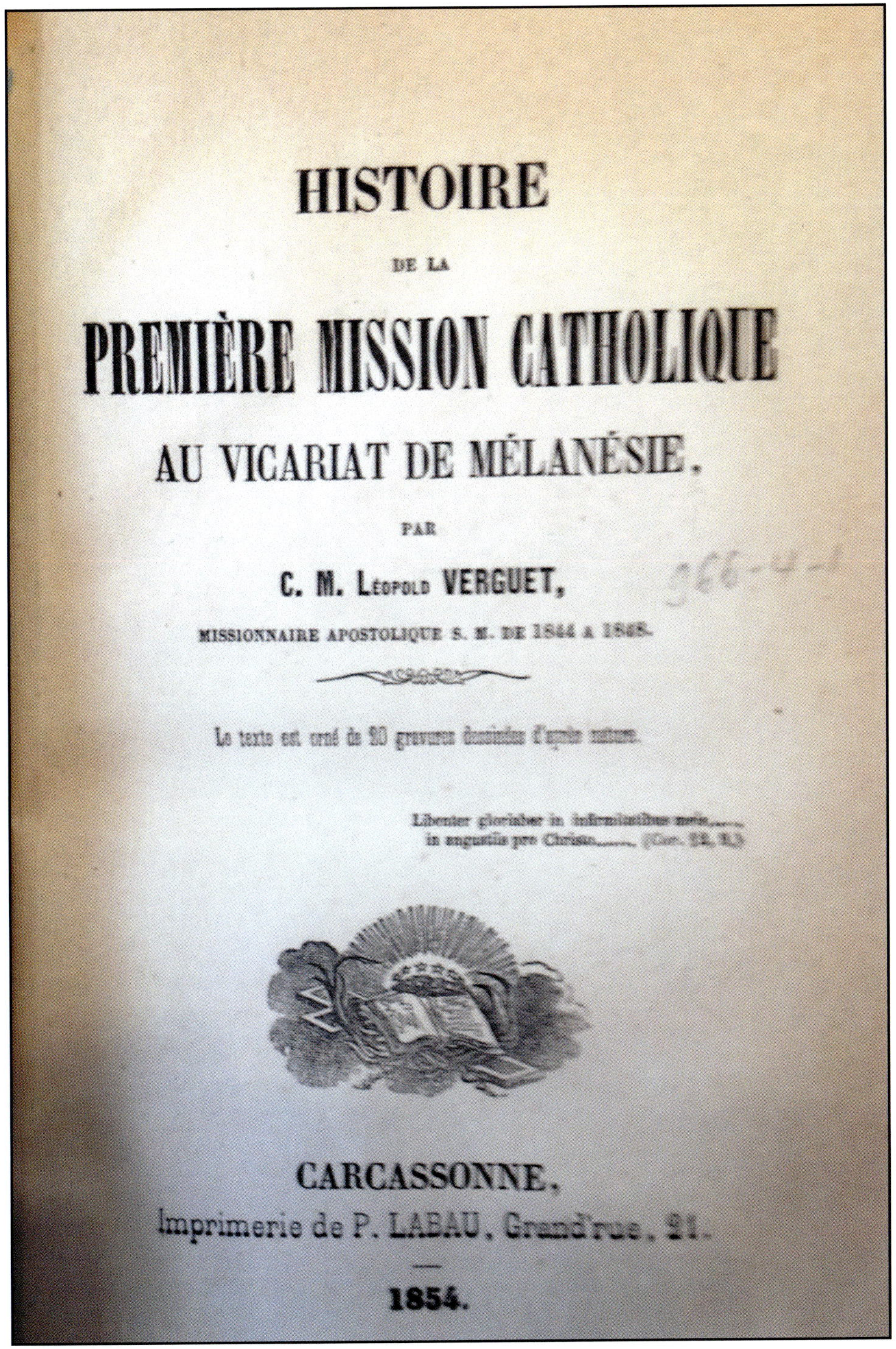

HISTOIRE

DE LA

PREMIÈRE MISSION CATHOLIQUE

AU VICARIAT DE MÉLANÉSIE,

PAR

C. M. LÉOPOLD VERGUET,

MISSIONNAIRE APOSTOLIQUE S. M. DE 1844 A 1848.

CARCASSONNE,

Imprimerie de P. LABAU, Grand'rue, 21.

1854.

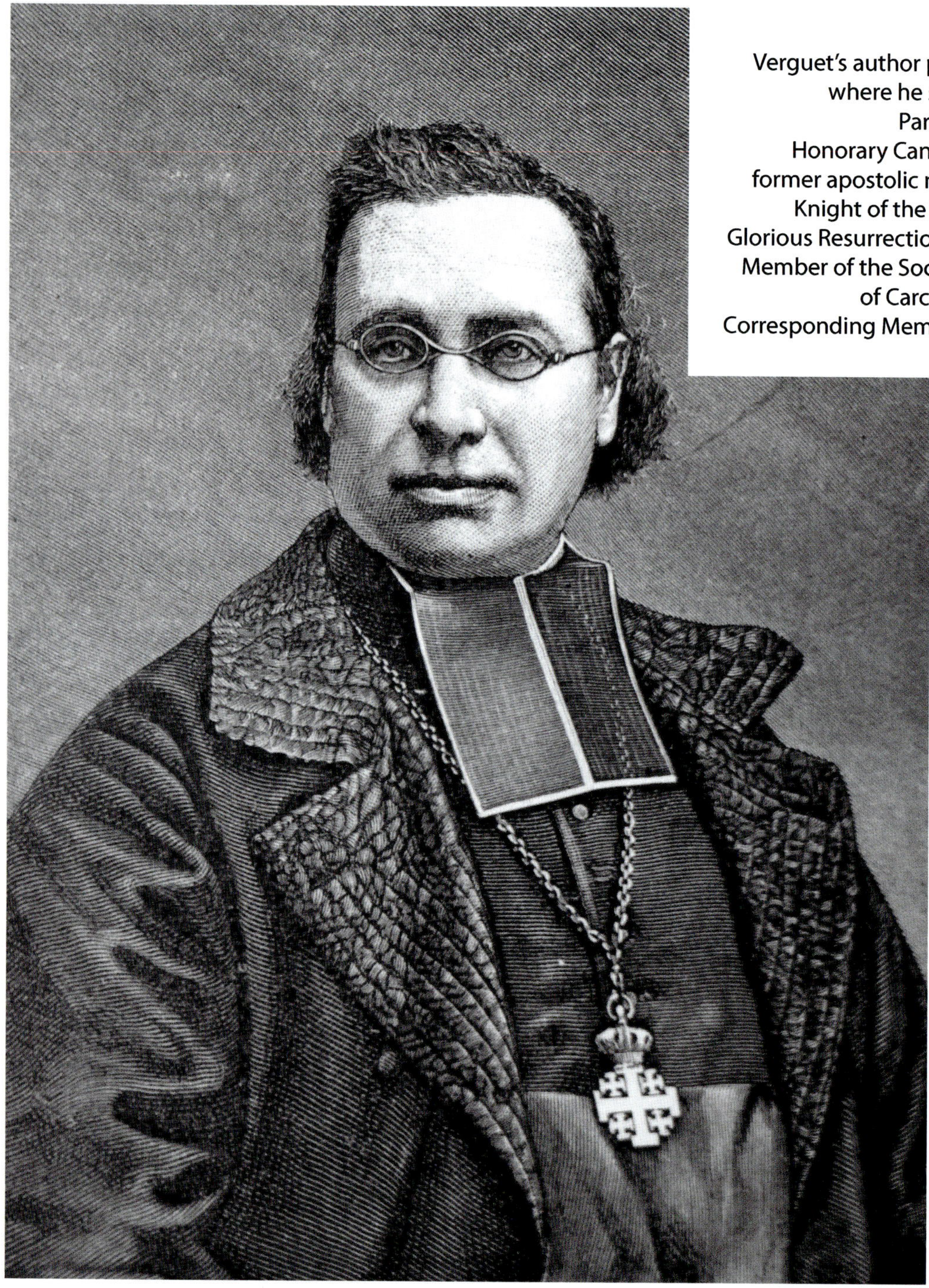

Verguet's author portrait for *Iles Salomon* where he styles himself as: Parish Priest, Honorary Canon of the Cathedral, former apostolic missionary in Melanesia, Knight of the Holy Sepulchre and Glorious Resurrection of Our Lord Jesus Christ, Member of the Society of Arts and Sciences of Carcassonne, and Corresponding Member of the Oriental Society

New Caledonia

Bishop Douarre made two further attempts to open the Catholic mission on New Caledonia. He died, probably of tetanus, during the third successful attempt on 27 April 1853, shortly before New Caledonia became a French colony on 24 September of that year.

Solomon Islands

Of the group of fourteen Frenchmen who had set out to bring the gospel to the Solomon Islands, Epalle, Jacquet, Hyacinthe and Paget had been killed; Montrouzier and Frémont had been seriously wounded in attacks; Br Prosper left the Society and remained in New Caledonia; Fr Chaurain and Br Gennade withdrew from the Solomons to work in the Procure in Sydney. The Marists withdrew from the Solomons in 1852, handing over the work to the Missionaries of Milan. That group lasted three years and then pulled their men out also because of disease, hostility and a sense of hopeless futility. In 1855 one of the missionaries of Milan, Giovanni Battista Mazzuconni was returning to the Solomons after recuperation in Sydney when the ship he was on ran aground near Woodlark Island and all on board were killed. He has since been declared 'Blessed' by the Catholic Church; a step on the path to being listed as a saint.

The Marists re-established the mission, successfully, in 1898.

Carcassonne

Back in France, Verguet maintained contact with the Society writing to the mission procurators Poupinel and Yardin, to the assistant general Monfat and to Montrouzier in the Pacific. He went into print about his experiences in the Pacific, publishing in 1854 *L'Histoire de la Première Mission Catholique au Vicariat de Mélanésie*, including etchings made from his sketches. This was the first major book on the Catholic Mission in the Solomons, written and illustrated by an eyewitness. The engravings were of such interest that they were also published separately in a cheaper edition in the same year as *Album de Mélanésie Océanie Occidental.*

In 1855, he became resident member of the *Société des Arts et des Sciences de Carcassonne*, then its active secretary. Verguet was one of the pioneers of photography in France, producing some of the earliest photographs of his town. In 1857 he published an eight-page pamphlet *Chapelle de Notre-Dame de la Santé rendue au culte de Marie.* In 1864 he applied photography to coin-collecting and published *Photographie appliquée a la numismatique: Monnaies romaines, monnaies consulaires et des familles romaines extraites de la Collection du Musée de Carcassonne.* A year later he produced a second similar publication: *Monnaies féodales; Monnaies des Comtes et des Vicomtes de Carcassonne; Photographie appliquée a la numismatique.*

In 1872 Verguet applied to join the Society of Mary once more. He seems not to have settled back easily into the life of a priest in the diocese. He was parish priest only briefly, the longest appointment he had was as chaplain to a girls' college. The Marist leadership said 'no' to his request in view of his age – he was then fifty-five.

In 1883 he published a small book entitled *Gran Archipel des Iles Salomon son Étendue sa Fertilité.* Two years later he wrote a forty-page article for the *Revue d'Ethnographe* entitled "Arossi ou San-Christoval et ses habitants" both with copious illustrations. At the age of 68 he was still reflecting on his experience of living among the peoples of Solomon Islands forty years previously.

In 1889 he was made an honorary Canon of the Cathedral in Carcassonne.

In 1893, when Verguet was 76, the Marists were preparing for their second attempt to evangelize the Solomon Islands. They requested and Verguet prepared a briefing paper on the conditions they were likely to encounter there. This fourteen page document, illustrated with watercolours of the various types of ship and with plans for a mission

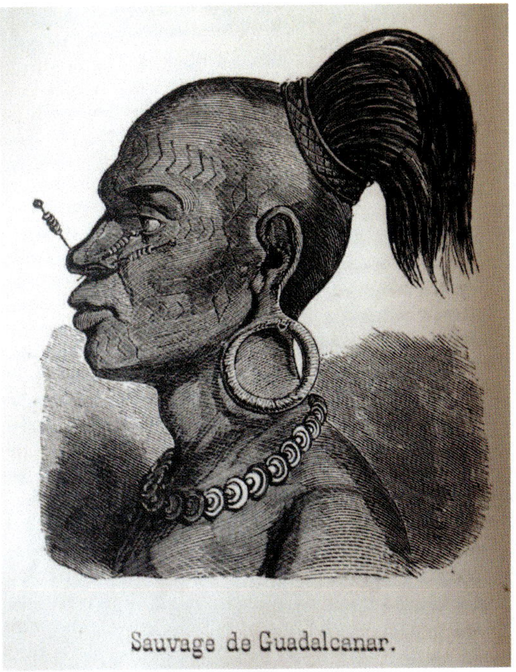

Engraving based on original in the Sketchbook (see page 33) used in *L'Histoire*

Island News.

Telegraph Press Association. Copyright. SYDNEY, November 12.

The Ringdove has concluded a six months' cruise amongst the islands of the Western Pacific. In one island of the Santa Cruz group the Union Jack had been hauled down by a native woman, she having commandeered it for wearing apparel. An earthquake in the group destroyed a number of houses. The officers succeeded in finding the grave of Bishop Epalle, who was murdered on Ysabel Island in 1845.

Feilding Star (NZ) 13 Nov 1900

GRAND ARCHIPEL

DES

ILES SALOMON

SON ÉTENDUE, SA FERTILITÉ

PAR

M. l'Abbé Léopold VERGUET

CHANOINE HONORAIRE DE CARCASSONNE
ANCIEN MISSIONNAIRE APOSTOLIQUE EN MÉLANÉSIE, CHEVALIER DU SAINT SÉPULCRE
DE LA TRÈS GLORIEUSE RÉSURRECTION DE N. S. J.-C.
MEMBRE DE LA SOCIÉTÉ DES ARTS ET SCIENCES DE CARCASSONNE
MEMBRE CORRESPONDANT DE LA SOCIÉTÉ ORIENTALE

Laudate Dominum omnes gentes.
Ps. 116.

MARSEILLE
TYPOGRAPHIE BLANC ET BERNARD
RUE SAINTE, 28 et 30

1883

Verguet's *Histoire* included copies of his sketches of how to find the grave of Epalle

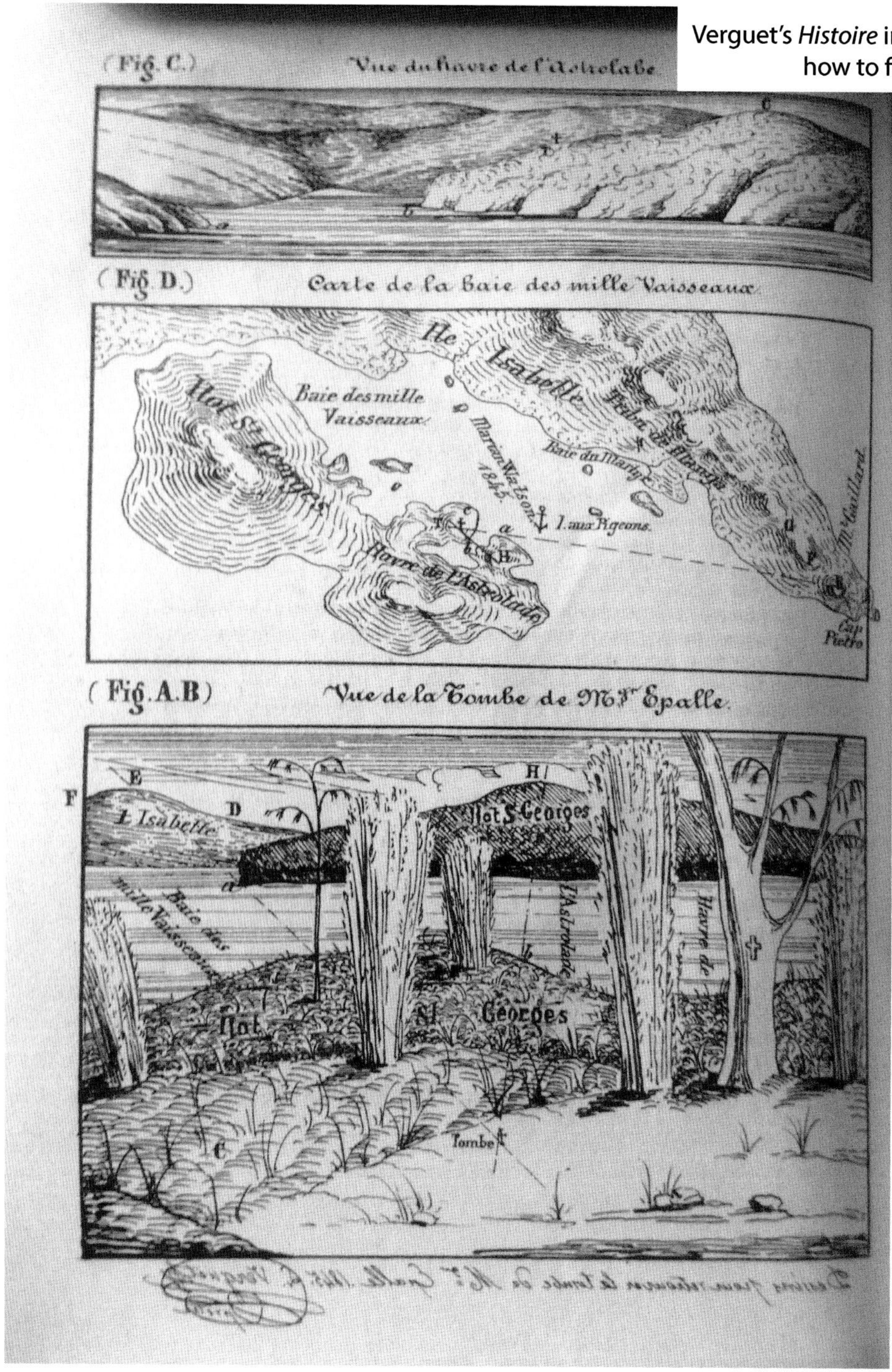

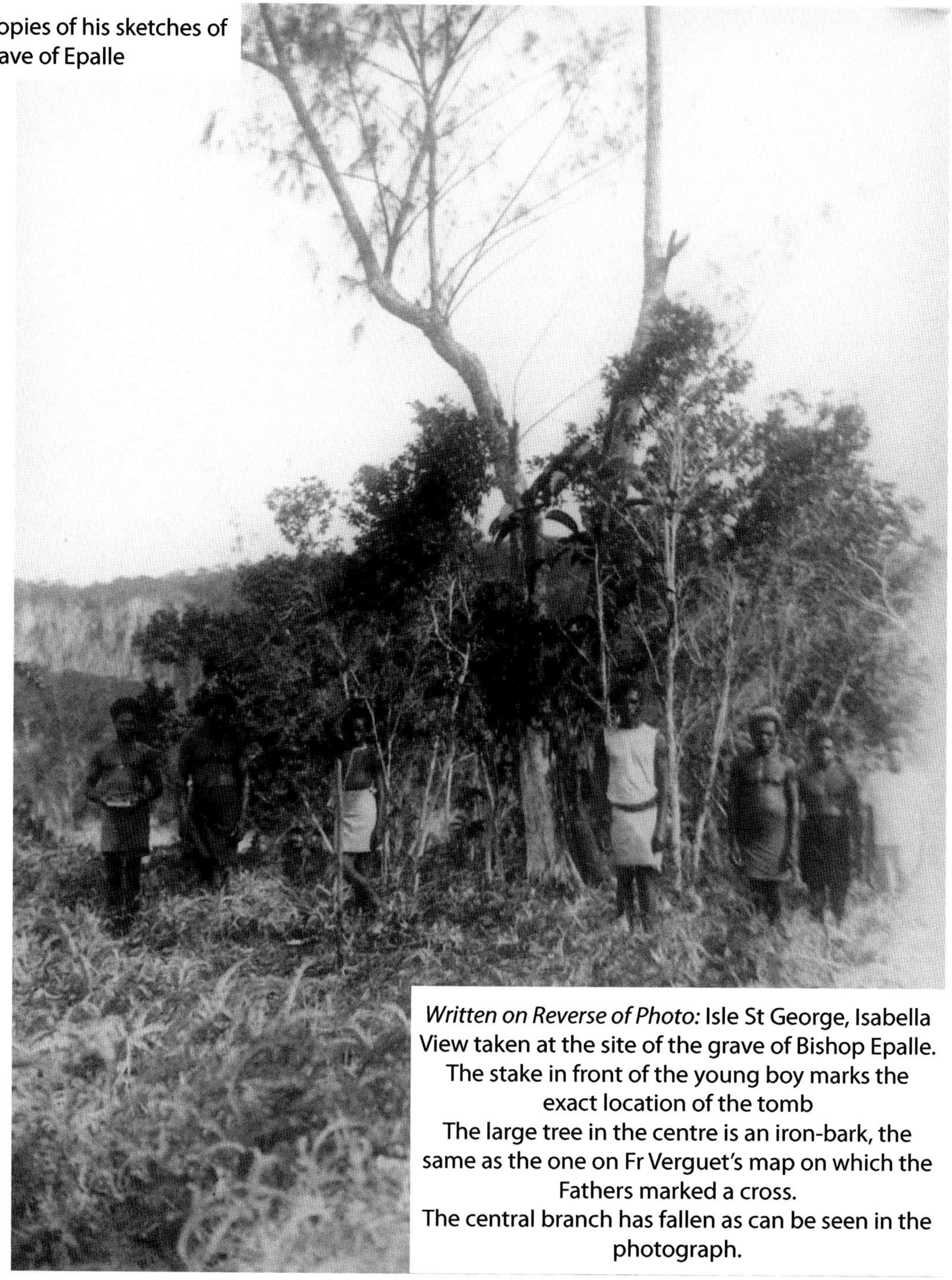

Written on Reverse of Photo: Isle St George, Isabella View taken at the site of the grave of Bishop Epalle.
The stake in front of the young boy marks the exact location of the tomb
The large tree in the centre is an iron-bark, the same as the one on Fr Verguet's map on which the Fathers marked a cross.
The central branch has fallen as can be seen in the photograph.

A SOLOMON ISLAND TRAGEDY.

Otago Daily Times, 23 March 1901

In 1845 a band of Roman Catholic missionaries, members of the Marist Order, set out from Sydney for the Solomon Islands, for the purpose of propagating Christianity amongst the savages of those regions. At their head was the Right Rev. Bishop Epalle.

Arriving at the Solomon Islands they cast about for a suitable place at which to effect their landing. They visited several islands, and finally decided on venturing ashore on the island of St. Isobel, as the natives appeared well disposed, and the island seemed suitable.

On landing, with Bishop Epalle at their head, they were received by hundreds of armed natives with great awe, as, in all probability, these were the first white men who had set foot on St. Isobel since Hernando Gallego discovered the Isles of Solomon hundreds of years before. It was not long, however, before their savage instincts got the better of their awe, and they attacked the party, who instantly began to retire towards their boat.

During the retirement the bishop received the full force of the attack, and when he was at last drawn into the boat he was bleeding copiously from five wounds in the head—three deep ones, and the remaining two scalp wounds. This occurred on December 16, and on the 19th of the same month Bishop Epalle breathed his last.

Afraid to bury the remains of their beloved leader on the island where he had met his death, the grief-stricken little band made their way to the island of St. John, to the northwest of Isobel, where the remains were tenderly laid to rest. Buried with the bishop were a crucifix, rosary beads, and several medals. A sketch of the position of the grave was made, and a report describing the wounds on the deceased was sent on to the head station of the Marist Order at Villa Maria, Sydney.

For 56 years the bones of the martyred bishop remained in their lonely grave in the midst of the savages, for whose spiritual welfare he laid down his life. During the whole of that time his religious brethren could never effect a landing, but four years ago a successful landing was made, and in January last the remains of the bishop were discovered and conveyed to Villa Maria, Hunter's Hill.

Last week (says the Sydney Telegraph), in the presence of his Eminence Cardinal Moran and all the Fathers of the Marist Order, Dr Sanderson Lloyd, Government medical officer for Ryde, made a minute examination of the skull wounds, and reported that they exactly corresponded with the description given 56 years ago. With the remains were found the cross, rosary beads, and medals, so, without any doubt, the bones now at Hunter's Hill must be those of Bishop Epalle.

station and maps of the islands is still in the General Archives of the Society of Mary in Rome. In 1898 the Marists returned to the Solomons, this time their mission succeeded in establishing the Church there.

In 1900 when Verguet was 83 he received the news that, using his maps and diagrams, the Marists had recovered the bones of Bishop Epalle. He was conclusively identified by the tomahawk marks on the skull precisely matching Verguet's sketch of his wounds. The bones were initially taken to the Marist base in Sydney and later returned to the Solomons to be reburied with honour in the bishop's chapel at Visale, on Guadalcanal. That island was to be the scene of significant conflict during the Second World War and the chapel and the tomb of Epalle were destroyed in a bombing raid in 1942.

Léopold Verguet lived on into the twentieth century, dying in 1914 at the age of 97.

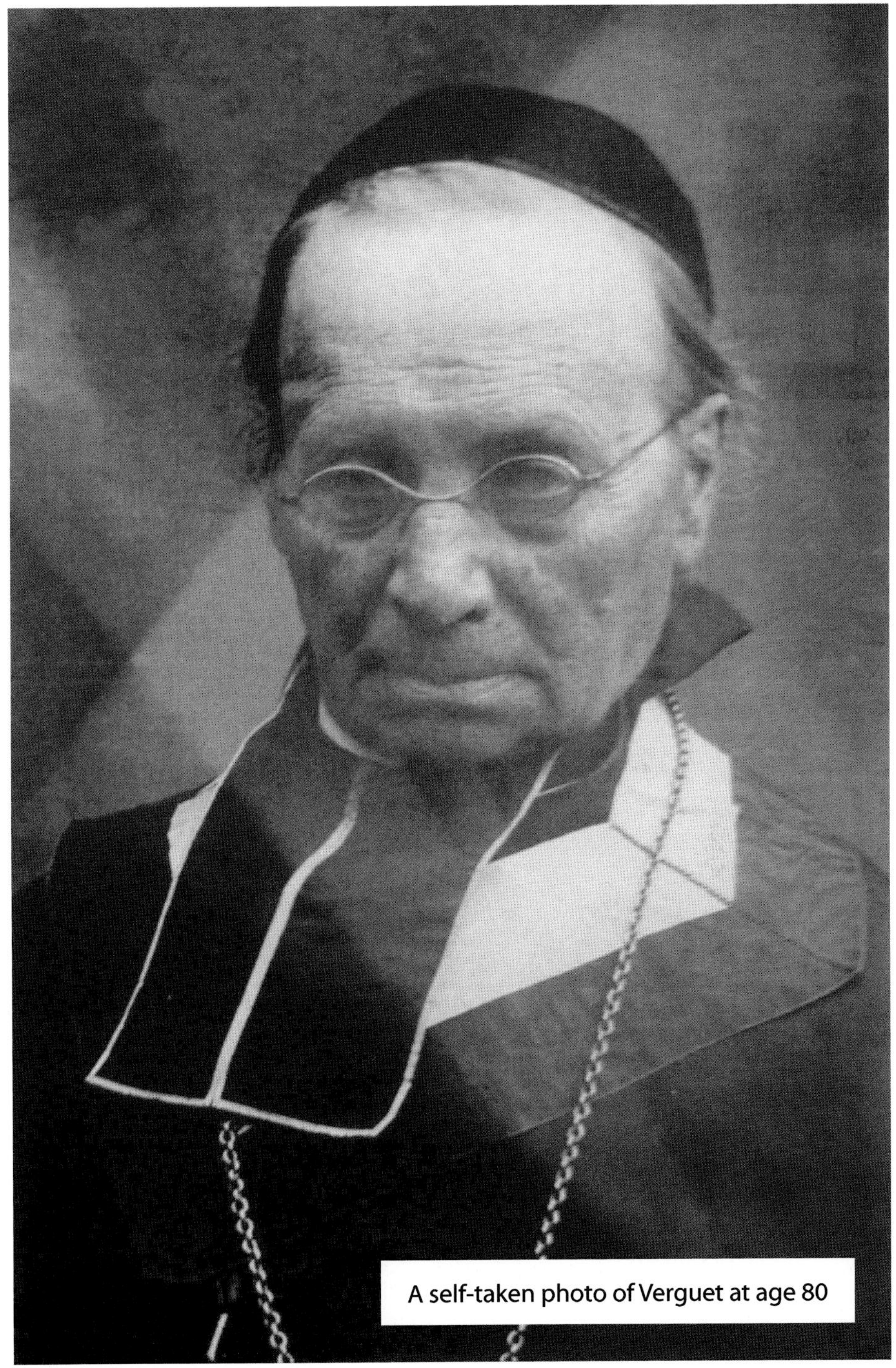

A self-taken photo of Verguet at age 80

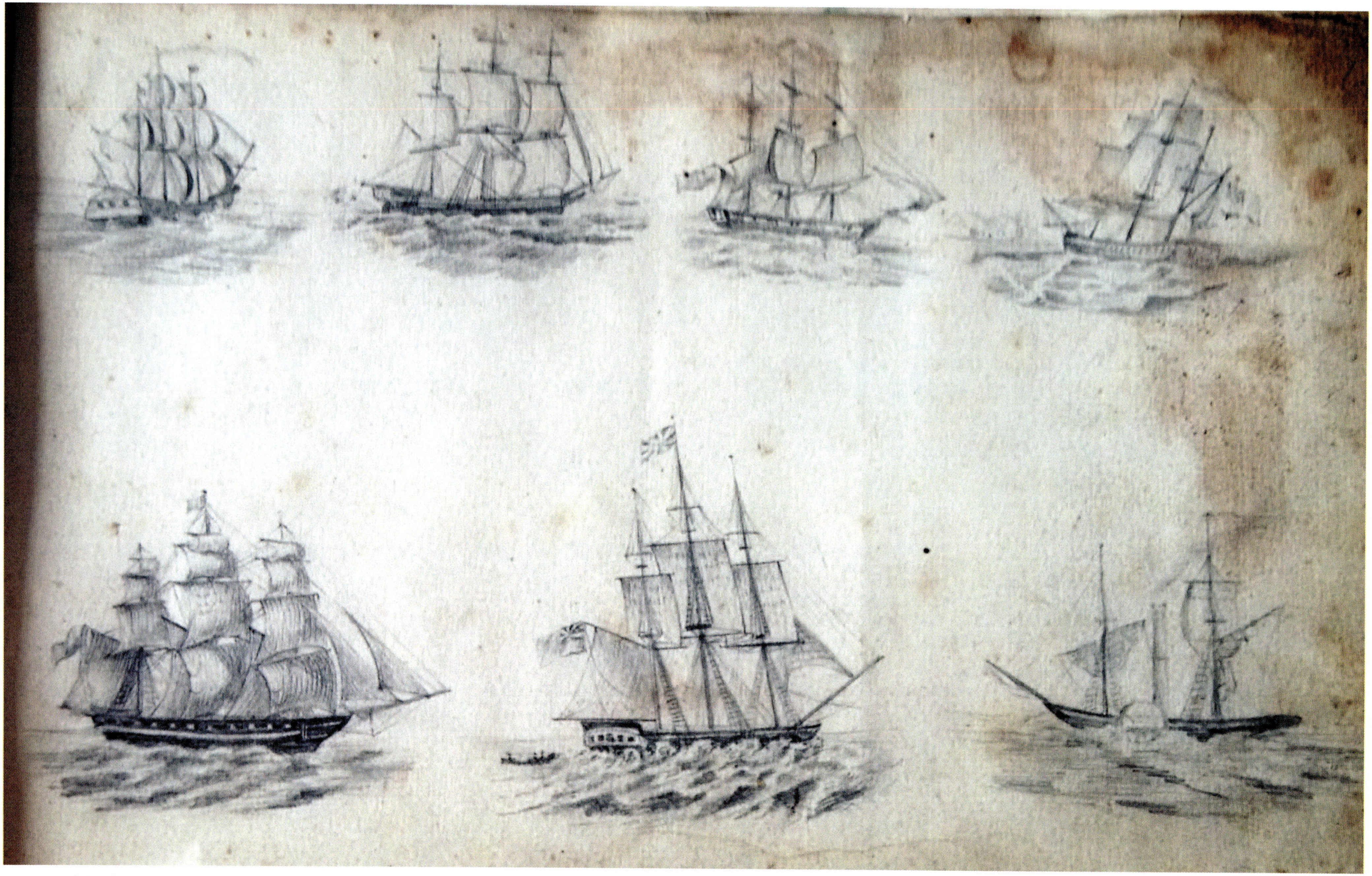

One of the first pages of the sketchbook shows seven ships. Some of them may be the *Bussorah Merchant* in different aspects.; the fifth strongly resembles a painting of that vessel. The presence of a steamship as the last image reminds us that Verguet travelled at the end of the era of the sailing ships.

Appendices

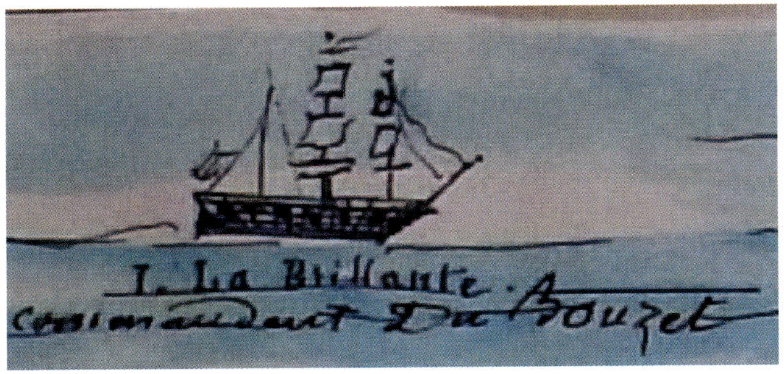

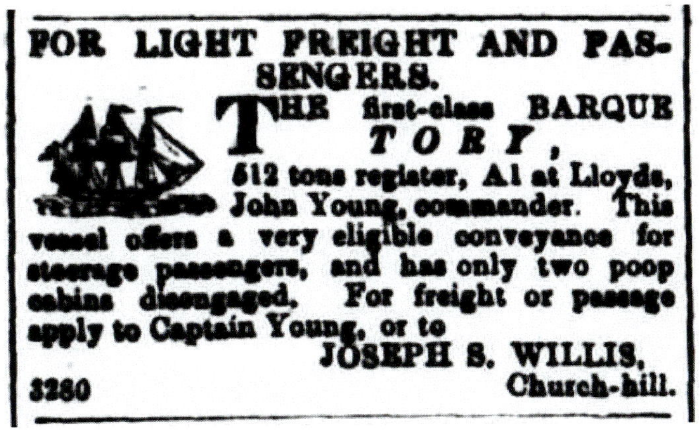
FOR LIGHT FREIGHT AND PASSENGERS.

THE first-class BARQUE *TORY*, 512 tons register, A1 at Lloyds, John Young, commander. This vessel offers a very eligible conveyance for steerage passengers, and has only two poop cabins disengaged. For freight or passage apply to Captain Young, or to

JOSEPH S. WILLIS,
Church-hill.

3280

Ships Verguet travelled on

From Le Havre to London
The packet boat *Wilberforce*

From London to Sydney
The *Bussorah Merchant*
with Captain Beal
550 ton barque; built in 1818 in India, running for over 35 years, in particular London – Australia

From Sydney to New Caledonia to the Solomons
The *Marian Watson*
with Captain Richards, an Englishman
140 ton schooner, spacious ship and 'one of the best ships in Sydney'

From San Cristobal to Sydney
L' Arche d'Alliance
with Captain August Marceau;
barque of 312 tons; run by the *Société de l'Océanie*

From Sydney to New Zealand to New Caledonia
The *Spec* (*Speculator*)
with Captain Burns
175 tons schooner.

From New Caledonia to Vanuatu and to Sydney
La Brillante,
with Commodore Le Comte Du Bouzet
French corvette 24 guns

From Sydney to London
The *Tory*
with Captain John Young, a Scot
512 ton barque

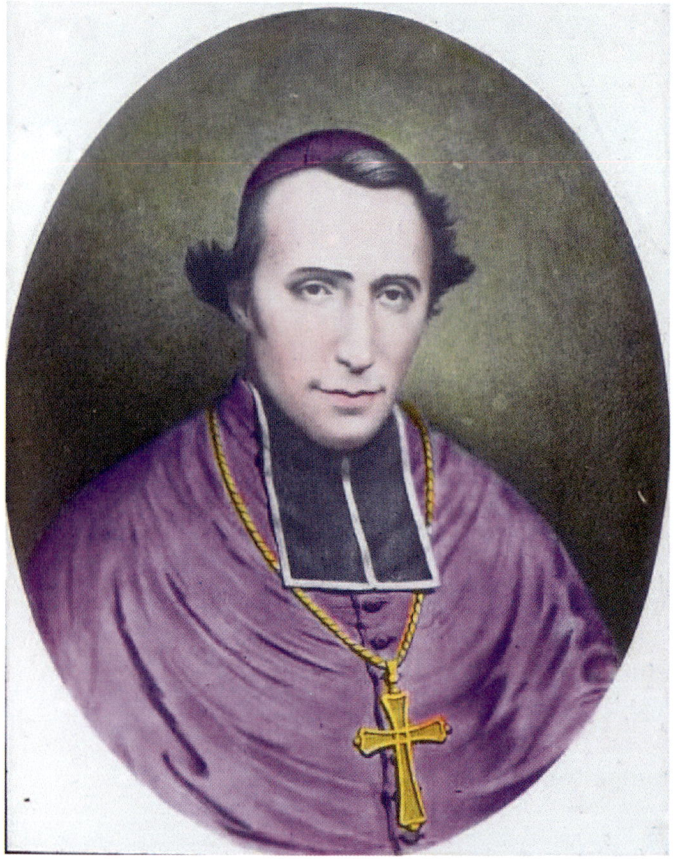

Colourised portrait of Bishop Epalle

Abbreviations in the Biographies

CS 1 Lessard, Gaston SM (ed.), *"Colin sup". Documents concernant le généralat du père Colin, volume I, De l'élection au voyage à Rome (1836-1842)*, Rome, 2007.

CS 2 Lessard, Gaston SM (ed.), *"Colin sup". Documents concernant le généralat du père Colin,* volume 2, *Du voyage à Rome au chapitre (1842-1845)*, Rome, 2009.

CS 4 Bourtot, Bernard SM (ed.), *« Colin sup ». Documents our l'étude du généralat de Jean-Claude Colin (1836-1854)*, volume 4, *De l'été 1848 à la démission (1848-1854)*, Rome, 2009.

LRO Girard, Charles SM (ed.), *Lettres reçues d'Océanie par l'administration générale des pères maristes pendant le généralat de Jean-Claude Colin, Textes revus, corrigés et ajoutés, 1836 – 1854*, Paris, Karthala – Rome, Société de Marie, ten volumes, 2009 and 2010.

Mayet Mayet, Gabriel-Claude, *Mémoires, Ms., 1837-1854,* APM, Rome.

Biographies

The Bishop and the other priests

Epalle, Jean-Baptiste (1808-1845), Marist priest, titular bishop of Sion in Asia Minor, first vicar apostolic of Melanesia and Micronesia (1844-1845)

Jean-Baptiste Epalle was born in Marlhes, the home village of Champagnat, on 8 March 1808. He was ordained a priest on 23 December 1837. Epalle began his Marist novitiate on 16 October 1837 and made profession on July 16, 1838. Epalle had joined the Society to go to the missions, but over time he gave more emphasis to the living of Marist religious life (Mayet 3, 148). Epalle left for the first time from Bordeaux on 9 September 1838 with the second band of Marist missionaries bound for Oceania. For three years he worked among the Māori, mainly at the Bay of Islands, also being provicar and administrator for Bishop Pompallier. In 1843 he returned to France to give an account of the missions. Before becoming bishop, Epalle made his vow of stability, in fact the first Marist to do so, to stress his identity as Marist (Mayet 6, 45). Cardinal Fransoni, assisted by Bonami SSCC, ordained Epalle bishop for Melanesia, on 21 July, in the chapel of Propaganda Fide, Rome. The next day the Marists had an audience with Gregory XVI. On 2 February 1845 he sailed from London with his missionaries to start the new vicariate. In Sydney, he was present at the talks with Bishop Pompallier. On 16 December Bishop Épalle and a small group landed on the island of San Isabel. He was almost immediately struck down but rescued by his confreres. Bishop Epalle died in consequence of the wounds on 19 December 1845, at the age of 37. His remains had been transferred to the church of Visale. The bombing of the church during World War II destroyed his tomb.

Archives: Archives of the Society of Mary, Via Alessandro Poerio 63, 152 Roma, Italy;

Bibliography: Antoine Monfat, *Dix Années en Mélanésie*; R. Poirier, 'Epalle, John Baptist', in N.A. Weber (ed.), *A Brief Biographical Dictionary of the Marist Hierarchy (1836-1953)*, private publication, Washington DC, 1953, 24-25; R.M. Wiltgen SVD, *The Founding of the Roman Catholic Church in Melanesia and Micronesia, 1850-1875*, Eugene, Oregon, Pickwick Publications, 2008.

Chaurain, Étienne (originally: Stéphane) (1819-1887), Marist priest, missionary

Étienne Chaurain was born in Marlhes (Loire), archdiocese of Lyon, on 6 June 1819. In October 1840 he joined the Society of Mary at Belley. On 25 September 1843, he was professed a Marist at Puylata. On 6 April 1844, he was ordained a priest. First he taught at Belley College. In 1845, he left with Bishop Epalle and the first group of Marists to go to the Solomon Islands. When they were attacked on Isabel, Father Chaurain courageously ran back to rescue wounded Epalle. The bishop, however, died a few days later. Chaurain became procurator at Sydney. On 11 November 1850, Chaurain and Brother Aristide left for France. Colin called Chaurain back to Europe. He was appointed among the first Marists to work in London, St. Anne's Parish, in September 1850. He arrived in London by the end of March 1851. Chaurain looked after the Irish and German Father Weber after the German Catholics. In 1864, Chaurain led the first Marist group to Jefferson College, Louisiana. After three years, he returned to London where he stayed until his death, except for a year of convalescence in France, 1884-85. On 22 August 1874 he made his vow of stability. Chaurain died on 3 November 1887.

Frémont, Jean-Pierre (1810-1864), Diocesan priest, Marist priest, missionary, apostolic prefect for Melanesia

Jean-Pierre Frémont was born on 19 August 1810 in Montigné (Maine-et-Loire), in the diocese of Angers. On 5 August 1841 he began his novitiate at Lyon, already a diocesan priest. He made Marist profession on 27 September 1842. On 2 February 1845 he left Eu-

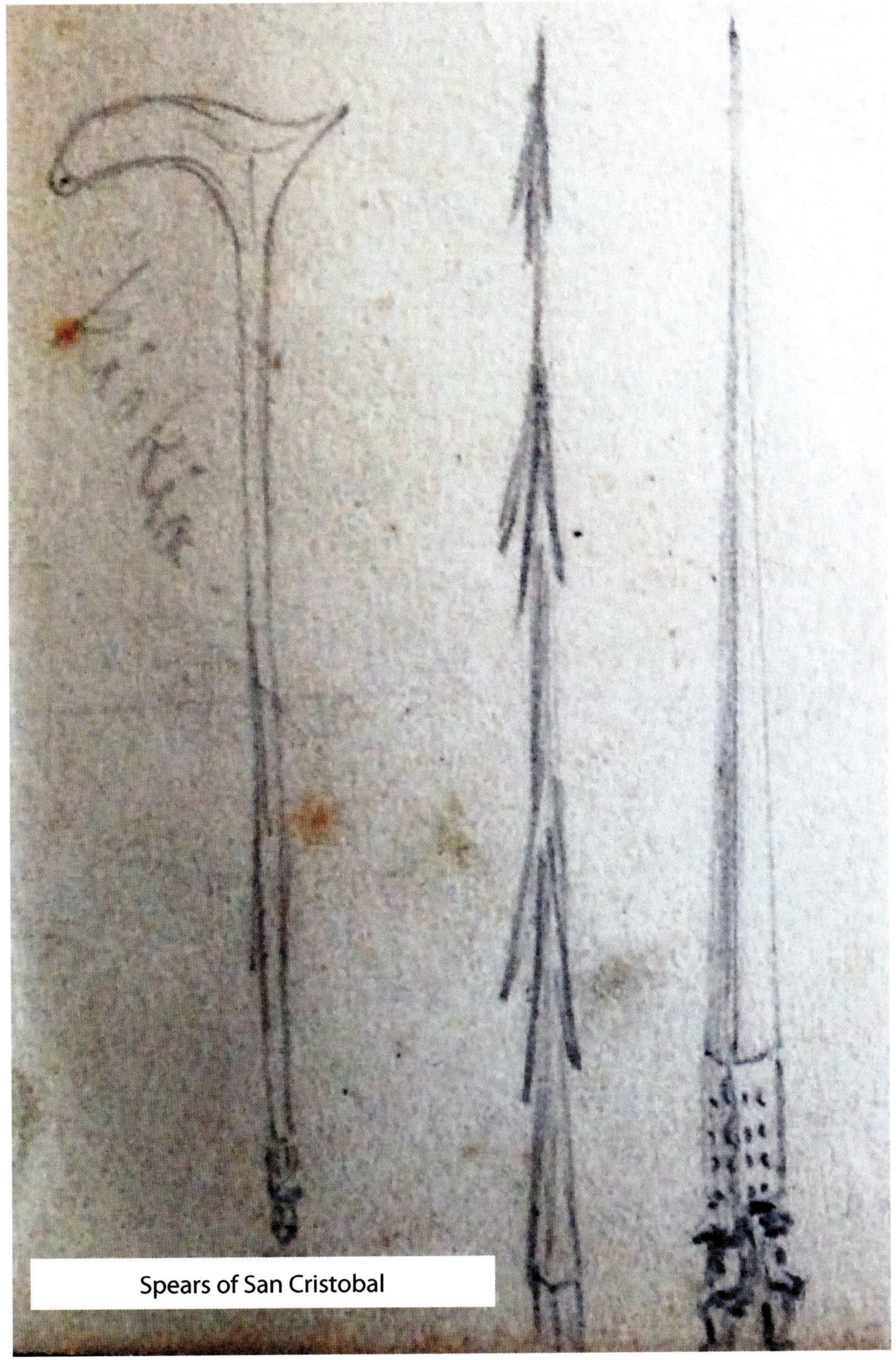

Spears of San Cristobal

rope from London with Bishop Epalle for Melanesia. After Montrouzier resigned in Sydney as pro-vicar, he was appointed pro-vicar. The group stopped at Balade (New Caledonia) on 16 November 1845. They went on to San Cristobal, arriving on 2 December 1845, from which they left on 6 December 1845 to go to Santa Isabel, arriving on 12 December. With Epalle he was attacked on Isabel but managed to rescue himself to the boat. He was wounded and carried the effects all his life. After Epalle's death, Frémont was elected provincial (LRO, doc. 479, 9) and had to lead the deliberations on what to do. The group returned to San Cristobal (Makira) Island. Two priests and a brother of their group were killed there in 1847. After two years, with Bishop Collomb arriving in August 1847, he decided to transfer the mission to Woodlark Island. After eight months at Woodlark, Frémont and Collomb founded a new mission on Rook Island near the mainland of Papua New Guinea. Within a short time the Bishop died together with another priest, leaving Father Frémont alone with a brother for eight months until the next boat came. He then returned to Woodlark where, in 1851, he was chosen by his confreres to be the new prefect apostolic. However, Colin had decided to withdraw the Marists from the vicariate of Melanesia. Frémont introduced the Milan Missionaries to the Woodlark mission in October 1852. In 1854 Frémont transferred to New Caledonia. There he was in charge of the central station of Port-de-France (Noumea) until his death on 2 March 1864. His remains were brought to the new cemetery of Saint Louis.

Jacquet, Claude-Antoine (1812-1847), Diocesan priest, Marist priest, missionary

Claude Jacquet was born in Belleville (Rhône) on 21 January 1812. Claude served as diocesan priest at Montbrison for eight years. He had met Colin's sister at Belleville. He had sought permission to join the Marists but was refused. In 1845 he left without permission with the group of Bishop Epalle for Oceania, informing his bishop, Cardinal de Bonald, only via letter from London. De Bonald ordered him to return, but this letter arrived too late - Jacquet was dead by then. Epalle explained that he had presumed Jacquet had permission and was kept from inquiries by the preparations in London (LRO, doc. 392). Colin had to apologize for Jacquet's departure. Jacquet made his testament at Sydney and his profession on San Cristobal on 19 March 1847. He was killed and eaten on San Cristobal on 20 April 1847, together with Father Paget and Brother Hyacinthe (LRO, Docs. 644, 667, 674). Jacquet was killed by an axe blow to the neck.

Montrouzier, Jean Xavier Hyacinthe (1820-1897), Deacon, Marist priest, missionary

Xavier Montrouzier was born on 3rd of December, 1820, in Montpellier (Hérault). He was a diocesan seminarian and deacon for his diocese. He was a scholar in the Natural Sciences at the Sorbonne when he joined the Society after a mission talk by Dubreul in his seminary in 1842. On 30 October 1843 he began his novitiate. On 14 July 1844, Bishop Devie ordained him a priest. On 22 September 1844 he made profession as Marist with a desire to go to the missions. He left with Bishop Epalle, as his pro-vicar, with the first group bound for the Solomon Islands, on 2 February 1845. After the death of Epalle at Santa Isabel, the group went to San Cristobal. There he narrowly escaped death in an attack. He was taken to New Caledonia to recuperate and returned the following year with Bishop Collomb. The group moved to Woodlark Island, where Montrouzier was superior for four years until he returned to Sydney in 1851. After writing a botanical book about Woodlark Island, he went to New Caledonia where he was present at the death of Bishop Douarre in 1853. He was named superior of the mission. With the coming of the French Governor in 1855, he became the first priest based in Nouméa. He began the mission on Belep on 1856, staying for two years, before founding the mission in Lifou, Loyalty Islands, in 1859. For four years he was chaplain to the convicts. He mainly worked on Belep. Montrouzier wrote many articles, mainly on the natural sciences and

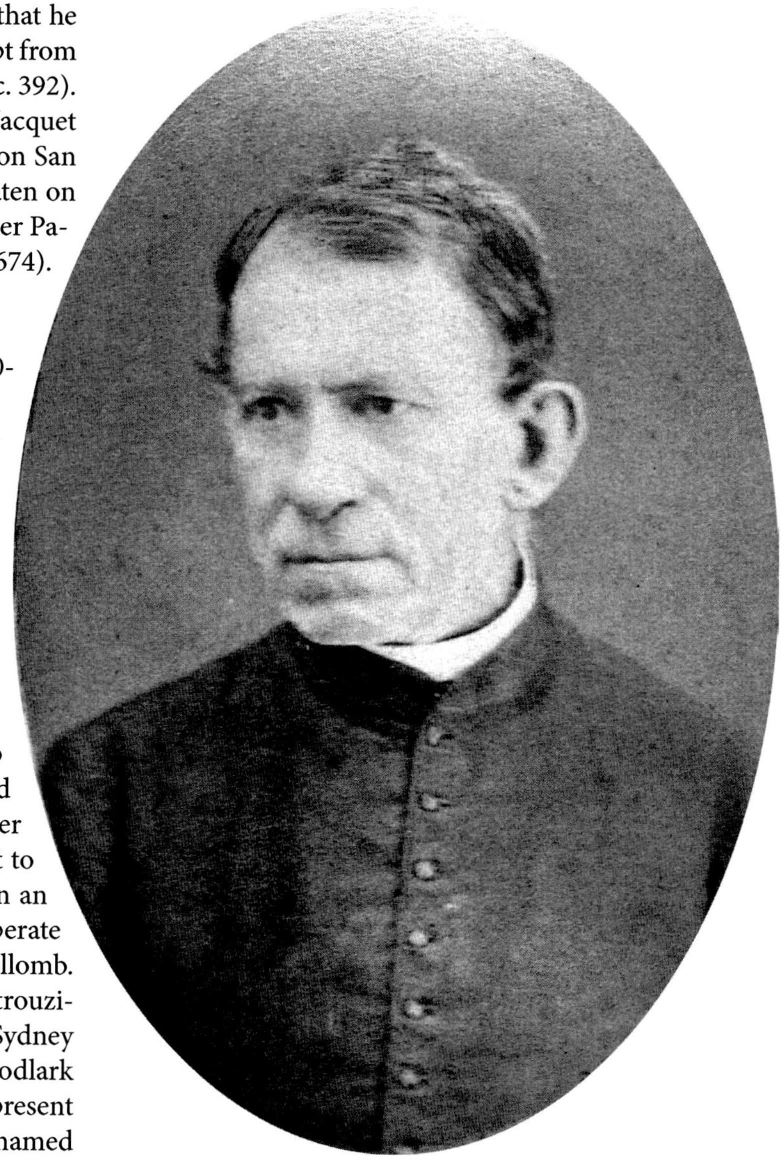

Jean Xavier Montrouzier

he discovered the vast mineral resources of New Caledonia. Montrouzier died at Saint-Louis, after 52 years in the mission, on 16 May 1897.

Montrouzier Writings: voluminous collection of letters to family and friends, 1843-1886, in APM; 'Notice historique, ethnographique et physique sur la Nouvelle-Calédonie, par le père X. Montrouzier, Paris, 1860, 52 pages;

Bibliography: H. Laracy, *Xavier Montrouzier, a Missionary in Melanesia*, in J. W. Davidson - D. Scarr (eds.), *Pacific Island Portraits*, Canberra, Australian National University Press, 1970, 127 – 145; Patrick O'Reilly, *Un missionnaire naturaliste. Xavier Montrouzier (1820 – 1897)*, in *Revue d'Histoire des Missions* (mars 1931); 'Notice sur le R.P. Montrouzier, botaniste, par le Dr G. Beauvisage', Paris, 1898, 60 pages; 'Deuxième note sur l'herbier du R.P. Montrouzier. Le genre Entrecasteauxia Montr., par le Dr. G. Beauvisage'; 'Revision de quelques genres de Plantes Néo-Calédoniennes du R.P. Montrouzier, par le Dr. Beauvisage', Paris, 1894; Léon Teissier, *Le pape des cévennes*, chez l'auteur, Montpellier, 1963, photocopy in APM, 7 pages; Gilbert P. Whitley, *Conchologists of the Past. 1. Father Xavier Montrouzier (1820 – 1897)*, in *Journal of the Malacological Society of Australia*, No. 11, 22 March 1968, 3 pages; P. O'Reilly, *Calédoniens: Répertoire bio-bibliographique*, p. 185; 'Pacific Characters come to Life', in *Pacific Islands Monthly* (November 1970), p. 85; *1858-2008. 150ème anniversaire de la mission Catholique à Lifou, Société d'études historiques* Nr. 155 (2008).

Paget, Jean-Marie (1816-1847), Diocesan priest, Marist priest, missionary

Jean-Marie Paget was born on 13 October 1816 in Sonnaz (Savoie), in the diocese of Chambéry. His parents, Donat Paget and Marie Bouvier, were modest farmers. Of their nine children, four became priests and five religious sisters. Jean-Marie studied at Saint-Louis-du-Mont and at the Major Seminary of Chambéry. In 1840 he was a sub-deacon and assisted his parish priest. On 21 May 1842 he was ordained a priest for the diocese of Chambéry. He served at the parish of Champagneux (Rhône). There they talked about the foreign missions and Oceania. Paget walked the 80 km to Lyon to see the Marist superior. He came back and decided to join the Society of Mary to go to Oceania. In October 1842 he left home for Lyon. There he met his compatriots Collomb, Villien, and Crey. Already trained as a diocesan priest, he made novitiate at Lyon for a year from 13 October 1842 and was professed as a Marist religious on 14 October 1843. On 2 February 1845 he left with Bishop Epalle for Oceania. On 20 April 1847 Paget, Jacquet and Hyacinth were killed on San Cristobal, Melanesia (LRO, docs. 644, 667, 674). Paget was killed by a lance in his chest.

Bibliography: Chanoine J. Paget, *Le P. Paget (1816-1847). De Sonnaz à San Christobal*, Chambéry, F. Gentil, 1915.

Thomassin, Joseph (1818-1891), Marist priest, missionary

Joseph Thomassin was born at Battigny (Meurthe-et-Moselle) on 21 May 1818 to Nicolas Thomassin and Elisabeth Moine. He did his schooling at the minor seminary of Pont-à-Mousson and the major seminary of Nancy. The historian Rohrbacher was his professor, confessor, and friend. Thomassin was interested in the foreign missions and read the Annales. Oceania was a topic. Epalle, looking for staff, visited major seminaries and also Nancy. In January 1844 Thomassin left for Lyon. Archbishop de Bonald ordained him a priest in Lyon cathedral on 1 June 1844. His Marist novitiate began on 2 March 1844. On 22 September 1844 he made profession at Puylata. On 2 February 1845 he left from London in the group led by Bishop Epalle. Thomassin was present at the death of Epalle. In December 1845, the group moved to San Cris-

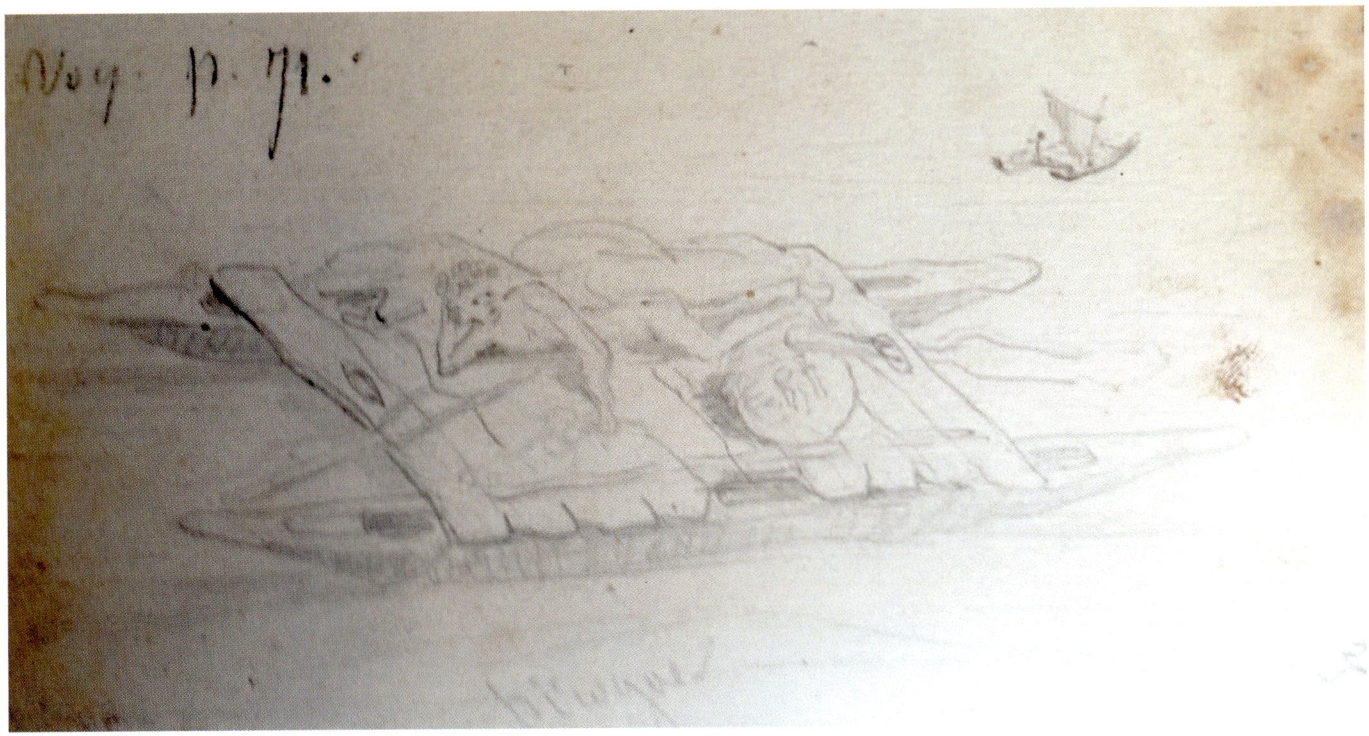

New Caledonian fishing from a double-hulled pirogue

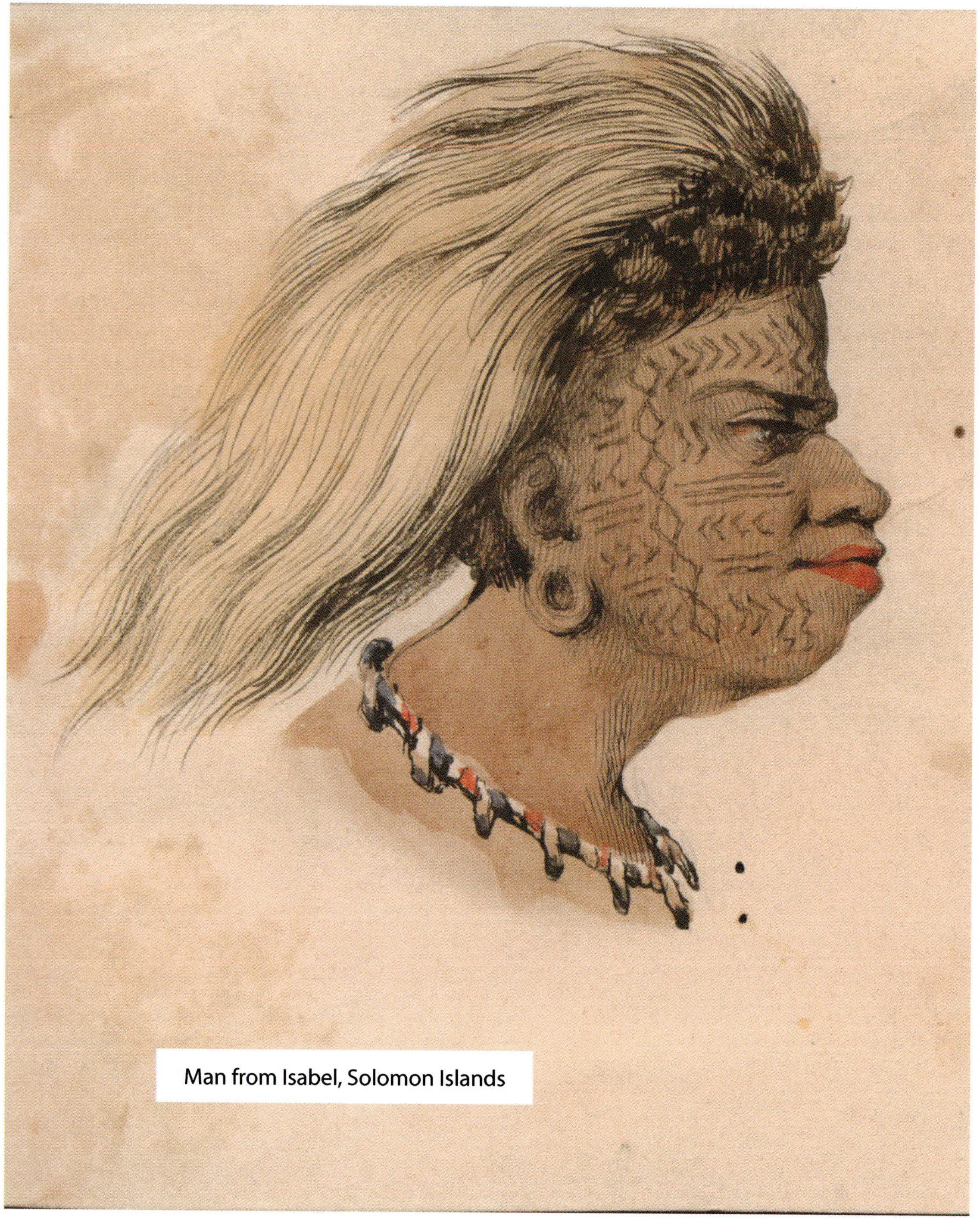

Man from Isabel, Solomon Islands

tobal, then in September on to Woodlark. There they had to give up in 1853. Thomassin drafted a dictionary of the local language. After introducing the Milan missionaries, the Marists reached Sydney in December. By the middle of 1854 he was back at Balade, followed by a year at Touho and a year at Pouébo. 1856-66, Thomassin lived at Touho, witnessing the destruction of the mission in 1862. 1866-67, Belep, and 1868 Païta were the next stations. In 1871 he came to the Procure at Nouméa. In 1874 he became parish priest at la Conception. On 27 September 1886 he made the vow of stability. Only away for short sojourns, he died at Conception on 28 June 1891.

Bibliography: [Xavier Montrouzier SM], *Notice sur le R.P. Joseph Thomassin. Missionnaire apostolique de la Société de Marie et sur les premières missions de la Mélanésie qui ont été le theatre de son apostolat*, Saint-Louis, Imprimerie Catholique, 1892.

The mission band: the Brothers

Besselles, Claude (1814-1890), coadjutor brother, missionary, **Brother Bertrand**

Claude Besselles was born at Valbenoîte (Loire) on 27 September 1814. He did his novitiate in 1842. On 8 December 1844, Bertrand made his final profession. On 2 February 1845 he left from London for the missions with the group heading for Melanesia guided by Bishop Epalle. Bertrand joined the station at Balade, New Caledonia, on 23 November, replacing Jean Taragnat. On 22 August 1847 they had to escape to Sydney, after Brother Blaise had been killed. From Sydney Bertrand reached Anatom on 14 May 1848 on the *Arche d'Alliance*. He left Anatom on 17 September 1849 for Ile-des-Pins and New Caledonia, the *reduction* at Yaté. On 14 January 1850 they had to leave New Caledonia again. Bertrand was sent to Sydney to recover. He came back during Douarre's third attempt in May 1851. From 1861 on he worked in New Caledonia (Hienghene, Ile-des-Pins, Ouen and Balade). He died at Nathalo, Lifou, on 1st of November 1890.

Brun, Jean (1821-1901), coadjutor brother, missionary, **Brother Aristide**

Jean Brun was born at La Chapelle-d'Aurrec (Haute-Loire), diocese of Le Puy, on 10 November 1821. On 13 June 1843, he made his vow of obedience and then final profession on the 8 December 1844. He was a tailor (Mayet). Aristide left Europe from London on 2 February 1845 (Mayet 5, 107). They reached Sydney on 22 June. In November, he stayed eight days with Douarre on New Caledonia. Aristide was in the group who accompanied Bishop Epalle to Ysabel in December 1845. They left for Makira, San Cristobal, on 10th January 1846. On 3 August 1847 the group left for Woodlark (arrival on 15 September). They had to give up on this island in June 1849. All returned to Sydney. Chaurain and Brother Aristide left Sydney for France on 11 November 1850 (CS 4, p. 430). On 24 November 1859 he returned to Oceania, posted in New Caledonia (Conception). With Rougeyron he stood before the tribunal in the gun-affair in 1864. Aristide died in Laita, New Caledonia, on 30 January 1901.

Châtelet, Joseph (1817-1847), **Brother Hyacinthe,** missionary

Brother Hyacinthe was born at Brandon (Saône-et-Loire), diocese of Autun, on 15 March 1817. He began his novitiate at Vauban on 25 July 1840, making his vow of obedience on 21 April 1842. He made final profession as Marist brother on 13 September 1843. Two years later, on 2 February 1845, Hyacinthe left Europe for Melanesia with Bishop Epalle. Again two years later, Hyacinthe, 30 years old, was with Fathers Claude Jacquet and Jean-Marie Paget looking for a site for a new station. They were attacked. Hyacinthe was pierced by a lance and decapitated by a tomahawk. The bodies were taken apart, roasted and eaten on Saint Cristobal, South Solomons, on 20 April 1847 (LRO, doc. 644, 667, 674).

Rolland, Jean-Pierre (1817-1898), coadjutor brother, missionary, **Brother Gennade**

Jean-Pierre Rolland was born at Saint Genis-Terrenoire (Loire) on 13 October 1817. His home is not far from Saint-Chamond and he claimed to have seen Champagnat while still at home. He joined in 1840 and began his novitiate on 29 January 1841. He made his final profession as Marist on 8 September 1844. On 2 February 1845 he left for Oceania in the group with Bishop Epalle bound for Melanesia. A smith and stonemason by trade, he worked as carpenter, blacksmith, gardener, and cook as necessary. Gennade seems to have been relatively immune to the malaria which periodically laid low his confreres. He was present at the death of the Bishop. Gennade helped in the establishment of the mission at Makira on San Cristobal, where another three Marists were killed. In September 1847 the community left San Cristobal with Bishop Collomb for Woodlark Island. Deprivations were extreme and Bishop Collomb and others in the community died. In 1852, when Colin decided to withdraw the Marists, Gennade stayed on for a further three years to help the newly arrived missionaries of Milan. He returned to Sydney in 1854 and remained in Villa Maria for the next 44 years, doing a great deal of building. He died there on 9 May 1898.

Rouesné, Prosper (1816- left 1859), coadjutor brother, missionary, **Brother Prosper**

Prosper Rouesné was born at Moisdon (Loire-Inférieure/ Loire Atlantique), diocese of Nantes, on 15 March 1816, to Adrien Rouesné and Marie Pouillé. In October 1843 he joined at la Favorite and joined the consecration to the Immaculate Heart of Mary at the retreat of the Brothers. On 22 September 1844, Prosper made profession before Colin. Prosper stayed at Puylata until he left for Oceania on 2 February 1845 (departure from London). He passed through Sydney, Balade, and Santa Isabelle. After the death of Bishop Epalle – Prosper was wounded in the attack - the group withdrew to Makira in January and to Sydney in March 1846. On 13 June 1846 he followed Bishop Douarre to Balade. On 22 August 1847 they had to flee again back to Sydney. Prosper came to Anatom on 14 May 1848 and L'île des Pins on 20 September. In August Prosper had asked to be released of his vows, but he stayed for the next eleven years. In 1854, he was seriously ill and received the last rites. In 1859, he left the Society of Mary (Letter 13 March 1859). He said he was scandalized by the behaviour of some brothers at Puylata who sold goods of the house so that they could afford the things the superiors had denied them. In March 1860 Prosper, still in New Caledonia, wrote to Poupinel offering to assist the mission at Pouebo as a lay person.

Vincent, Charles (1803-1853), coadjutor brother, missionary, **Brother Charles**

Vincent was born in 1811. The date of his religious profession is not known. On 2 February 1845 he set out from London with the group led by Bishop Epalle (Mayet 5, 107). Via Sydney and New Caledonia, they reached Ysabel Island. After the death of Epalle, they withdrew to Makira and then Woodlark. Verguet left a drawing of a garden planned by Brother Charles. On 21 December 1847 they left Woodlark for Sydney. Charles worked in Oceania from 1845 until 1848 (Solomon Islands). In 1848 he was ill and withdrew from the missions. On 21 April he left Sydney to return to France. He died in 1853.

Archives and Bibliography

APM Artworks by Léopold Verguet (1817-1914)

Léopold Verguet (1817-1914) was a member of the Society of Mary and Oceania missionary from 1844 to 1850. The general archives of the Society of Mary, Rome (APM) keep a dossier on his person and a collection of his works.

Verguet added information to many of his drawings either on the design or in reference to his book on the first Catholic mission in Melanesia. In this book, he tells his story as a missionary and his travels, 1845-1849. He included various drawings and designs:

C. M. Léopold Verguet, missionnaire apostolique S.M. de 1844 à 1848, *Histoire de la première mission catholique au vicariat de Mélanésie*, Carcassonne, Imprimerie de P. Labau, Grand rue, 21, 1854. Reprinted by Montpellier, Collection Arts et Traditions rurales, 2012.

APM = Archivio Padri Maristi, Padri Maristi, Via Alessandro Poerio, 63, 00152 Roma, Italia

APM Dossier Personnel Léopold Verguet

Scatola APM 961

Scatola 962

APM Dessins Verguet (green album)

APM Dessins Verguet (pages in plastic cover)

APM Dossier Causa Marmoiton

APM 2313 / 12463

APM 2313 / 12468

APM 2314 / 12472

Other publications use material from the Marist archives or other archives with material by Verguet. We give some examples:

Hésiode, Garae, *L'arpenteur des nostalgies. Léopold Verguet (1817-1914)*, catalogue of the exhibition July 2008 at Carcassonne.

Catalogue of the exposition *Mer de Corail, terres de mission. Les Maristes en Océanie. 1836-1936*. Service historique de la Défense, Toulon. Musée Balaguier, La Seyne sur Mer, 3 April-31 March 2006.

Girard, Charles SM (ed.), *Lettres des missionnaires maristes en Océanie 1836 – 1854*. Préface de Claude Prudhomme. Introduction historique de Claire Laux (mémoire d'églises) Paris, Editions Karthala, 2008.

Girard, Charles SM, *Presentation of Lettres reçues d'Océanie*, in A. Greiler (ed.), *Catholic*

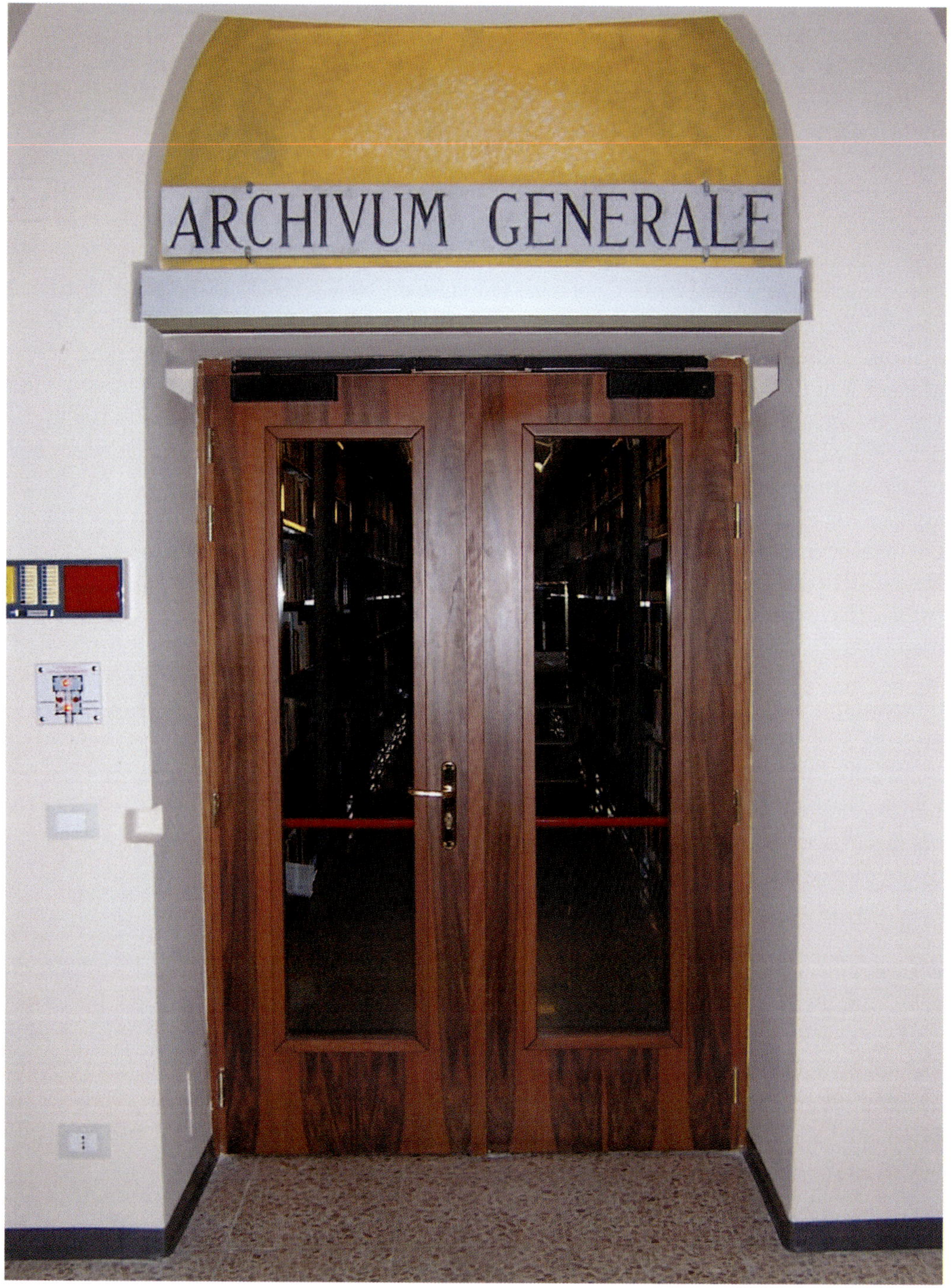

Beginnings in Oceania. Marist Missionary Perspectives, Adelaide, ATF, 2009, 23 – 25.

Girard, Charles SM (ed.), *Lettres reçues d'Océanie par l'administration générale des pères maristes pendant le généralat de Jean-Claude Colin, Textes revus, corrigés et ajoutés, 1836 – 1854*, Paris, Karthala – Rome, Société de Marie, ten volumes, 2009 and 2010 (= LRO).

Lessard, Gaston SM (ed.), *"Colin sup". Documents concernant le généralat du père Colin,* volume I, *De l'élection au voyage à Rome (1836-1842)*, Rome, 2007 (= CS 1).

Lessard, Gaston SM (ed.), *"Colin sup". Documents concernant le généralat du père Colin,* volume 2, *Du voyage à Rome au chapitre (1842-1845)*, Rome, 2009 (= CS 2).

Bourtot, Bernard SM (ed.), *« Colin sup ». Documents our l'étude du généralat de Jean-Claude Colin (1836-1854),* volume 4, *De l'été 1848 à la démission (1848-1854)*, Rome, 2009 (= CS 4).

Website 'www.mariststudies.org': From this site we took the English translations of the letters edited in LRO. Our gratitude goes to the different translators.

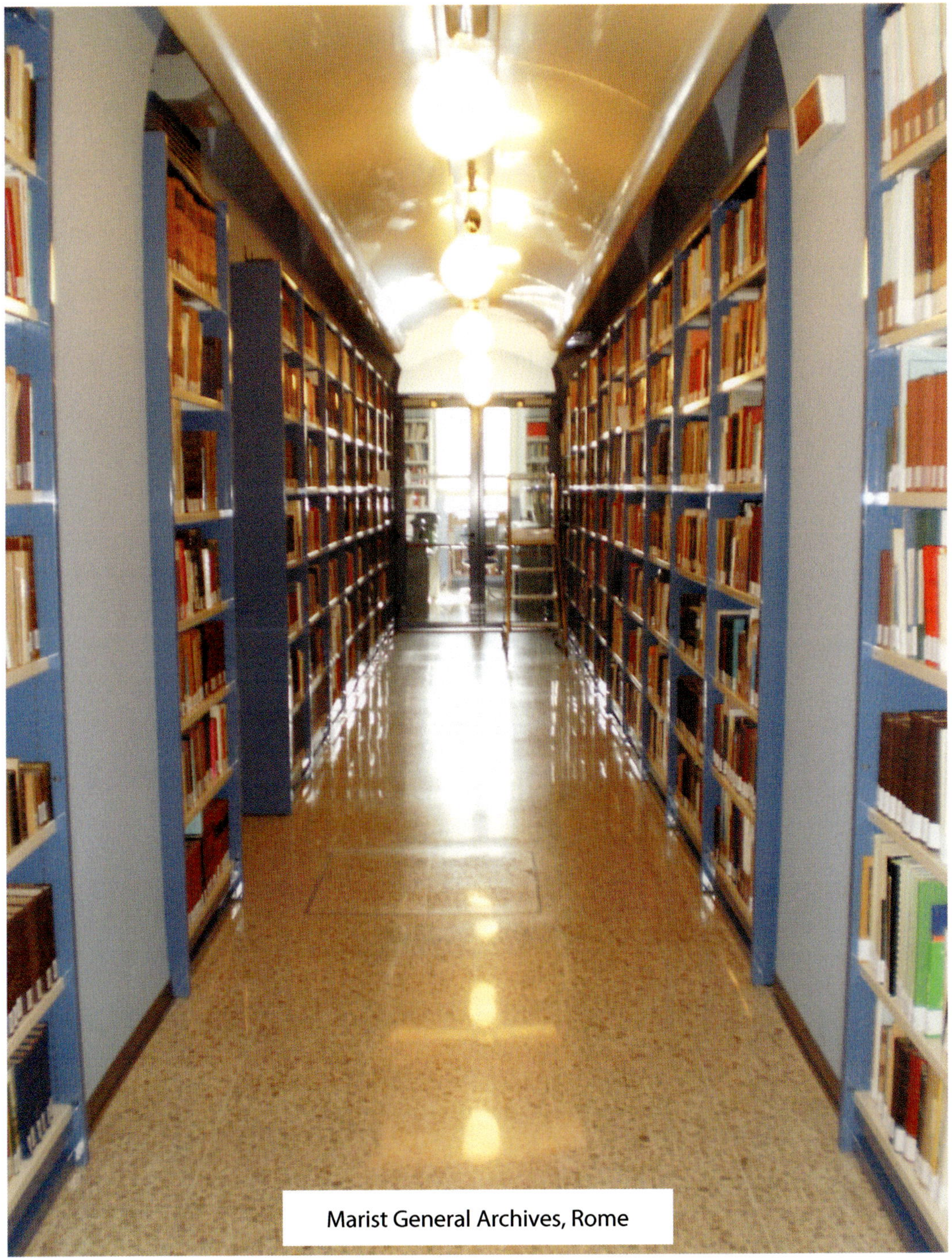

Marist General Archives, Rome

Secondary Literature

Coste, Jean SM, *Lectures on Society of Mary History (Marist Fathers). Part I, The Beginnings, 1786 - 1836; Part II, Fr Colin's Generalate, 1836 - 1854*, Rome, 1965.

Delbos, Georges MSC, *The Catholic Church in New Caledonia. A Century and a Half of its History*, translated by Derek Finlay SM, Suva, Cepac, 2000.

Gnecchi-Ruscone, Elisabetta, 'A School of Iron, Vexation and Blood, but a School Nonetheless', *The Journal of Pacific History*, 47:3, 2012, 389-403.

Greiler, Alois SM (ed.), *Catholic Beginnings in Oceania. Marist Missionary Perspectives*, Hindmarsh, ATF, 2009.

Kerr, Donal SM, *Jean-Claude Colin, Marist. A Founder in an Era of Revolution and Restoration: The Early Years 1790 – 1836*, Dublin, The Columba Press, 2000.

Knox, Margaret, *Voyage of Faith. The Story of the First 100 Years of Catholic Missionary Endeavour in Fiji and Rotuma*, Suva, Archidiocese of Suva, 1997.

Laracy, Hugh, *M. Xavier Montrouzier, a Missionary in Melanesia*, in J. W. Davidson - D. Scarr (Ed.), *Pacific Island Portraits*, Canberra, Australian National University Press, 1970, 127 - 145.

Laracy, Hugh, *Marists and Melanesians: a History of Catholic Missions in the Solomon Islands*, Canberra - Honolulu, 1976.

Laracy, Hugh, *Leopold Verguet and the Aborigines of Sydney 1845*, in *Aboriginal History* 4, 1-2 (1980) 179 - 183.

Laracy, Hugh, *Marists and Mariners. The Solomon Island Story*, in *International Journal of Maritime History* 3, 1 (1991) 59 - 80.

Laracy, Hugh, *Le R.P. Colin, les maristes et le vicariat de Mélanésie (1845-1853)*, in *Société d'Etudes Historiques de la Nouvelle-Calédonie*. Bulletin N° 154 (2008) 65 – 86.

Laracy, Hugh, *Colin and Melanesia*, in A. Greiler (ed.), *Catholic Beginnings in Oceania. Marist Missionary Perspectives*, Adelaide, ATF, 2009, 87 – 103.

Laracy, Hugh, *Of Missionaries and Mariners: Marists, Milanese and the Vicariate of Melanesia, 1845-1859*, conference Wellington, April 2009.

Laux, Claire, *Les missionnaires et la mémoire des civilisations polynésiennes*, in *Revue d'Histoire de l'Église de France* 89 (2003) 69 – 80.

O'Reilly, Patrick SM, *La Société de l'Océanie (1844 - 1854)*, in *Revue d'histoire des missions* 7, 2 (1930) 227 – 262.

Richard, Jean-Claude – Alain Saussol, *Deux dessins de Léopold Verguet (1817-1914), missionnaire mariste en Océanie et chanoine à Carcassonne, sur les tragiques événement de Nouvelle-Calédonie en juillet-août 1847*, Cahiers 20, Arts et Traditions Rurales, 2009, p. 341 – 366; / see: www.artstraditionsrurales.fr.

Roach, Kevin SM, *Venerable Jean-Claude Colin and the Mission in New Zealand, 1838 - 1848*, Thesis, Rome, Gregorian University, 1963.

Roach, Kevin SM, *Jean Claude Colin and the Foundation of the New Zealand Catholic Mission*, in *New Zealand Journal for History* no 1 (1969) 74 - 83.

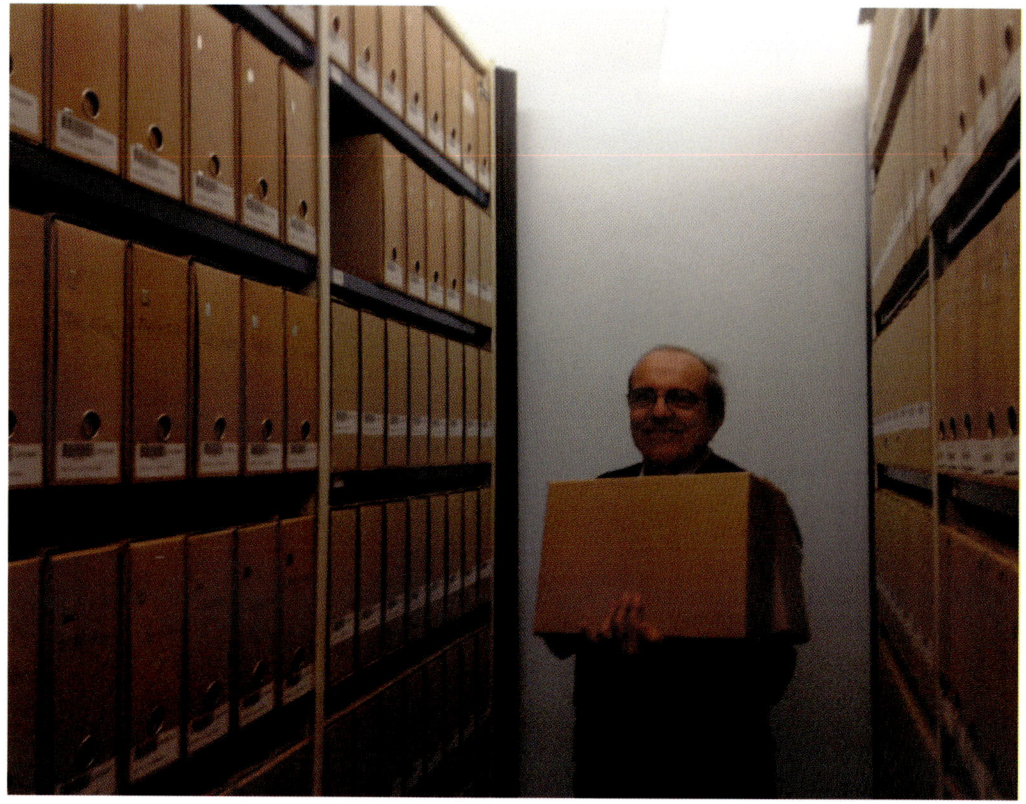

Marist Archivist, Carlo Maria Schianchi, with some of the Verguet material

Verguet, C.M. Léopold, missionnaire apostolique S.M. de 1844 à 1848, *Histoire de la première mission catholique au vicariat de Mélanésie*, Carcassonne, Imprimerie de P. Labau, Grand rue, 21, 1854 (Verguet, *Mélanésie*); second edition Paris 1861.

Verguet, C.M. Léopold, *Arossi ou San-Christoval et ses habitants*, in *Revue d'ethnographie*, separatum, Paris, 1885.

Verguet, C.M. Léopold, *Grand Archipel des Iles Salomon, son étendue, sa fertilité*, Marseille, Blanc et Bernard, 1883.

Verguet, C.M. Léopold, *Dissertation sur une deuxième mission aux iles Salomons*, 13 p, et album géographique s'y rapportant, 1893, 23 pages;

Wiltgen, Ralph M. SVD, *The Founding of the Roman Catholic Church in Oceania. 1825 to 1850*, Canberra - London - Norwalk, Australian National University Press, 1979.

Wiltgen, Ralph M. SVD, *The Founding of the Roman Catholic Church in Melanesia and Micronesia, 1850 – 1875* (Princeton Theological Monograph Series), Eugene, Oregon, Pickwick Publications, 2008.

Index of Names

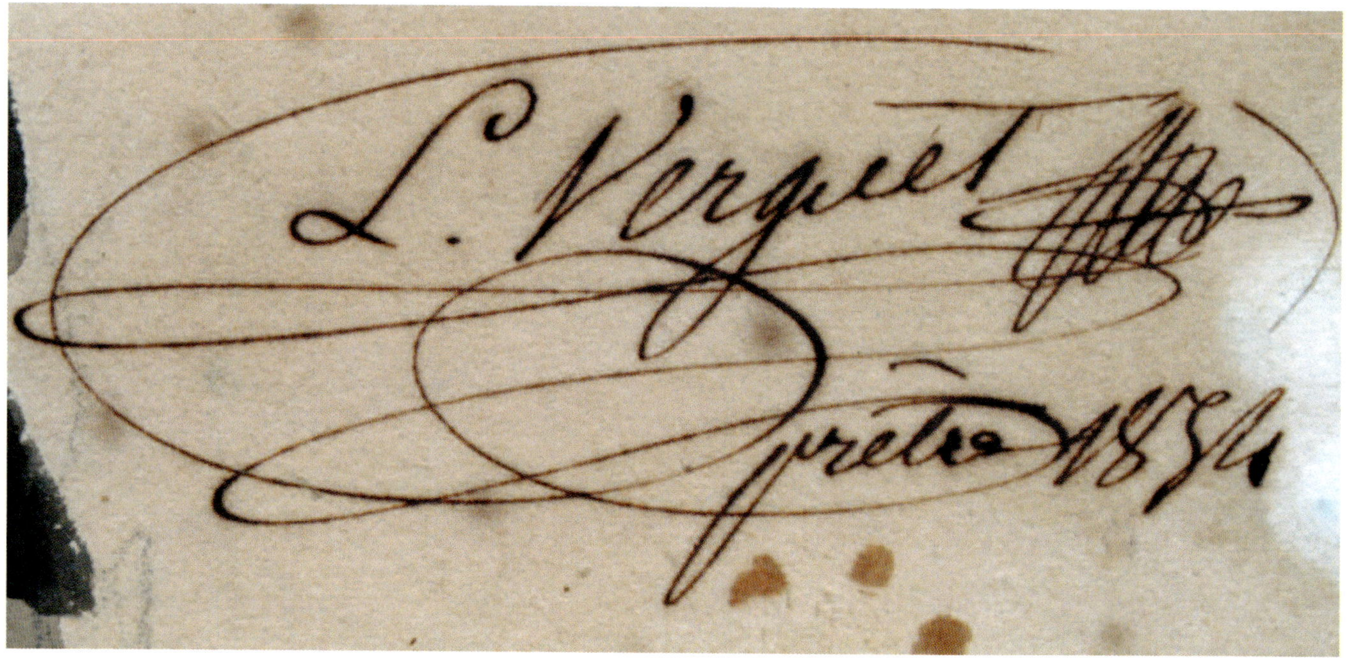

L. Verguet
Priest, 1854